A Weak Messianic Power

A Weak Messianic Power

Figures of a Time to Come
in Benjamin, Derrida, and Celan

Michael G. Levine

FORDHAM UNIVERSITY PRESS
NEW YORK   2014

Copyright © 2014 Fordham University Press

All rights reserved. No part of this publication may be reproduced, stored in a retrieval system, or transmitted in any form or by any means—electronic, mechanical, photocopy, recording, or any other—except for brief quotations in printed reviews, without the prior permission of the publisher.

Fordham University Press has no responsibility for the persistence or accuracy of URLs for external or third-party Internet websites referred to in this publication and does not guarantee that any content on such websites is, or will remain, accurate or appropriate.

Fordham University Press also publishes its books in a variety of electronic formats. Some content that appears in print may not be available in electronic books.

Library of Congress Cataloging-in-Publication Data is available from the publisher.

ISBN 978 0 823 25511 5

16 15 14   5 4 3 2 1
First edition

For Gabriel and Emmanuelle

CONTENTS

List of Figures ix

Acknowledgments xi

1. A Time to Come: Hunchbacked Theology, Post-Freudian Psychoanalysis, and Historical Materialism   1

2. The Day the Sun Stood Still: Benjamin's Theses, Celan's Realignments, Trauma, and the Eichmann Trial   14

3. *Pendant*: Celan, Büchner, and the Terrible Voice of the Meridian   37

4. On the Stroke of Circumcision I: Derrida, Celan, and the Covenant of the Word   63

5. On the Stroke of Circumcision II: Celan, Kafka, and the Wound in the Name   80

6. Poetry's Demands and Abrahamic Sacrifice: Celan's Poems for Eric   97

Notes 125

Bibliography 165

Index 173

FIGURES

1 Manuscript of "Ô les hableurs" 122
2 Paulownia Leaf Underlying Manuscript Page of "Ô les hableurs" 123

ACKNOWLEDGMENTS

Many people and institutions have helped me as I worked on this book, and I want here to express my gratitude and appreciation. I would first like to acknowledge the support of my wonderful colleagues in German at Rutgers: Nicola Behrmann, Fatima Naqvi, Nicholas Rennie, and particularly Martha Helfer. I have been fortunate to work with students like Gabriela Belorio, Christophe Koné, Barbara Natalie Nagel, Shambhavi Prakash, Christopher Powers, Chadwick Smith, Eric Trump, and Nicole Zeftel, who have consistently challenged me with their unsettling questions and startling insights.

There are those luminaries whom I have read religiously over the years but have not known very well on a personal level, people whose writings have profoundly stirred and inspired me from afar. Among them I count the late Barbara Johnson and Jacques Derrida, but also Werner Hamacher, Shoshana Felman, and Judith Butler. I have been fortunate to make new friends in recent years whose company has enriched me greatly and whose ideas have found their way—directly and indirectly—into this book: Elisabeth Weber, Gabriele Schwab, Barbara Hahn, Eric Downing, Alexander Gelley, Paul North, Bertrand Badiou, and Michael Sherringham. I would not know who I was or how to orient myself intellectually without the continuing friendship of Ulrich Baer, Bella Brodzki, Cathy Caruth, Peter Demetz, Susan Derwin, Michael Holquist, Richard Klein, Elissa Marder, John Michael, Rainer Nägele, Gerald Pirog, Russell Samolsky, Samuel Weber, Sharon Willis, and especially Jared Stark. This book is also deeply indebted to conversations—both real and imagined—with Peter Demetz, Anna Glazova, Jason Groves, John Hamilton, Carol Jacobs, Dori Laub, Vivian Liska, Gerhard Richter, Avital Ronell, Thomas Schestag, and Richard Sieburth.

I am grateful to have had the opportunity to work again with my editor, Helen Tartar, who brings such dedication, vision, and integrity to her work. I would also like to thank the fine staff at Fordham University Press—particularly Thomas Lay; Eric Newman; Kem Crimmins; Kathleen Sweeney; my copy editor, Emily Williams; and the indexer, Johnna VanHoose Dinse. The book is much improved thanks to their efforts. I am also grateful to my tireless and highly enterprising research assistants Carlos Gasperi and Danica Savonick. Essential administrative support was provided by Stefanie Toye, Maria Guerroro-Reyes, and Elizabeth deWolfe. I am extremely grateful to the Camargo Foundation for generously supporting my research with a residential fellowship and especially to its co-directors Connie Higginson and Leon Selig for their many kindnesses to my family during our stay in Cassis. Finally, I would like to thank my children, Gabriel and Emmanuelle, to whom I dedicate this book, and my wife, Juliann Garey, for their amazing grace, their unconventional approach to projects big and small, and the pyrotechnics of their conversation.

Earlier versions of Chapters 2–6 appeared in various journals: Chapter 2 in *MLN* German Issue, 126:3 (2011): 534–560; Chapter 3 in *MLN* German Issue, 122:3 (2007): 573–601; Chapters 4–5 in *Diacritics*, double issue on "Derrida and Democracy," 38.1–2 (2008): 64–91; Chapter 6 in *MLN* Comparative Literature 126 (2011): 1014–48. I thank these publishers for permission to use this material.

A Weak Messianic Power

ONE

A Time to Come: Hunchbacked Theology, Post-Freudian Psychoanalysis, and Historical Materialism

> Redemption depends on the tiny fissures in the continuous catastrophe.
> —WALTER BENJAMIN, *Central Park*

There is often in writing a secret place around which thoughts—around which what is less than, not yet, and perhaps never to be thought—may gather. Walter Benjamin alludes to such a place in an April 1940 letter to his friend and confidante Gretel Adorno. Referring to the thoughts that would secretly coalesce around the writing of his now-famous theses on the concept of history, he notes, "The war, and the constellation that brought it about, led me to set down some thoughts of which I can say that I kept them to myself—kept them indeed from myself—for some twenty years." (Der Krieg und die Konstellation, die ihn mit sich brachte, hat mich dazu geführt, einige Gedanken niederzulegen, von denen ich sagen kann, dass ich sie an die zwanzig Jahre bei mir verwahrt, ja, verwahrt vor mir selber gehalten habe.)[1] The pressures of the war and of being made to flee first from his homeland and then, in turn, from his second home in Paris (which he would be forced to abandon shortly after this letter was sent) give the theses a tremendous sense of urgency. Under such pressures, thoughts that had heretofore been held back and kept apart began to find their way to each other, coming together with and against Benjamin's knowledge in a kind of clandestine rendezvous.

That the theses are themselves the place where thoughts held incommunicado for some twenty years would begin to converse, engaging in a secret colloquy whose codes and protocols would have to be learned *sur place* from indications provided by the text itself, is suggested not only in the letter to Gretel Adorno but also in a key passage of the second thesis. The passage appears in *Walter Benjamin: Selected Writings*, volume 4 as follows:

> The past carries with it a hidden index [führt einen heimlichen Index mit] by which it is referred to redemption. Doesn't a breath of the air that pervaded earlier days caress us as well? In the voices we hear isn't there an echo of now silent ones? Don't the women we court have sisters they no longer recognize? If this is so, then there is a secret agreement [eine geheime Verabredung] between past generations and the present one. Then our coming was expected on earth. Then, like every generation that preceded us, we have been endowed with a *weak* messianic power, a power on which the past has a claim.[2]

This passage will be discussed at greater length in Chapter 2. For the moment I wish only to draw attention to the language of secrets and hidden indications to which Benjamin has recourse, noting in particular the phrase *eine geheime Verabredung*, which is rendered as "a secret agreement" in both the initial English translation of the theses that appeared in *Illuminations* and the revised edition of the text published in *Selected Writings*. What is obscured in this translation is the sense of an "appointment" and, moreover, through the root *Rede*— from which the term *Verabredung* is formed—the sense of a call or address. Telling in this regard is the translation of the phrase *eine geheime Verabredung* that Benjamin himself provides in a French version he composed of the text. There it is rendered as *un rendez-vous mystérieux* (GS 1.3: 1260).

The secret meeting of which the theses speak is in a sense the one to which Benjamin appears to have felt himself called. Called in secret, called under the pressure of the war and the constellation it brought about, but also perhaps called under the pressure of a rapidly approaching end that would soon overtake him, he set down thoughts about a secret appointment between past generations and the present one. As a closer reading of the theses reveals, what speaks to us out of the past, what summons us to a secret rendezvous with it, is strictly speaking that which *will have never belonged to it* or that which will have belonged only as a missed possibility and unrealized potential. Evident in the passage cited above is the proximity of the notion of a secret appointment (*eine geheime Verabredung*) to that of a hidden or secret index (*einen heimlichen Index*) that the past carries along with it. It is by means of such an index, Benjamin says, that the past is "referred to redemption" (durch den sie auf die Erlösung verwiesen wird).

Yet what does the theologically charged term "redemption" (*Erlösung*) mean in the context of these secrets? According to Hamacher, the term should be understood "most prosaically"—as *Einlösung* more than *Erlösung*. Itself a prosaic term, *Einlösung* is usually associated with the cashing of checks and the redemption of deposits or coupons. Understood in this way, *Erlösung*, according to Hamacher, would mean,

> a redeeming of possibilities which are opened with every life and are missed in every life. If the concept of redemption points towards a theology—and it does so without doubt and *a fortiori* in the context of the first thesis, which mentions the "little hunchback" of theology—then this is not straightforwardly Judeo-Christian theology, but rather a theology of the missed or distorted—hunchbacked—possibilities, a theology of missed, distorted or hunchbacked time. Each possibility that was missed in the past remains a possibility for the future, precisely because it has not found fulfillment. For the past to have a future merely means that the past's possibilities have not yet found their fulfillment, that they continue to have an effect and demand their realization from those who feel addressed by them. When past things survive, then it is not lived-out (*abgelebte*) facts that survive; rather what survives are the unactualized possibilities of that which is past. There is historical time only insofar as there is an excess of the unactualized, the unfinished, failed, thwarted, which leaps beyond its particular Now and demands from another Now its settlement, correction and fulfillment.[3]

What remains unactualized, Benjamin suggests, stays with us, remaining not merely as a lingering echo but as a secretly insistent appeal. Because such appeals do not pass through normal channels of communication, because they are not transmitted via publically sanctioned, consciously recognized ways of speaking, they seem to require from the addressee a special attunement, perhaps even a certain mode of unconscious receptivity.

Indeed, as Benjamin suggests in *A Little History of Photography*, the peculiar mode of address in question here speaks both from and to a certain otherness. "It is another nature," he writes, "which speaks to the camera rather than to the eye [Es ist ja eine andere Natur, welche zur Kamera als welche zum Auge spricht]: 'other' above all in the sense that the space informed by human consciousness gives way to a space informed by the unconscious" (*SW* 2: 510; *GS* 2.1: 371).

What does it mean for something to speak to the eye, let alone to the camera? What is this speech of another nature? If it is indeed speech addressed to the unconscious, speech addressed from one unconscious to another, it communicates only to the extent that it speaks through the lapses and slips of another. It speaks to the camera through the aperture of the eye—that is, through openings in the space informed by human consciousness, through blind spots in its field of vision. According to Benjamin, the photographic devices of slow motion and enlargement dilate the space informed by human consciousness, and it is through such dilations that the optical unconscious speaks. Not only does this unconscious speak out of turn—speaking in place of another, speaking where the space informed by human consciousness gives way to it[4]—but it also speaks out of time, speaking, as Benjamin says, from a place where the future nests eloquently in the immediacy of a long-forgotten moment ("im Sosein jener längstvergangenen Minute das Künftige . . . so beredt nistet").

Just as it is necessary to underscore the root *Rede*, and with it the element of address implicit in the phrase *eine geheime Verabredung*, so too is it important to stress the term *beredt*, which Benjamin uses here to describe the peculiar eloquence of this nesting future, this future that will have found itself in the nest of another time. Benjamin's remarks are occasioned by his reflection on a picture of the nineteenth-century French photographer Dauthendey and his fiancée taken at the time of their engagement. Viewing the photo while knowing of the woman's subsequent suicide, Benjamin remarks that her husband-to-be would one day, shortly after the birth of their sixth child, find her lying in the bedroom of their Moscow house with her veins slashed. In the photo, Benjamin says,

> He seems to be holding her, but her gaze passes him by, absorbed in an ominous distance [saugend an eine unheilvolle Ferne geheftet]. Immerse yourself in such a picture long enough and you will realize to what extent opposites

touch, here too: the most precise technology can give its products a magical value, such as a painted picture can never again have for us. No matter how artful the photographer, no matter how carefully posed his subject, the beholder feels an irresistible urge to search such a picture for the tiny spark of contingency, of the here and now, with which reality has, so to speak, seared the complexion of the image [den Bildcharakter gleichsam durchgesengt hat], to find the inconspicuous spot where in the immediacy of that long-forgotten moment the future nests so eloquently that we, looking back, may rediscover it. For it is another nature that speaks to the camera [. . .].

(*SW* 2: 510; *GS* 2.1: 371)

Like the past of which Benjamin speaks in the theses—which is not so much a past reality as an unrealized possibility—the future in question here will, from the first, have stood out from its immediate surroundings.⁵ Just as the photo is said to be shot through with tiny sparks of contingency, with blind spots seared into the artist's field of vision, so too is the past riddled with moments that will never have belonged properly to it. What speaks to the beholder of this photo not only addresses him from a locus of contingency but also speaks, as it were, only by accident. Speaking as and from a tiny spark of happenstance, it speaks the language of sparks, a language *that* sparks. Not only is this the language with which "reality has, so to speak, seared the complexion of the picture," it is also the language that ignites in the beholder an irresistible urge or unconscious compulsion; the beholder, Benjamin says, "fühlt unwiderstehlich den Zwang."⁶

As though summoned to a clandestine meeting, the beholder is driven to search the picture for a hidden location, to find "the inconspicuous spot" (die unscheinbare Stelle) where, in the immediacy of that long-forgotten moment, the future is said to nest so eloquently. Addressed by this future of the past as though touched by a tiny spark of contingency, the beholder is moved not only to seek out in the picture that moment of blindness with which reality has seared it, that site of an accident ("das winzige Fünkchen Zufall"), but moreover, to locate himself, find himself, and render himself there. The addressee only first comes to be in that place where, in being called out of himself, he is called into another relationship with the past, into what in the theses is called a secret rendezvous.

The temporality of "a time to come" developed in the following chapters, is not merely that of a future time or a coming present, but that of the future anterior, a time in which future and past do not so much come together as come about one another, doing so in a way that circumvents conventional modalities of presence and holds time open to the coming of another. In this regard, it is no doubt telling that Benjamin's theses themselves draw to a close around a certain opening of time. Their final words thus speak of a second, describing it not as a positive temporal unit but as a narrow aperture—as the strait gate (*die kleine Pforte*) through which the Messiah might enter. "We know," Benjamin writes,

> that the Jews were prohibited from inquiring into the future; the Torah and the prayers instructed them in remembrance. This disenchanted the future, which holds sway over all those who turn to soothsayers for enlightenment. This does not imply, however, that for the Jews the future became homogeneous, empty time. For every second was the small gateway in time through which the Messiah might enter. [Denn in ihr war jede Sekunde die kleine Pforte, durch die der Messias treten konnte.]
>
> (*SW* 4: 397; *GS* 1.2: 704)

What Benjamin proposes in the theses is a way of thinking the present as something other than a bridge, other than a mediating link between past and future presents. Thus, he writes, "The historical materialist cannot do without the notion of a present which is not a transition [die nicht Übergang ist], but in which time takes a stand (*einsteht*) and has come to a standstill (*und zum Stillstand gekommen ist*)" (*SW* 4: 396; *GS* 1.2: 702).

That the new English translation of the theses contained in *Selected Writings* takes pains to emphasize the element of standing that links the German terms *einstehen* (taking a stand) and *Stillstand* (standstill) is telling. For the stand in question is related not only to a pause, suspension, or holding open of time, but also to a spatial shift, a change in orientation from the horizontal axis to the vertical one. That this stand is to be understood as a reworking of familiar temporal-spatial coordinates—and, by extension, as an unsettling of the language to which we have recourse when speaking about the movement and stasis of time—is apparent in Benjamin's famous definition of an origin (*Ursprung*) in the first chapter of his *Origin of the German Tragic Drama*. There, he writes, "the origin stands in the flow of becoming as a maelstrom" (steht im Fluß des Werdens als Strudel). As the ensuing discussion makes clear, this maelstrom interrupts the horizontal flow of time not only as a vertical descent but also, and above all, as a swirling movement of coming-to-be and passing-away.

Origin, although an historical category through and through, has nevertheless nothing in common with emergence [Entstehen]. In origin what is meant is not the becoming of something that has sprung forth [das Werden des Entsprungenen], but rather the springing-forth that emerges out of coming-to-be and passing away [dem Werden und Vergehen Entspringendes]. Origin stands in the flow of becoming as a maelstrom [Strudel] that irresistibly tears [reißt] the stuff of emergence into its rhythm. In the bare manifestation of the factual, the original is never discernible, and its rhythm is accessible only to a dual insight. It is recognizable on the one hand as restoration, as reinstatement, and on the other, precisely therein as incomplete, unfinished.[7]

(GS 1.1: 226)

What stands in the flow of becoming (*Werden*) stands still only to the extent that "coming-to-be and passing away" (*Werden und Vergehen*) come about one another, spiraling vertiginously toward one another in the vortex of a present no longer conceived of as a mere transition. This vortex, or *Strudel*, to which the origin is compared may thus be said to figure a circumvention of presence, a whirling, abyssal movement of return in which past and future circle around one another, without the bridge or mediation of the present, in a temporal relationship most closely associated with the future perfect tense.

As noted above, this temporal dimension of Benjamin's thought stands in close proximity to his meditations on the unconscious—on that speech of another nature to which he refers in *A Little History of Photography*, that speech that addresses us in such a way as to call us out of ourselves, summoning us to a secret appointment with that which, strictly speaking, will never have belonged to the past. That Benjamin introduces such a mode of address in conjunction with both the notion of a hidden index by which the past is referred to redemption and the notion of a *weak* messianic power on which the past has a claim (*Anspruch hat*), a claim so urgent and imperious that it cannot be ignored or avoided—"Pas moyen d'éluder sa Sommation," as he writes—all this suggests that the unconscious marks a critical, if largely implicit, intersection in his effort to bring together a "little hunchback" of theology that, as Hamacher notes, is "not straightforwardly Judeo-Christian theology, but rather a theology of the missed or distorted—hunchbacked—possibilities, a theology of missed, distorted or hunchbacked time" with an equally unconventional sense of historical materialism.[8]

As a critical articulation between theology and materialism, the notion of the unconscious implicit in Benjamin's theses unsettles what it brings together, making it possible to read the theological in more prosaic terms while giving the materialist historian unable to evade the summons of what speaks to him or her from a certain future of the past ways of heeding its address, ways of attuning himself or herself to a certain historical unconscious.

It is at such an intersection, moreover, that prevailing theories of the unconscious may themselves be unsettled, that the opportunity arises to view psychoanalytic approaches to history—as well as the history of psychoanalysis itself—in new ways that make explicit the ties linking the temporality of the future perfect, the structure of address integral to it, and the movements of repetition associated with it in Benjamin to post-Freudian theories of belatedness. Let us recall in this regard Benjamin's definition of an origin (*Ursprung*) as that which "stands in the flow of becoming as a maelstrom that irresistibly tears the stuff of emergence into its rhythm." This rhythm, he adds, is accessible only to a dual insight: "recognizable on the one hand as restoration, as reinstatement, and on the other, precisely therein as incomplete, unfinished" (*GS* 1.1: 226).[9]

In psychoanalytic terms, this movement of restoration and reinstatement may be understood as the direction of the French "return to Freud," associated most notably with Lacan, Laplanche, and Derrida. Rather than going back to the founding father and foundational concepts, rather than returning to that very sense of an origin from which Benjamin seeks to depart, it was a "return" to aspects of Freud's work that had remained undeveloped and insufficiently theorized; a "return" that sought to make contact not with established concepts, but with energies and processes *silently at work*; with something unacknowledged and unassimilated in the past; with what one might describe, *pace* Benjamin, as "citable" fragments that, at the time of their initial inscription, could not be integrated into a context of significance. In a sense, what the French reading of Freud discovered was a certain belatedness of Freudian thought, a certain future nesting eloquently within it, something—at once meaning and force—that exceeded Freud's own grasp and that, in its very excessiveness, secretly continued to drive his thought, making it possible for later generations to inherit a certain way of thinking with and beyond him. If, as Benjamin suggests, a *weak* messianic power is first and foremost an endowment ["uns . . . mitgegeben"], the

French return to Freud gives us a sense of how such a gift may be passed on. For what is transmitted is not a positive content or "power" in the strong sense so much as a certain excess.[10] In Benjamin's second thesis, which is discussed at greater length in the next chapter, this excess is associated with the insistence of the signifier *mit-* in the pivotal verbs *mitführen, mitschwingen* and *mitgeben*.[11]

The Day the Sun Stood Still

This next chapter argues that focusing on the rhythms of Benjamin's own language, on the repetition of the prefix *mit-* and on a certain cadence and anaphoric élan of his prose, provides otherwise inaccessible insight into this dimension of excess. More generally, the chapter will argue that rhythmic repetition, as Benjamin conceives it, the kind of rhythm into which the stuff of emergence is said to be torn, is to be understood as an incomplete and unfinished movement of restoration and reinstatement—that is, as a movement of return that never comes full circle; that in turning back, leaves itself open at each and every turn, at each and every second, to the coming of another.

To put it in more psychoanalytic terms, the following chapters view repetition less as a single, imperious *Zwang* than as a double and divided compulsion, as a movement of return inhabited by contradictory pressures and driven by competing impulses. Such an understanding owes much to recent work in trauma studies, itself a future of psychoanalysis made possible by the French return to Freud and its belated discovery of belatedness. While informed by this work, the following chapters' approach to repetition takes as its more immediate point of departure Paul Celan's 1960 *Meridian* address delivered on the occasion of his reception of the Büchner Prize.

Pendant

In this speech, generally regarded as his most extensive reflection on "poetry today" and his own poetic thinking, Celan draws a distinction between two modes of coming: "coming back" and "coming between." "Die Kunst," he notes in the first line of the second paragraph, "kommt wieder." He contrasts this movement of artistic recurrence directly with another mode of coming described in the preceding sentence. There it is "coming" in the sense of an intervention or interruption: "Es kommt etwas dazwischen." In ways that subsequent chapters will explore, there is, Celan suggests, in art's recurrence another pulse at work, some other impulse beating within it. Celan never names this impulse, though he suggests at certain points that is associated with the Hölderlinian notion of a caesura and a certain movement of poetic intercession.

That this impulse remains unnamed is telling. For Celan's more general endeavor, as I see it, is to trace all the impasses of traumatic recurrence—all those moments of stasis, fixation, and compulsive repetition; all those instances of linguistic paralysis, of being made to stand tongue-tied and immobilized on a highly invested frontier that is at once the threshold of speech, the limit of a body cultivated to speak in particular ways, and the border of a carefully patrolled politico-military entity at which an unpronounceable password, a shibboleth one mispronounces on pain of death, is demanded. At the same time and in those same precarious moments, one has the sense that Celan is feeling his way toward the pulse of that which beats otherwise and perhaps comes only in the meantime, coming as the linguistic intervention of a mistake, slip, or lapsus, as the unconscious proffering of a secret password. This is perhaps why—in contrast to art, which is said to come back—that which "comes between" remains unnamed.

Here "a time to come" is once again related not only to the future perfect tense but also to the structures of repetition and address with which it is associated in Benjamin. Nowhere is this more apparent in Celan's *Meridian* speech than in his discussion of a seemingly insignificant error committed by Karl Emil Franzos, editor of the first critical and complete edition of Georg Büchner's works and posthumous writings. While Celan's reading of this mistake will be discussed in detail in Chapter 3, it is important to note at this point the connection he makes between citation and repetition as he views Franzos' *mis*quotation of a key passage in Büchner not as just an act of repetition gone awry, but as evidence of something else faintly beating at the heart of repetition. That this slip involves misquoting the word *commode* (commodious) as *kommende* (coming) is, of course, important to Celan; for this "coming" word, coming in the meantime and in the place of another, functions as a silently tendered shibboleth that gives access to an altogether different level of textual functioning, a dimension of belatedness silently at work in a text whose main character asserts at one point, "*A posteriori*—that's how everything begins."

The question Celan poses about this "coming" word suggests that the editorial parapraxis also has the structure of an address.

> Is *Leonce and Lena* [the Büchner text in question] not full of words which seem to smile through invisible quotation marks, which we should perhaps not call *Gänsefüßchen*, or goose feet, but rather rabbit's ears, that is, something that listens, not without fear, for something beyond itself, beyond words?[12]

Needless to say, the term "shibboleth"—used above to describe words unconsciously proffered and silently tendered; words that come only by accident and in place of others; words whose comings seem inadvertently to open the frontiers of language to something else going on in the texts and religious traditions in question (for it is now, since the Franzos lapsus, also the question of "a coming religion" that poses itself)—this term receives its most patient elaboration in Derrida's "Shibboleth: For Paul Celan."

On the Stroke of Circumcision

Discussed at length in Chapter 4, "Shibboleth" is strategically positioned on the threshold of a time to come. Divided into seven sections, each of which may be said to correspond to a day of the week, it breaks off just before coming to the eighth day of which it speaks, that day on which, according to Jewish tradition, the act of circumcision is supposed to be performed on a male infant. Thus, the text begins: "One time alone [Une seule fois]: circumcision takes place but once [n'a lieu qu'une fois]."[13] Stopping just in time, Derrida seems not only to postpone his appointment with what is said to take place at "an absolutely specific date" but also, in doing so, to stave off the act itself.

Yet it quickly becomes apparent that such a deferral makes possible a different, more circuitous approach to what he calls "the tropic of circumcision" in Celan. Putting off an encounter with circumcision as such, with the kind supposed to take place only on the eighth day, Derrida's text gives place to another, more circularly repetitive performance, one that will have taken place many times and on many different parts of the Celanian corpus without ever being definitively carried out, without ever being enacted as such. Such is the tropic of circumcision. For if circumcision is already in the Bible, and even before Saint Paul, not confined exclusively to the male member, if it is already, as Derrida observes, a matter of the circumcision or uncircumcision of the lips, of the tongue (Exod. 6:12, 30), of the ears (Jer. 6:10), and of the heart (Lev. 26:41), then the tropical or figurative dimension of it will have preceded any allegedly literal or proper sense. This is precisely the kind of allegation Saint Paul makes when calling for a spiritual, metaphorical circumcision of the heart rather than for a literal one of the foreskin.

If Derrida restores to circumcision its tropicality, the sense that it may take place on many parts of the body—but also and especially in the Celanian corpus on the body of words, names, and poems—without any one of them being viewed as its proper locus, he does so in view of a circumcision to come. In reclaiming for circumcision its tropicality—its irreducible multiplicity, figurality, and improperness—he seeks also and above all to open the closed circle of the rounding cut: sign at once of Jewish exclusivity and of Jewish exclusion. This is why circumcision is itself a trope for Derrida, a way of speaking in the aftermath of the Shoah but also with an eye to contemporary identity politics about practices of Jewish exclusion and the relation of these practices to the closed circle of traumatic repetition, related in its turn to the circular return of dates and anniversaries in Celan's poetry—"the dates," as he says in *The Meridian*, "from which and toward which we write" (47, 196). The tropic of circumcision is itself a figure, then, for the way these various circles will have been joined together in the Celanian corpus, like links in a chain of mutually defining and circularly redefined signifiers. Derrida's indirect approach and roundabout way of speaking about the tropic of circumcision are thus, I argue, necessitated by the instability of his object of study and its entanglement in a complex network of relationships, a network that is the very warp and woof of the Celanian text.

Yet, as Derrida himself is acutely aware, even in the most densely woven and tightly constructed of Celan's poems there are the tears and rents of unstitchable wounds, the traces of unfillable voids and unfathomable silences. Indeed, it is no exaggeration to say that his poems often gather like scar tissue around such wounds and are significant not only for what they say but also, and perhaps above all, for the silences and secrets they keep. Chapter 5 engages in extended readings of such poems. These are not only poems to be read but also ones that read, and what they read is *Kafka*—meaning not just the author and the body of his work but moreover the wound that will have gathered in the place of this notoriously improper proper name.

Poetry's Demands and Abrahamic Sacrifice

The final chapter focuses on three poems Celan wrote for his son, Eric, in the spring and summer of 1968. Among them is the only poem Celan ever wrote entirely in French. Tracing the movement from German to French in the successive composition of these poems, the chapter explores what it might have meant for Celan to write poems to his son at this time, a time not only of great revolutionary fervor in Paris but also of tremendous personal turmoil for the poet. As we know from oral testimony given by his wife, Gisèle Celan-Lestrange, and reported to André du Bouchet, Celan felt himself faced at this time with a choice between his poems and his son, claiming in moments of delirium that poetry was demanding of him that he "re-perform 'the sacrifice of Abraham.'"[14]

The last of the three poems dedicated to Eric, the one written entirely in French and the only one never included in any of Celan's planned publications, may be read as a paternal legacy and poetic testament. Like Benjamin's theses on the concept of history, itself often read as a suicide note and philosophical last will, this poem makes a special place for the *seconde*, which is conceived not as a positive unit of time but rather as a narrow opening in it, as an aperture through which another, perhaps even "an altogether other," might come.

TWO

The Day the Sun Stood Still: Benjamin's Theses, Celan's Realignments, Trauma, and the Eichmann Trial

> Der entscheidende Augenblick der menschlichen Entwicklung ist immerwährend.
>
> —KAFKA, *Aphorismen*

Even the most sensitive and persuasive readings of Benjamin's much-discussed last, unfinished text, his untitled theses on the philosophy of history, fail to focus sufficiently on a number of its key stylistic traits and its status within the body of his work as yet another in a series of meditations on the genre of "the last will and testament."[1] Perhaps the most definitive reading of Benjamin's theses to date, Werner Hamacher's essay "'Now': Benjamin on Historical Time," focuses on the second thesis as the key to its understanding of time and the ways in which Benjamin brings together theological and materialist approaches in his notion of "a *weak* Messianic power."[2]

While agreeing in many respects with Hamacher's reading, this chapter begins with two seemingly minor stylistic aspects of the second thesis that he does not address. The first has to do with Benjamin's use of the prefix *mit-* in three pivotal terms; the second concerns a shift from the present perfect tense to the subjunctive. The passage in question is all the more interesting because an earlier version of it had already been drafted as part of *The Arcades Project*. There Benjamin writes, "Happiness for us is thinkable only in the air that we have breathed, among the people who have lived with us" (Das Glück ist uns nur vorstellbar in der Luft, die wir geatmet, unter den Menschen, die mit uns gelebt haben).[3] When returning to this meditation on happiness in the theses, a meditation that is also occasioned by a passage from Rudolf Hermann Lotze's *Mikrokosmos*, Benjamin speaks again of a certain atmosphere. Yet the air in the later text is somehow thicker and the breathing more labored. In place of the respiratory rhythm of the present perfect tense, a temporal continuum in which the present reaches back into a past that in turn extends forward into the present, Benjamin shifts to the subjunctive.

Here, then, is the passage from the second thesis, in my own translation:

> There is happiness—such as could arouse envy in us—only in the air we have breathed [nur in der Luft, die wir geatmet haben], among people we could have talked to [mit Menschen, zu denen wir hätten reden], among women who could have given themselves to us [mit Frauen, die sich uns hätten geben können]. In other words, the idea of happiness is so intimately bound up with that of redemption that the former may be said to carry the latter as an abiding resonance [Es schwingt, mit anderen Worten, in der Vorstellung des Glücks unveräusserlich die der Erlösung mit]. The same applies to the idea of the past, which is the concern of history. The past carries with it a secret index [führt einen heimlichen Index mit] by which it is referred to redemption. Doesn't a breath of the air that pervaded earlier days caress us as well? In the voices we hear, isn't there an echo of now silent ones? Don't the women we court have sisters they no longer recognize? If this is so, then there is a secret appointment [eine geheime Verabredung] between past generations and the present one. Then our coming was expected on earth. Then, like every generation that preceded us, we have been endowed with a *weak* messianic power, a power on which the past has a claim.
>
> (*SW* 389; *GS* 1.2: 693–4)

Not only does the passage shift from the present perfect to the subjunctive, moving from the "air we have breathed" to "people with whom we could have spoken, women who might have given themselves to us"—from the verbs *geatmet haben* to *hätten reden* and *sich uns hätten geben können*—but, as was noted earlier, the shift is itself accompanied by the introduction of terms formed with the prefix *mit-*: the verbs *mitschwingen*, *mitführen*, and *mitgeben*. At stake in this shift is the hint of something else hanging in the air, a faint suggestion that is carried over in the phrase "the idea of happiness is so intimately bound up with that of redemption that the former may be said to carry the latter as an abiding resonance." (Es schwingt [. . .] in der Vorstellung des Glücks unveräusserlich die der Erlösung mit.)[4]

The series of tentative questions that follows, questions about a light touch, a faint echo, and an unacknowledged kinship, represent different ways, in different senses, of *releasing* something into the air, of letting something resound through this series of questions, of holding open a fragile, tremulous space of "what might have been" in the air of "what has been." Rather than just letting something linger in the air like a faint echo or resonate in the idea of happiness like that of redemption, Benjamin's series of open-ended questions has the effect of potentiating possibilities, of sounding out the unrealized potential, the latent potency, and the weak messianic power of the subjunctive.[5]

The following sentence, beginning with the conditional "If this is so [. . .]" (Ist dem so [. . .]), pursues this suspensive and potentiating movement, continuing to accumulate potential in the very rhetoric of suspense. Rather than closing off the aforementioned pointedly open-ended series of questions with a definitive answer, Benjamin lets it continue in the *possibility* of "if this is so, then [. . .]."[6] With a kind of anaphoric élan, the term "then" beats out the beginning of three new clauses.

> If it is so, then there is a secret appointment between past generations and the present one. Then our coming was expected on earth. Then, like every generation that preceded us, we have been endowed with a *weak* messianic power, a power on which the past has a claim.
>
> (SW 4: 389; GS 1.2: 694)

Benjamin not only lets accumulating potentials resound in these lines but, as in his discussion elsewhere of a doorbell whose ring is said to be too powerful (*zu durchschlagend*) for its surroundings and that breaks like shock waves into wider areas, he lets the thrice repeated "then" of the second thesis ring out like a call for a "secret appointment," for a *rendez-vous mystérieux* or *geheime Verabredung* between past generations and our own.[7] And it is this reverberating call hanging in the air, this demand ringing almost imperceptibly in our ears, that endows us with a *weak* messianic power: "dann ist uns eine *schwache* messianische Kraft mitgegeben" (GS 1.2: 694).[8]

That Benjamin again employs a verb with the prefix *mit-* in this instance is telling. For it seems to indicate a different mode of endowment, one that cannot be described in straightforward, positive terms as a natural gift or a positive bequest, as a transmission of property, or of what might be said to belong properly to the past. Benjamin's strategic use of the prefix *mit-* in the second thesis instead has a way of drawing attention to that which hangs virtually about the gift, to that which is *borne along with it*, given as a supplement, as a supplementary gift that is not directly donated or bequeathed.[9]

The prefix *mit-*, which appears to have such marginal significance at the beginning of the theses, working insistently from the margins to shift accents and unsettle familiar notions of power, potential, and potency, gradually moves to the center, in the end informing Benjamin's key notion of a constellation. In turning to this much-quoted, if still largely misunderstood notion, I want first to stress the ways in which the signifier *mit-* of the second thesis continues to resonate in later sections of the text, and second to demonstrate how the enigmatic notion of a "secret appointment" between past generations and the present one, touched on in the second thesis, only really becomes comprehensible when read in conjunction with the notion of a constellation. When introducing this notion, Benjamin pointedly avoids the more traditional term *Sternbild* which, as *Bild*, seems to suggest an all-too-static and fixed image of the stars in the heavens.[10] By opting instead for the Latinate *Konstellation*, he not only allows the German *mit-* to resonate in the Latin *Kon-* but also introduces a highly dynamic and elliptical thought figure.

To elaborate on these two dimensions of the Benjaminian *Konstellation*, it is necessary to turn briefly from his theses to Derrida's "Shibboleth: For Paul Celan" and in particular his reading of the Celan poem "IN EINS" ("IN ONE"). While Derrida never explicitly mentions Benjamin in "Shibboleth," his extended meditation on the question of the date and his location of "IN ONE" as the singular site of a multiple gathering help us understand what exactly is at stake for Benjamin in his use of the term "constellation."[11]

Here then is Celan's poem "IN ONE," quoted first in German and then in John Felstiner's English translation.

IN EINS

Dreizehnter Feber. Im Herzmund
Erwachtes Schibboleth. Mit dir,
Peuple de Paris. *No pasarán.*

Schäfchen zur Linken: er, Abadias,
der Greis aus Huesca, kam mit den Hunden
über das Feld, im Exil
stand weiss eine Wolke
menschlichen Adels, er sprach
uns das Wort in die Hand, das wir brauchten, es war
Hirten-Spanisch, darin,

im Eislicht des Kreuzers "Aurora":
die Bruderhand, winkend mit der
von den wortgrossen Augen
genommenen Binde—Petropolis, der
Unvergessenen Wanderstadt lag
auch dir toskanisch zu Herzen.

Friede den Hütten!

IN ONE

Thirteenth of February. In the heartmouth
an awakened Shibboleth. With you,
Peuple
de Paris. *No pasarán.*

Little sheep to the left: he, Abadias,
the old man from Huesca, came with his dogs
over the field, in exile
white hung a cloud
of human nobility, he spoke
into our hands the word that we needed, it was
shepherd-Spanish, in it,

in icelight of the cruiser "Aurora":
the brotherly hand, waving with
the blindfold removed from
his word-wide eyes—Petropolis, the
roving city of those unforgotten,
lay Tuscanly close to your heart too.

Peace to the cottages![12]

 In approaching Benjamin's notion of a constellation through Celan's poem, it is important to recall the poet's own reference to stars in his 1958

Bremen address. Speaking about a certain way of thinking that accompanies not only his own endeavors but also those of a younger generation of lyric poets, he reflects,

> These are the efforts of someone who, overarced by manmade stars, unsheltered even by the traditional tent of the sky, exposed in an unsuspected, terrifying way [der, überflogen von Sternen, die Menschenwerk sind, der, zeltlos auch in diesem bisher ungeahnten Sinne], and thus most uncannily in the open, goes with his very being to language, stricken by—and in search of—reality.
>
> (SPP 396; GW 3: 186)

Here Celan is referring not just to the 1957 launch of Sputnik but, more tragically, to the incinerated and still somehow airborne remains of those who were made to wear the yellow star whether they identified themselves as Jews or not. Overarced (*überflogen*) by stars that no longer guide him, the poet goes to language in an effort to orient himself. Yet, as he stresses in his 1960 *Meridian* speech, to get his bearings in a world whose coordinate system has been radically altered, he must also in a sense shift from spatial to temporal coordinates and write poems in which the attempt is made to remain mindful of certain dates, of precisely those dates by which every poem may now be said to be marked. As Celan proposes in a series of open-ended questions:

> Perhaps we may say that every poem has its "20th of January" inscribed upon it? Perhaps what's new for poems written today is just this: that here the attempt is clearest to remain mindful of such dates?
>
> But do we not all write ourselves from and as of such dates? And what dates do we write toward, to what dates do we ascribe ourselves?[13]

When Celan speaks of every poem having its "'20th of January' inscribed upon it," he is alluding not only to the beginning of Georg Büchner's *Lenz* but also and above all to the date of the 1942 Wannsee Conference at which the so-called Final Solution of the Jewish Question was planned by Nazi leaders. That the reference is at least double suggests that the return of the one date be read through the other. For the thing about dates is that they return. Circling back as anniversaries, they also circle around one another.

"Perhaps what is new about poems written today," Celan suggests, "is just this: that here the attempt is clearest to remain mindful of such dates [solcher Daten eingedenk zu bleiben]" (*GW* 3: 196). What then does it mean "to remain mindful"? Here again the circularity of the date is crucial. For mindfulness means not only actively commemorating an anniversary or keeping a date consciously in mind but also at the same time being passively and unconsciously *minded by* such returns. Indeed, in suggesting that "every poem has its '20th of January' inscribed upon it," Celan is reminding his audience that the returns in question are traumatic, that traumatic moments have a way of minding *us*, of holding us in their thrall, of making us turn incessantly and unwittingly around them. January 20th, 1942, Celan is saying, is just such a date. Not only does it keep returning, but it keeps us, in our turn, revolving around it. Thus, perhaps what is new about "poems written today" is their particular mindfulness of the way they are held in thrall by certain traumatic events and are forced to orbit compulsively around them.

Yet, the orbital paths traced by Celan's poems do more than simply mark the points and dates on which they remain stuck. They also provide a new kind of orientation in a world "overarced by manmade stars." "Unsheltered even by the traditional tent of the heavens" and "exposed in an unsuspected, terrifying way," Celan turns to the revolutionary movement of dates rather than to any static configuration of stars to get his bearings. Moreover, the dates of greatest importance to him are ones that involve political rather than stellar realignments.

These realignments are clearly in evidence in the 1963 poem, "IN ONE." Written on the very frontier between civil war and international conflict, between internal strife and warfare between nations, the poem's first words suggest that all of these conflicts turn in some way around the date February 13. The conflicts in question include first the Franco-Algerian struggle and the events of February 13, 1962. On that date, hundreds of thousands of people gathered in Paris to protest against the French police for the deaths of eight people during an anti-OAS demonstration at the Métro Charonne. Expressing his solidarity in a mix of French and German, Celan writes, "Mit dir,/*Peuple*/*de Paris*" (*GW* 1: 270). The second conflict, as Derrida notes, fell "on February 12, 1934, after the failure of the attempt to form a common Front of the Right, with Doriot, after the riot of February 6, a huge march took place, bringing together the masses and the leadership of the parties of the left. This was the origin of the *Front Populaire*" (*S* 24; *SPC* 45). Third is the *Action Française*'s attempted assassination of Leon Blum, leader of the *Front Populaire*, on February 13, 1936. Fourth is the February 1936 electoral victory of the *Frente Popular* on the eve of the Spanish Civil War, a conflict that would pit the Republican government, supported by the International Brigades, against Franco's *Frente Nationale*, which was backed by Mussolini's troops and Hitler's Condor Legion. Again standing with the left and this time in Spanish, Celan takes up the Republican rallying cry *No pasarán* (They shall not pass). Fifth is the 1917 February Revolution in Russia and the beginnings of the October Revolution—both of which are associated with the cruiser *Aurora*, which was undergoing major repairs at the time in Saint Petersburg. In February part of her crew joined the first revolution, and on October 25 the cruiser refused to carry out an order to put to sea, sparking the second revolution. Sixth, and certainly not finally, is the last line of the poem, the italicized exclamation: "*Peace to the cottages!*" (*Friede den Hütten!*) (*GW* 1: 270).

Commenting on this line, Derrida notes only that its "terrible irony must surely aim at someone" (*S* 23; *SPC* 46). While that someone may well have been Heidegger, to whom Celan would later address the poem "Todtnauberg" after a 1967 visit to the thinker's cottage, because the poem was published in 1963, in the collection *Die Niemandsrose* (*The No-one's-Rose*), the target remains uncertain. What is clear, however, is that the poem does not so much end with this line as break off in the midst of a citation of the opening lines of Georg Büchner's 1834 revolutionary pamphlet *The Hessian Messenger*, the second half of which reads: "War on the Palaces!" (Krieg den Palästen!). This strategically interrupted quotation not only leaves the poem on the brink of a yet-to-be-declared war but is also itself a slightly altered citation of the French revolutionary motto "Guerre aux châteaux, paix aux chaumières" coined by Chamfort. Celan's citation of Büchner's revolutionary pamphlet is telling; for, as he well knew, after its publication the author was forced to flee across the border to Strasbourg, where over the next few years he would write all of his major works: three plays and a prose piece that would all one day be seen as masterpieces of German literature.[14]

So how does all this help one to understand the notion of a constellation? In Thesis XVII Benjamin associates this notion with a certain arrest of thought.

> Thinking involves not only the movement of thoughts, but their being brought to a standstill [Stillstellung] as well. Where thinking suddenly comes to a stop in a constellation saturated with tensions, it gives that constella-

tion a shock, by which thinking is crystallized into a monad. The historical materialist approaches a historical object only where it confronts him as a monad. In this structure he recognizes the sign of a messianic arrest of happening, [. . .] a revolutionary chance in the fight for the oppressed past. He takes cognizance of it in order to blast a specific era out of the homogenous course of history.

(*SW* 4: 396 trans. mod.; *GS* 1.2: 702–3)

Celan's poem "IN ONE" does the work of the historical materialist described by Benjamin, blasting certain moments out of the course of history. It does so in order to bring them into another kind of alignment, to make them revolve not only around a particular date but also and above all around each another.[15] And it is in this doubly revolutionary movement that thinking suddenly comes to stop in what Benjamin calls "a constellation saturated with tensions." To arrest a movement of thought, for Benjamin, is thus not to stop thinking but rather to remain thoughtfully suspended in a pregnant pause, in a moment held in suspense, held open by the competing pull of various forces.

Having discussed the various events brought into alignment in the poem, I would like to turn now to the way the poem itself is structured as a highly dynamic constellation. To appreciate its dynamism, one must keep a number of things in mind: first, the many times gathered under the collective title "IN ONE" or "ALL IN ONE" ("IN EINS"); second, the constellation of dates orbiting around the same date, "thirteenth of February," which opens the poem and marks the second of its gravitational centers; third, the numerous political watchwords, rallying cries, and passwords gathered around the third focal point of the poem, the "Hebrew" word *Schibboleth* that appears in line two; and fourth, the four languages of the poem—French, Hebrew, German, and Spanish—which are associated not only with particular international and intranational alliances and the shibboleths that mark them but also with the question of inter- and intralingual translation, the fourth crux of the poem introduced by the end of the first strophe.

Not only does the poem effectively begin again with the entry of each of these four gathering centers, but, held open by the pull exerted by each of them, it traces the contours of a decentered constellation in which each of these mutually defining, circularly redefined gatherings appears to orbit elliptically around the others. Whereas the term "ellipsis" is commonly used to describe an oval-shaped orbital path traced around two fixed points or gravitational centers, here it is a question of four points whose positions are only first "fixed" through their differential relations to the others around which they turn and which, in turn, circle around them. It is this latter, more radical notion of an elliptical movement, a movement involving an incessant, open-ended process of circular redefinition that is condensed into Benjamin's notion of a constellation and is taken up by Celan in his own related notion of a *Kontur*.

A *Kontur* for Celan is at once a *con-turning* movement of multiple gatherings and the shifting *contours* of their mutating interrelationship.[16] As is the case in his 1960 *Meridian* address, such a movement is "elliptical" not only in the orbital sense of circularly con-turning points but also in the way that each gathering "center" of the poem is itself a *point of suspension*, an elliptical mark defined less by what and where it is than by the place it holds open in relation to the others. While "IN ONE" may be said to gather a number of related gatherings into itself, into one, it does so precisely to open each one (including itself) to the difference of the others.

As may be inferred from Derrida's reading of Celan, a poet who was himself a sensitive reader of Benjamin and who cited him at strategic moments in his own work, the accent in the Benjaminian notion of a *Konstellation* falls as much on the prefix *Kon-* (echoing the *mit-* used earlier) as on the stellar, reminding us of the *multiple suns* that hang in the heavens of the theses, hovering over them like a constellation of elliptically revolving, mutually recontextualizing citations.[17] Among the cited suns and mutually illuminating citations convoked in the course of the theses are the figure of the "citation à l'ordre du jour" (*SW* 4: 390; *GS* 1.2: 694); the reference to the end of days in the mention of the Last Judgment ("welcher Tag eben der jüngste ist") (*SW* 4: 390; *GS* 1.2: 694); the figure of a "secret heliotropism" (eines Heliotropismus geheimer Art) (*SW* 4: 390; *GS* 1.2: 694); and perhaps most enigmatically Benjamin's citation of a verse penned in French during the July Revolution of 1830. This citation appears in the fifteenth thesis and is prefaced by the following remarks:

> On the first evening of fighting, it so happened that the dials of the clocktowers were being fired at simultaneously and independently from several locations in Paris. An eyewitness, who may have owed his insight [seine Divination] to the rhyme, wrote as follows:

> Qui le croirait! On dit, qu'irrité contre l'heure,
> De nouveaux Josués, au pied de chaque tour,
> Tiraient sur les cadrans pour arrêter le jour.
>
> (Who would believe it! It said that, incensed at the hour,
> Latter-day Joshuas, at the foot of every clocktower,
> Were firing on clock faces to make the day stand still.)
>
> (*SW* 4: 395; *GS* 1.2: 702)

As Benjamin notes, the insight of this eyewitness, his "divination" of the deeper significance of this strange coincidence, may be indebted to a poetic exigency, to a certain reason of rhyme. Coupling *jour* and *tour*, the poet links an utterly unforeseeable, truly historical event, the simultaneous and spontaneous firing upon different clock towers around Paris, to another moment in which time is said to have been brought violently to a halt, the moment recounted in Joshua 10:13 in which the sun is said to have kept its place in the *middle of the heavens* and, *waiting*, did not go down for the space of a day. There was, as the biblical passage continues, "*no day like that, before it or after it.*"[18]

For Benjamin, as for Derrida and Celan, these poetically related moments are linked not only with a break in time, but moreover with an explosion of the continuum of history, an explosion that is itself associated with the inauguration of a revolutionary calendar and the introduction of ways of keeping time different from the "homogeneous, empty time" (*SW* 4: 395; *GS* 1.2: 701) so scathingly critiqued by Benjamin throughout this text.[19] Of particular relevance here is the way that time speeds up over the course of Benjamin's own theses, an acceleration reflexively marked by the introduction of the figure of time-lapse photography at the beginning of the fifteenth thesis. More importantly, as time speeds up in the movement from one thesis to the next, the temporal units to which Benjamin refers not only become smaller and smaller but also, at the same time, more concentrated, more explosively charged.[20] It is no accident in this regard that the theses end somewhat belatedly with two appendices, both of which speak of seconds and split seconds, the latter and more famous one concluding with a description of the second as "the strait gate through which the Messiah might enter" (die kleine Pforte, durch die der Messias treten konnte) (*SW* 4: 397 trans. mod.; *GS* 1.2: 704).[21]

Like Celan, Benjamin understands the "second" (*Sekunde*) not so much as a positive moment in time but rather as a cut, division, or opening within it. Like its English cognate, the German *Sekunde* derives from the Latin *secunda minuta*, the second minute, itself the "result of a second operation of sexagesimal division."[22] It is through such divisions within divisions—of hours into minutes, minutes into seconds, and seconds into split seconds—Benjamin suggests, that the Messiah might enter.[23]

In other words, rather than coming full circle with the completion of a revolutionary orbit around the same gravitational center, around the same fixed point or temporal unit, time may be opened, at each and every turn, to another order. Such openings may be said to split the present moment—understood as a positive, discrete unit of time, be it an hour, minute, second, or "now"—in the same way that the method of Benjamin's *Arcades Project* is said to split the atom or nucleus (*Kern*). "This work," he commented to Ernst Bloch of *The Arcades Project*, "comparable, in method, to the process of nuclear fission, liberates enormous energies of history that are bound up in the 'once upon a time' [es war einmal, or 'it was at one time'] of classical historiography" (*AP* 463; *GS* 5.1: 578).[24]

For Benjamin, the coming of the Messiah is thus associated less with the irruption of another temporal order, less with a time of redemption, an awakening of the dead or the piecing back together of a shattered world, than with a break in time that is also a lapse of consciousness, a gaping of the present that is also a lack of presence of mind.[25] It is through such moments freed from conscious control, through moments blasted out of the empty, homogeneous continuum of time, that pent up historical energies are released and we are given fleeting access to a certain historical unconscious. Such is the time frame of the clandestine appointment, or *geheime Verabredung*, of which Benjamin speaks, a time frame or mode of coming that will have been less a meeting, rendezvous or coming together, than a *circumvention* of the categories of presence in the future perfect tense.[26] This is no doubt why Benjamin refers to it as a *secret* appointment.

Benjamin, Suicide, and the Circumvention of Presence

The theses are themselves, of course, a historically charged text in which the author's tragic suicide in September 1940 at the French–Spanish frontier is itself inscribed.[27] In what follows I want to extend my very selective reading of the theses in two directions, discussing it first, in biographical terms, as the last in a series of "last wills and testaments" Benjamin wrote, wills that are themselves not by chance associated with the act of taking one's life. The second direction involves Benjamin's materialist reinterpretation of the theological, his understanding of Judgment Day as a revolutionary break in time, the kind of break to which an *unprecedented legal proceeding* might give place. Such a proceeding, Shoshana Felman has argued, was the 1961 Eichmann Trial.

I begin then with the biographical dimension, reading Benjamin's theses in the context of his other last wills and testaments. As Felman has already noted in *The Juridical Unconscious*, a text to which I will be returning often in what follows, Benjamin's 1932 autobiographical work, *Berlin Chronicle*, is not only explicitly dedicated to his son, Stephan, but is also implicitly addressed to him as a last will and testament. While Felman's pathbreaking work on Benjamin is an important touchstone for what follows, my interest in it is also motivated by a certain perplexity concerning her conspicuous and repeated use of terms like "prophecy," "clairvoyance," and "foresight."[28] Such terms rarely, if ever, appear in her writing—with the significant exception of her discussion of Mallarmé's *Crise de vers* in her book on testimony. There she writes, "In a way, Mallarmé suggests that he speaks too soon, before he is quite ready, before he quite knows what his subject is about [. . .]. He [. . .] speaks in advance of the control of consciousness; his testimony is delivered 'in breathless gasps': in essence, it is a *precocious testimony*."[29] At stake in what follows then is an attempt to understand various relations to the future—"prophecy," "clairvoyance," "foresight," and "speaking in advance of the control of consciousness"—in terms of trauma theory and, more specifically, in the temporal terms of the future perfect tense. Felman, I believe, uses this theologically loaded vocabulary in a pointedly ironic way, the only way perhaps to articulate the complex interaction of the theological and materialist dimensions of Benjamin's thought. Such an approach is reflected in my own notion of Benjaminian "ghostwriting" developed below.

"Upon writing *Berlin Chronicle*," Felman notes, "Benjamin had an imminent suicide plan in mind [. . .]. This is why, as a correlative or counterpart to the autobiographical *Chronicle*, Benjamin also left a will" (*JU* 51). The will contained two requests: first, that a portion of the proceeds from a posthumous edition of the author's own writings be sent to his son; second, that the writings of the brothers Fritz and Wolf Heinle—which Benjamin had edited after the suicide of his dear friend Fritz, who along with his girlfriend had taken his life in an act of uncompromising resistance against German militarism at the outbreak of World War I—find their way through another dear friend, Gershom Scholem, to the library of the Hebrew University of Jerusalem. "I think it would be nice," Benjamin wrote in a farewell letter to his cousin Egon Wissing in 1932, "if the manuscript department of the library of the University of Jerusalem [sic] accepted the posthumous writings of two non-Jews from the hands of two Jews—Scholem's and mine."[30]

Thus, the will concerns the future of two related editions of posthumous writing: Benjamin's own and that of the brothers Heinle, which he himself had edited. In his letter to his cousin Benjamin is particularly concerned with the hands through which the latter edition will pass. Let us dwell for a moment on the movement of these hands and the scene of transmission of which they are a part. On one level, this scene is very straightforward and involves only a linear passage of the posthumous writings of two non-Jews through the hands of two Jews en route to a final resting place in the Hebrew University of Jerusalem. Yet, on another level, the movement of these hands gestures toward another scene—*einen anderen Schauplatz*, as Freud would call it—in which an unconscious act of transmission is being performed, an act involving not just the transmission of posthumous editions but also the performance of a kind of ghostwriting.

To bring this scene into focus, it is necessary to read a number of texts together and, moreover, to read them in terms of what Benjamin would call a constellation, to read them, in other words, as textual fragments wrenched out their original context, out of a context in which they will never quite have fit. Yet, such an approach also, at the same time, means reading them as ill-fitting fragments brought into orbit around each other, as traumatic moments blasted out of the so-called continuum of history and left to be interpreted only in terms of their mutually unsettling, mutually illuminating relation to one another.

As was suggested earlier, the challenge in reading such constellations is to grasp them in their simultaneity, in their "all at once," their "now time"—or *Jetztzeit*, as Benjamin would call it—as out-of-place memory fragments standing in for and being circularly redefined by their mutually unsettling interrelationship. To be more specific, it is a question here of reading parts of Benjamin's autobiographical *Berlin Chronicle* in conjunction with the last will and testament he wrote at that time; the posthumous writings—both his own and those of his friends—mentioned in that will; Benjamin's theses on the philosophy of history, at once his final text and another last will and testament; and Scholem's biography of Benjamin, which is subtitled *The Story of a Friendship*.

Written in memory of his dear friend, Scholem's biography may also be read as a text haunted by the story of another friendship, a story Benjamin himself tries to tell in *Berlin Chronicle*, the story of his friendship with Fritz Heinle. Like Scholem's biography, Benjamin's autobiographical text is the story both of a friendship and of a friend's suicide. Unlike the biography, Benjamin's *Berlin Chronicle* is also a text written on the verge of suicide. It takes a number of hands to transmit this complicated story of double friendships and double suicides. As was noted earlier, it involves first and most obviously the passage of the posthumous writings of two non-Jews through the hands of two Jews. Yet it also involves a kind of writing from beyond the grave, a kind of ghostwriting, writing done not just on the verge of suicide but also as though the act had already been committed. It is in this sense that we may view Scholem's biography of Benjamin as a ghostwritten text: with one hand Scholem writes the story of a friendship, his own with Benjamin, while with another ghostly hand an Other writes itself under his name, secretly transmitting the story of another friendship, that of Benjamin and Heinle.[31]

I would like to turn now to the story of that other friendship, focusing on the moment in *Berlin Chronicle* when Benjamin describes his friend Heinle's August 8, 1914 suicide, four days after the German invasion of Belgium. Like the ill-fitting textual fragments to which I referred earlier, this traumatic moment stands out narratively and temporally from its surroundings. As Felman observes, "*Berlin Chronicle* cannot go directly either to the proper name of the dead friend or to the actual story of his death. Temporally as well as spatially, the story keeps moving in circles, as though around an empty, silent center. The word *suicide* does not figure in the text. Heinle's name is introduced as though in passing: it vanishes as soon as it is mentioned; and so does the event. Throughout the text, the name and the event keep vanishing" (*JU* 39).

That the moment of Heinle's suicide is indeed an "empty, silent center" in *Berlin Chronicle*, a gaping hole in time around which "the story keeps moving in circles," is nowhere more clearly marked than in the tense structure Benjamin uses to describe how he first received news of the event. "Later," he writes, "after the morning when an express letter awoke me with the words 'You *will find us lying* in the Meeting House'—when Heinle and his girlfriend *were dead*—the district remained for a period the central meeting place of the survivors" (Später—als der Morgen gekommen war, zu dem ein Eilbrief mich mit den Wörten geweckt hatte: 'Sie *werden uns im Heim liegen finden*'—als Heinle und seine Freundin *gestorben waren*, blieb diese Gegend noch eine Weile die Mitte für die Begegnungen der Überlebenden.) (*SW* 2: 604–5, trans. mod. and emphasis added; *GS* 5.1: 478).

As Felman notes, the "unnamed suicide takes place in the blank, the interval between a future—'you will find us'—and a past: 'were dead.'" (*JU* 41). This "interval" between a future and a past opens, in other words, as the gaping absence of a present, suggesting that this wound in time, this missing present, is also a gap in consciousness, an "unforgettable" moment. Yet, it is "unforgettable" not in any normal sense but rather in the way that memory fragments are, according to Freud, "most enduring when the incident that left them behind never entered consciousness" (*JU* 190, fn. 70). As was suggested in Chapter 1, the interval opened in Benjamin's text between a future—"you will find us"—and a past—"were dead"—gives us to understand the future perfect tense in a new way—namely, as the time frame of a relationship between past and future that is not mediated by the present. The present, as Benjamin says in the theses, is not a "transition" or "bridge" (*Übergang*) (*SW* 4: 396; *GS* 1.2: 702). Instead, the future perfect is the time frame of a past in which a future is already inscribed, in which Benjamin's subsequent suicide will in a sense have already taken place. Benjamin's writing on suicide, I would suggest, is always couched in the "now time" of the future perfect tense.[32] Like *Berlin Chronicle*, it is writing on the verge of a suicide already committed.

It is this strange temporal contortion to which Felman draws our attention when she writes, "[Benjamin's] own suicide *will repeat*, therefore, *and mirror* the suicide of his younger friend, *his alter ego*, at the outbreak of the First World War" (*JU* 48). In describing Heinle as Benjamin's "alter ego," Felman suggests that he is not just a close friend, double, or other self, but, more literally, that he marks a space of alterity within the self, keeping it from ever being one with or fully present to itself, and leaving it, as such, open, exposed, and vulnerable to the solicitations of the other, to that "secret appointment," *rendez-vous mystérieux*, or *geheime Verabredung* of which the second thesis speaks.

Apropos of the story of double friendships and double suicides we have been following, it is important to note that Heinle and his girlfriend—themselves already a double suicide—never get a *proper burial*. As Benjamin writes in *Berlin Chronicle*,

> And when, finally, after August 8, 1914, the days came when those among us who were closest to the dead couple did not want to part from them until they were buried, we felt the limits in the shame of being able to find refuge only in a seedy railway hotel on Stuttgart Square. Even the graveyard demonstrated the boundaries set by the city to all that filled our hearts: it was impossible to procure for the pair who died together graves in one and the same cemetery.
>
> (*SW* 2: 606; *GS* 5.1: 480)

Commenting on this passage, Felman suggests that Benjamin here circles back to the traumatic suicide of his friends by way of their improper burial, the one wound held open, amplified, and in a certain sense interpreted through its relation to the other. Thus, Felman writes,

> The most traumatic memory that Benjamin keeps from the war is [. . .] the added insult, the accompanying shame of the impossibility of giving the beloved corpse a proper burial, the shame of the incapability of taking leave of the dead bodies by giving them the final honor of a proper grave. It is because the bodies cannot be appropriately buried that the corpse of youth becomes a ghost that never will find peace. The grave, symbolically, cannot be closed. The event cannot be laid to rest. (*JU* 44)

Here as elsewhere in Felman's writings, the symbolically open grave stands as the figure of an unmournable loss, as the sign of the survivor's ongoing identification with the deceased, of an identification, one should note, that will be uncannily repeated in Benjamin's own *improper burial*. We know that Benjamin is buried in Port Bou on the French–Spanish border, but "nobody," writes Peter Demetz, "knows where."[33] In 1992, a monument was built. But Benjamin's body is not in the grave where the monument now stands (*JU* 49).[34] Not only does the one improper burial mirror and repeat the other, not only is the one implicated in and amplified by the other, but the two in turn also stand in their very lack of properness for those killed in the two World Wars, for those buried in anonymous mass graves, for those mass murders of the Holocaust and its airborne, unburied dead. These are the "stars of human making," the stars by which we are "overarched" that Celan describes in his Bremen address.[35]

The Eichmann Trial, K-Zetnik, and the Awakening of the Dead

At this point and in conclusion I would like to return to Benjamin's materialist reinterpretation of the theological and his understanding of Judgment Day as a revolutionary break in time, the kind of break to which an unprecedented legal proceeding might give place. Such a proceeding, Felman has argued, was the 1961 Eichmann Trial. Conducted in the new Jewish homeland of Israel, it differed in many significant ways from the Nuremberg Trials held in the immediate postwar years in occupied Germany. With this trial there is a shift from an international military tribunal to a national court action of international significance; from a multilingual trial conducted in German, English, French, and Russian to one whose official language was Hebrew; from a trial in which the prosecution's case was based overwhelmingly on written evidence and documents generated by the alleged perpetrators to one in which oral testimony and a historical narrative told from the victims' perspective played a crucial role; from a proceeding in which the defendants were tried under international law to one in which the accused was judged according to the law of one nation; from a trial in which the extermination of European Jewry was subsumed to a large extent into legal categories and historical narratives of a more political and military nature to one in which the Holocaust and crimes committed against the Jewish people were the primary concern.[36]

The central conflict of the trial may be seen as the struggle to reconcile the need to present a legally cogent indictment against a single defendant, Adolf Eichmann, with the need to dramatize the spectacular nature of the crimes of which he was accused (*JU* 102). Or as the chief Israeli prosecutor Gideon Hausner put it, "we needed more than a conviction, we needed a living record of a gigantic human and national disaster" (*JU* 106). In contrast, Hannah Arendt strongly objected to the use of the trial for purposes other than the strict administration of justice. "Justice," she writes in *Eichmann in Jerusalem*,

> demands that the accused be prosecuted, defended, and judged, and that all the other questions *of seemingly greater import*—of "How could it happen?" and "Why did it happen?," of "Why the Jews?" and "Why the Germans?," of "What was the role of other nations?" and "What was the extent of coresponsibility on the side of the Allies," of "How could the Jews through their own leaders cooperate in their own destruction?" and "Why did they go to their death like lambs to the slaughter?"—be left in abeyance. Justice insists on the importance of Adolf Eichmann [. . .]. On trial are his deeds, not the sufferings of the Jews, not the German people or mankind, not even anti-Semitism and racism.[37]

"Justice," she continues, "demands seclusion, it permits sorrow rather than anger, and it prescribes the most careful abstention from all the nice pleasures of putting oneself in the limelight" (*EJ* 6). At stake for Arendt is the very legitimacy of the proceedings, which she sees as being severely compromised by the pedagogical zeal of the prosecution. Its will to educate, to teach younger Israelis about "the ways in which their own flesh and blood had perished," to teach an oblivious world about "the horrors that occurred before its eyes," was precisely what Arendt objected to. For it risked turning the proceedings into a theatrical spectacle and, even worse, into a show trial (*EJ* 4). It is this danger that Arendt seeks to conjure in her repeated description of the house of justice as a theatrical space.

> Whoever planned this auditorium in the newly built *Beth Ha'am*, the House of the People, had a theater in mind, complete with orchestra and gallery, with proscenium and stage, and with side doors for the actors' entrance. Clearly, this courtroom is not a bad place for the show trial David Ben-Gurion, Prime Minister of Israel, had in mind [. . .]. And Ben-Gurion, rightly called "architect of the state," remains the invisible stage manager of the proceedings. (*EJ* 4–5)

In contrast to Arendt's reading of the trial in which its most famous moment of rupture, the falling unconscious of a witness known as K-Zetnik on the stand is treated with scorn and derision, Felman reads this moment as the emergence of meaning from the historical unconscious, as an unconscious rupture of the legal framework and, moreover, as the unprecedented advent of a legal narrative. Of significance to Felman is not only the fact that K-Zetnik lost consciousness on the witness stand but that this moment, "captured on film, left an indelible mark on the trial and has impressed itself on visual and historical memory. The courtroom scene," she notes,

> has since been broadcast many times on radio and television. Despite the repetition, the power of this legally compelling moment does not wane and its force of astonishment does not diminish and does not fade. It has remained a literally unforgettable key moment of the trial, a signal or a symbol of a constantly replayed and yet ungrasped, ungraspable kernel of collective memory. (*JU* 135)

For Felman, the constant replaying of this moment is indicative of its status as a traumatic flashback. It is a scene like the footage of Flight 175 striking the second of the Twin Towers on September 11, 2001, a shot played over and over again in the media, that has yet to be grasped and that continues to address us in its very ungraspability, an incessant address symbolized by its constant replaying.[38] It is the element of compulsive repetition, I would suggest, and not any mere polemic with Arendt, that draws Felman to this moment and causes her to analyze it as a symptom of something much larger. Thus, while K-Zetnik's fainting and his default as a witness illustrates for Arendt, as Felman puts it, "the folly of the prosecution in both its disrespect for legal relevance and in its narcissistic and misguided predilection for witnesses of prominence" (*JU* 143), Felman views K-Zetnik as a fragile human bridge spanning two utterly heterogeneous worlds. It is this bridge that collapses when demands placed on the witness from each side become too great, and it is at this moment that K-Zetnik falls into a coma.

As Felman notes, just

> prior to his fainting spell K-Zetnik had been trying to define Auschwitz by re-envisaging the terrifying moment of Selection, of repeated weekly separation between inmates chosen for an imminent extermination and inmates arbitrarily selected for life. This moment is ungraspable, the witness tries to say 'And the inhabitants of that planet had no names. They had neither parents nor children... They did not live, nor did they die, in accordance with the laws of this world. Their names were their numbers... They left me, they kept leaving me, left... for close to two years they left me and always left me behind... I see them, they are watching me, I see them.' (*JU* 147)

As the reader will have noticed, the witness uses only negative terms to describe "that planet" and the state of limbo in which its "inhabitants" were suspended, shifting at a significant moment in his testimony from the past into the present tense. Rather than simply bringing the past into the present, this shift marks a break in time, a sudden burst of "now time," a caesura in which an exchange of looks holds time open and at a standstill. "I see them, they are watching me, I see them," he says. What his words bear witness to is thus an unbreakable bond between seer and seen, held together in a vertiginous flash.[39]

Remaining bound to those departing through his constant reliving of this exchange of looks, K-Zetnik remains bound as well to a moment in which, as Felman observes, "life and death are separating but still tied up together" (*JU* 147). This is, in short, not a memory of the past but the ongoing reliving of a scene of departure that never leaves K-Zetnik, a scene in which he sees himself visually and existentially bound to those still watching him.

It should be noted that this witness who seeks to bridge the gap between the living and the dead in the course of his testimony goes by two names: the first, K-Zetnik, is like the inhabitants of the planet of which he speaks, no name but merely a generic term colloquially used to refer to concentration camp inmates; the second, Yehiel Dinoor, was a name he adopted upon emigration to Israel, the last name Dinoor meaning "a residue from the fire." It is by this latter name that one of the judges addresses him at the very moment in his testimony when he is giving an account of his other, adopted name "K-Zetnik." "*Mr. Dinoor*, please, please listen to Mr. Hausner and to me," says the presiding judge (*JU* 149). It is at this moment that K-Zetnik faints, a collapse Felman interprets as follows:

> K-Zetnik faints because he cannot be interpellated at this moment by his legal name, Dinoor: the dead still claim him as *their* witness, as K-Zetnik who belongs to them and is still one of them. The court reclaims him as *its* witness, as Dinoor. He cannot bridge the gap between the two names and the two claims. He plunges into the abyss between the different planets. On the frontier between the living and the dead, between the present and the past, he falls as though he himself were a corpse. (*JU* 149)

To complicate matters even further, the Israeli judge who addresses the witness by his Hebrew name and summons him in a sense to return to his place among the living, is for K-Zetnik an authority figure in whose voice he hears that of another. As Felman explains,

> When the judge admonishes Dinoor from the authoritarian position of the bench, coercing him into a legal mode of discourse and demanding his cooperation as a witness, K-Zetnik undergoes severe traumatic shock in re-experiencing the same terror and panic that dumbfounded him each time when, as an inmate, he was suddenly confronted by the inexorable Nazi authorities of Auschwitz. The judges' words are heard not as an utterance originating from the present courtroom situation but as a censure uttered from within "the other planet," as an intrusive threat articulated right out of the violence of the traumatic scene that is replaying in K-Zetnik's mind. The call to order by the judge urging the witness to obey—strictly to answer questions and to follow legal rules—impacts the witness *physically* as an invasive call to order by an SS officer [. . .]. Panicked, K-Zetnik loses consciousness.
> (*JU* 146)

Yet, tellingly and I think most importantly for Felman, this moment of breakdown in the trial, this loss of consciousness of a witness on the stand, is also at the same time the moment when meaning emerges from the historical unconscious as an unconscious rupture of the legal framework, and, moreover, as the unprecedented advent of a legal narrative. Such a narrative, she argues, does not simply *give voice* to what had heretofore been silenced, to the history of the oppressed, but, more radically, it *gives place* to the silent shadow or negative of the proceedings, doing so in such a way that the presences and voices of the trial are suddenly set in *counterpoint* to its absences and silences. The Auschwitz survivor K-Zetnik's falling silent and unconscious on the witness stand not only marks a limit of legal speech and the conscious parameters of the trial, it also inadvertently "awakens the dead" (*SW* 4: 392; *GS* 1.2: 697).[40]

In contrast to more traditional notions of Judgment Day, of messianic coming and the end of time, here the "awakened dead" do not simply come back, resurrected and restored into life. Instead, awakened paradoxically *as the dead*, the *Schmattes* and *Figuren* heretofore denied the dignity of burial—the "rags" and "puppets" heretofore refused the linguistic status even of corpses and human remains—return as revenants whose very absence and silence become for the first time hauntingly "present" and mutely "resonant" in the Israeli courtroom. It is the ghostly presence and resonant silence of the awakened dead that transform the proceedings into an unprecedented dialogue between speech and silence, between consciousness and the unconscious, the living and the dead.

It is this type of dialogue, Felman suggests, to which Benjamin seems to allude in his early text on "The Metaphysics of Youth" when he writes,

> Conversation strives toward silence, and the listener is really the silent partner [*der Schweigenspartner*, a term coined on the model of—and in pointed contrast to—the more familiar term for interlocutor, *Gesprächspartner*]. The speaker receives meaning from [this silent partner]; the silent one is the unappropriated source of meaning.
>
> (*SW* 1: 6; *GS* 2.1: 91)

THREE

Pendant: Celan, Büchner, and the Terrible Voice of the Meridian

A posteriori—that's how everything begins.
— BÜCHNER, *Leonce and Lena* (1.3)

In his 1960 *Meridian* address, delivered on the occasion of receiving the Büchner Prize for Literature, the poet Paul Celan pinpoints a central organizing moment in the work of the nineteenth-century writer and dramatist in whose name the award was given. While winners of the Büchner prize are generally expected to reflect in their acceptance speeches on their relations to the writer, Celan's address goes well beyond the level of artistic reflection, turning repeatedly about a pivotal moment in Büchner's work, a moment with which it makes contact and on which it in many ways remains stuck. That moment, as the title of Celan's speech suggests, is associated with the time of day when the sun is directly overhead, standing majestically at the zenith of its movement across the heavens.[1]

It is a moment that recurs at critical points in Büchner's plays and prose works. Yet its value is not always the same. Indeed, what is gathered together at this privileged point in time, what is brought to a head in the punctuality of this moment are at least three competing values, three mutually exclusive ways of understanding the significance of this moment. In Büchner's work the noontide meridian is at once a moment of absolute sovereignty, a point of stasis and traumatic fixation, and the site of a possible opening toward what is yet to come.

The focus of this chapter will be twofold. I propose to approach Büchner through Celan, concentrating both on that overdetermined highpoint in his work to which the poet draws our attention, and on that moment in Celan's own speech when questions of sovereignty and temporality come together and ultimately usher in a very different notion of poetic majesty. I am referring to that moment in Celan's *Meridian* address when he discusses the famous last words of Büchner's 1835 play, *Danton's Death*.

To understand the effect of these last words, it is necessary to recall the specific context in which they are uttered. At this point in the play Danton and many of his circle, including the pamphleteer and journalist Camille Desmoulin, have already been sent to their deaths at the Place de la Révolution by Robespierre. In the scene immediately following their execution, Desmoulin's bereaved widow, Lucille, appears alone on stage. Isolated in her grief, she is painfully cut off from the comprehension of her surroundings. Her world has effectively come to an end, yet, as she observes,

> Everything else is allowed to go on living [. . .]. Everything's astir; clocks tick, bells ring, folk pass, water flows, everything continues just as before, for ever and ever. —But no! It mustn't happen, no! I shall sit on the ground and scream, so everything stops, shocked into stillness, not a flicker of movement. [She sits down, covers her eyes, and screams. After a pause, she stands up.] It makes no difference. Things are just as they were. The houses, the street. The winds blow, the clouds drift. —Perhaps we just have to bear it [Wir müssen's wohl leiden].[2]

Just as Lucille's words have no impact whatsoever on the world around her, so too is she herself now absorbed into the crowd of women joining her on stage. Yet, the speech act that so badly misfires in this scene—the cry that was to have shocked everything into stillness and brought time itself to a halt—will be performed again in the next scene. Whereas Lucille's first scream fails to stop anything, her last words—"Long live the King!," (*CPLOW* 4.7: 73; *WBMA* 133) hurled in the direction of a patrol entering the Place de la Révolution—lead to her immediate arrest. These words, which will in fact be her self-imposed death sentence, also effectively stop the play itself dead in its tracks.

For Celan, these suicidal words uttered at the edge of silence, these cutting words on which a curtain of silence falls like the guillotine, stand in sharp contrast to the prolixity and grandiloquence of the only other scene set at the Place de la Révolution. "They are all there," Celan says of this scene, "Danton, Camille, and the rest. They do not lack words, even here, artful, resonant words, and they get them out. Words—in places Büchner need only quote—about going to their death together" (*CP* 39; *GW* 3:189). Whereas these all too theatrical deaths are for Celan nothing more than a "triumph of 'puppet' and 'string,'" Lucille's last cry is described by him as a *Gegenwort*, a "word against the grain," a razor-edged word that, as he says, "cuts the 'string,' and does not bow to the 'bystanders and old warhorses of history.' It is an act of freedom. It is a step" (*CP* 40; *GW* 3:189).

It is at this point in Celan's speech that the questions of sovereignty and temporality, to which I referred at the outset, come together. "True," Celan concedes, "Lucille's 'Long live the King' sounds at first like a profession of faith to the 'ancien régime.' But it is not . . . this is not homage to any monarchy, to any yesterday worth preserving. It is homage to the majesty of the absurd which bears witness to human presence [Gehuldigt wird hier der für die Gegenwart des Menschlichen zeugenden Majestät des Absurden]. This, ladies and gentlemen," he adds, "has no definitive name, but I believe that it is . . . poetry" (*CP* 40 trans. mod.; *GW* 3:190).

Thus, according to Celan, Lucille's apparent homage to the king must also be read as an act of betrayal. Indeed, what it betrays, what it lets slip, is a secret allegiance to another majesty, to one, moreover, that appears to have no definitive name and that perhaps can only be hailed in the guise of another.[3] Lucille's counterword is thus not only sharp enough to cut the strings of theatrical artifice, but sufficiently doubled-edged to inscribe within an avowed movement of return to the old regime a tentative opening toward a new majesty, an opening, Celan suggests, that could not have been made in any more decisive or direct way. What, precisely, is promised or announced through this opening in Büchner's drama?

To trace the contours of this uncertain opening, it is necessary to focus more directly on those meridianal moments that play such a capital role in Büchner's work. As his 1836 comedy *Leonce and Lena* makes abundantly clear, the meridian is itself a sovereign moment. Indeed, high noon marks the point in the play at which a number of mutually reinforcing values associated with a very traditional, decidedly *ancien régime* notion of majesty come together. Telling in this regard is the way the monarch of the play, King Peter, makes plans to have his son's wedding—his *Hochzeit*, literally his "high time"—start punctually at the stroke of noon.[4] The timing of the ceremony is all the more significant given the fact that, upon marriage, Prince Leonce is immediately to take his father's place on the throne. "It is the supreme royal will," Leonce is told, "that on the day of your wedding all the instruments of the most supreme royal will shall pass into your Highness's hands." (An dem Tage ist ein höchster Wille gesonnen, seine allerhöchsten Willensäußerungen in die Hände Eurer Hoheit niederzulegen.) (*CPLOW* 1.3: 89; *WBMA* 170). The wedding ceremony is thus also in effect to be a rite of succession.

As the crowning moment approaches, however, the prince is nowhere to be seen. Growing ever more anxious, the king turns to his master of ceremonies and asks whether the borders of the realm are being watched. "Yes, your Majesty: the view from this room here allows us to keep the most rigorous watch" (*CPLOW* 3.3: 103; *WBMA* 184). This act of surveillance performed on the monarch's behalf reminds us of his own synoptic perspective, of the way he stands not only at the head of state but also literally at the highest point in the land. While the task of keeping watch over the borders of the realm may be delegated to others, it is the king's all-encompassing look that first defines those frontiers, actively gathering the kingdom together in the embrace of a sovereign eye. Not only does King Peter thus stand in the same structural position as the sun directly overhead, but the analogy between them also implicitly serves to elevate and naturalize his position of authority.[5]

Of course, the prince and princess of the play do eventually come into view. In one of those odd theatrical scenes that endeared Büchner to the Expressionists and Brecht alike, the prince and the princess appear not as themselves but as actors playing actors, as automata mechanically reciting words put in their mouths by others. Bearing in mind Celan's remarks about Lucille and her double-edged way of hailing a new majesty of the absurd in the guise of pledging allegiance to an old sovereign, consider the fool Valerio's introduction of the masked prince and princess. "What I really wanted to do," he says, was to announce to this noble and venerable company the arrival of these two world-famous automata. I would have added that I am perhaps the third and the oddest of them all—*if*, that is, I myself actually knew for certain who I am, though no one by the way should be surprised that I don't, since I myself know nothing of what I say, and don't even know that I don't know, so that it's highly probable that I am simply being *made* to talk like this [daß man mich nur so reden l ä ß t], and that in reality it is nothing but cylinders, pipes, and windbags speaking these words of mine.

In a mechanical, rasping voice, he then adds, "Ladies and gentleman, you see before you two persons of opposite sex, a male and a female, a gentleman and a lady. Nothing but cunning clockwork, nothing but springs and pasteboard" (*CPLOW* 3.3: 105; *WBMA* 186).

One begins to get a sense here of how problematic that "human presence" of which Celan speaks may be, that *Gegenwart des Menschlichen* to which the majesty of the absurd is said to bear witness. Indeed, as we have already begun to suspect, what may perhaps come to define the human in both Büchner and Celan is precisely its lack of self-presence, its constitutive openness to the other, its way of coming upon another in the very place of a sovereign self, upon the uncanny otherness of this self.

Telling in this regard is the way the moment of the meridian in Büchner stands not merely as a sovereign gathering point, but also, at the same time, as an open wound, a gash in the heavens, out of which a terrible voice begins to speak. I am referring to that moment in *Woyzeck* when the title character asks the physician, who had just been chastising him for answering a call of nature in public, whether he has ever caught sight of the other side, or doubleness, of nature: "Doktor, haben Sie schon was von der doppelten Natur gesehen?" "Sometimes," Woyzeck continues, "when the sun's up high in the middle of the day and it seems like the world is bursting into flames, this terrible voice starts talking to me." The English translation does not capture Woyzeck's startling and ungrammatical speech that goes beyond a simple representation of dialect: "Wenn die Sonn in Mittag steht und es ist als ging die Welt in Feuer auf hat schon eine fürchterliche Stimme zu mir geredt!" (*CPLOW* 8: 122; *WBMA* 243).

Here something appears to intervene—or to have already intervened—at the very instant when the sun, closing yet another cycle, returns to its sovereign point of origin. It is through this momentary gap in time that a voice begins to talk—or has already spoken, as Büchner seems to imply. This voice addresses Woyzeck as though it itself were now speaking through lips opening in the sky above. We will return to this uncanny pairing of human faces and heavenly countenances in a moment.[6] Yet before asking with Woyzeck what it might indeed mean to catch sight of the doubleness of nature, it is necessary to consider the peculiar timing of this scene. That the voice in question starts talking at the instant when, as Woyzeck says, "the sun's high up in the middle of the day," is particularly telling given the course of the title character's own life. "Slow down, Woyzeck, slow down: one foot after the other," [Langsam, Woyzeck, langsam; ein's nach dem andern!] a captain in his regiment tells him as the poor and obviously very high-strung soldier gives him an uncomfortably close and rapid shave *(CPLOW* 5: 164; *WBMA* 239). Apparently more concerned about the time than his own skin, the captain continues,

> You're making me quite giddy. What on earth am I to do with the spare ten minutes if you finish too early today? Woyzeck, just think, you've still got a good thirty years to live, thirty years! That's 360 months, not to mention the days, the hours, the minutes! What are you going to do with all this vast expanse of time? Pace it, Woyzeck, pace it! [Teil Er sich ein, Woyzeck.] I really get frightened for the world when I think of eternity. Activity, Woyzeck, activity! Eternal means eternal, it means *eternal*, you must see that; and yet again it's not eternal, it's an instant, a single instant [ein Augenblick]—Woyzeck, it makes me shudder when I think that the world revolves in a single day, what a waste of time, where's it all going to end? Woyzeck, I can't bear to see a millwheel turning any more—it makes me melancholic.
> (*CPLOW* 1: 18–9; *WBMA* 239–40)[7]

If it is important to know at this point exactly how much time Woyzeck still has to live, if the mention of his remaining thirty years leads to such complex and seemingly absurd calculations on the part of the captain, it is because, as we later learn from Woyzeck himself, he already has a good thirty years behind him—thirty years, seven months, and twelve days, to be exact (*CPLOW* 20: 132; *WBMA* 250). The captain's calculations thus place Woyzeck precisely at the midday of his life.[8] What is more, to be situated in this way is to find oneself halfway to sixty, suspended between two incompatible interpretations of thirty: it is either, as the captain says, an eternity or a single instant.⁹ The point, however, is that it is impossible to choose between these alternatives, a point the captain himself seems to make when he asks Woyzeck in another apparent digression what the weather is like that day. "Bad, sir, bad wind," Woyzeck says. "Yes, yes," the captain replies. "I can tell: it's all sort of rushing by out there [s'ist so was Geschwindes draussen]. Gives me such a turn, a wind like that does . . . I reckon it's a southerly-northerly" "Ja wohl, Herr Hauptman!" "Ha! ha! ha! Southerly-northerly," the captain repeats *(CPLOW* 6: 119; *WBMA* 240).

The joke is bad and even worse for having been made at Woyzeck's expense. Its point, however, is to suggest that Woyzeck is himself suspended at the midday of life, held in place by forces, like the southerly-northerly winds blowing through the play at this moment, that come from two opposing directions at once. He is forced, in other words, to experience this moment of suspension as an eternal instant, as an eternity compressed in an instant, in one so intense it seems to go on forever, in one so traumatic it seems never to let go or to admit of any closure.¹⁰

To be suspended at the midday of his life is thus, for Woyzeck, to be ceaselessly exposed to the terrible voice of the meridian. If we know less at this point about what this voice says than what it does, it is because its saying is itself a doing. And indeed what it does is bear down on Woyzeck as though with the full weight of the sun overhead, inflaming and provoking him to no end. "It seems," as he says, "like the world is bursting into flames." The voice is itself a shadowless illumination, one that penetrates Woyzeck's innermost places and leaves him with nowhere to hide. So inescapable is the call of this voice, so viciously circular is it in its relentless pursuit of him that the more Woyzeck runs away from it, the closer he appears to get to it.

To see what this voice does to Woyzeck is also, as he himself suggests, to begin to view nature in a different way. "Doctor," he asks, "have you ever caught sight of the doubleness of nature" *(CPLOW* 8:122; *WBMA* 243)? To view nature in this way, Büchner implies, is to see it first as a nightmarish landscape, as a place where haunting voices begin to speak through disembodied lips opening in the clear countenance of the heavens. Yet, we might also understand this doubleness in terms of Woyzeck's flight *toward* a voice he cannot avoid, a voice from above that he is bound to hear again in what speaks to him from below. Consider in this regard the scene in which he finds himself all alone on an open field at night. Bending toward the ground, he asks, "Ah, what's that? What's that you say? Louder, louder—stab, stab the wolf bitch dead? [stich, stich, die Zickwolfin tot?] [. . .] Shall I? Must I? Can I hear it there too? Does the wind say it too? Will I go on hearing it over and over: stab, stab,—stab her dead?" *(CPLOW* 14: 129; *WBMA* 248).

In the following scene this imperious voice returns, speaking to Woyzeck now through the walls of his room. "Can't you hear it?" he asks his friend Andres. "'Stab! Stab!' it keeps on saying and there's a feeling between my eyes like a knife cutting through [und zieht mir zwischen den Augen wie ein Messer]" *(CPLOW* 15: 129; *WBMA* 248). Like all the cuts in Büchner's work, the voice Woyzeck hears at this point is itself double-edged, doing repeatedly to him precisely what it tells him over and over again to do to another. So intense is the doubling, so reversible are the positions of self and other, that there is no longer any difference between active and passive voice, between being stabbed by a piercing command and being driven by that command to knife another.[11]

Whereas in *Leonce and Lena* the meridian is a majestic high point in time, in *Woyzeck* it is a kind of puncture wound, a gaping hole in time. Looking up at the heavens as though contemplating the significance of this moment, the title character says, "the sky has such a nice, firm, rough-cast look, it makes you want to bang a nail into it and hang yourself, just because of the tiny line—the *Gedankenstrichel*—between yes and no, d'you see, sir, yes and no? Is no to blame for yes or yes for no? I'll have to think it over" *(CPLOW* 9: 124; *WBMA* 245).[12] Here the meridian is figured as an overdetermined locus of suspension: while the nail hole suggests a gap in time inscribed on the face of the heavens, the rope dangling from it is one from which a person could hang himself, a tiny line—a *Gedankenstrichel*—upon which yes and no themselves appear to hang uncertainly and reversibly from each other.

Another such meridianal moment is to be found in *Danton's Death*. Only here, in the place of the sun, it is the "fiery star" (*Haarstern*) of the *stella syphilitica* that stands directly overhead; in place of the hanging line of the *Gedankenstrichel*, a human spinal cord. Thus, Collot tells Barrère, "your spinal cord is shriveling in [the] scorching radiance [of this star]" *(CPLOW* 3.6: 56; *WBMA* 117). Emphasizing the rope-like status of this cord, Billard adds immediately, "Before long the pretty little fingers of his delightful mistress Demahy will yank it from its casing and dangle it down his back like a pigtail" (Nächstens werden die niedlichen Finger der reizenden Demahy es ihm aus dem Futteral ziehen und es als Zöpchen über den Rücken hinunter hängen machen) (*CPLOW* 3.6: 57; *WBMA* 117).

Büchner's figuration of the meridian as a *Gedankenstrichel* in *Woyzeck* and as a spinal cord in *Danton's Death* serves not only to underscore its status as an overdetermined moment of suspension and traumatic fixation in his plays but also to forge an unexpected link between his literary and scientific work. Of particular relevance here is his 1836 anatomical treatise, *Mémoire sur le système nerveux du barbeau* (*Treatise on the Nervous System of the Barbel*). With the choice of this topic for his doctoral dissertation, Büchner sought to contribute to the solution of a silent but nonetheless poignant problem in early nineteenth-century brain anatomy. The problem was that the cerebral spheres were generally seen as symmetrical, but no adequate reason for this symmetry had yet to be found. Apropos of the figure of the spinal cord as a dangling *Gedankenstrichel*, it should further be noted that what was in dispute with regard to the *barbeau* was not only the question of symmetry or the number of nerves that connect the fish's brain to the rest of its nervous system but also where exactly the fish's brain begins and how its relationship to the spinal cord should be understood.

Büchner's anatomical study of the *barbeau* helps bring into focus a more general preoccupation with the place of the head in the body of his work. Of note are not only the decapitated and upside-down hanging heads of *Danton's Death* but also the author's peculiar way of opening each of his other literary works with a reference to the place, function, or precarious status of the head. Thus, *Lenz* begins with an expression of the title character's frustration at not being able to walk on his head ("nur war es ihm manchmal unangenehm, daß er nicht auf dem Kopf gehn konnte") (*CPLOW* 141; *WBMA* 137), while *Leonce and Lena* opens with the prince's wish to see himself on his head ("O wer sich einmal auf den Kopf sehen könnte!") (*CPLOW* 1.1: 79; *WBMA* 161). Though the exact sequence of scenes in *Woyzeck* remains open to dispute, it is not uncommon for editors to place the main character's description of a spoke-like, quill-covered head rolling over the grass at the very beginning ("da rollt Abends der Kopf, es hob ihn einmal einer auf, er meinte es wär ein Igel") (*CPLOW* 1.1: 113; *WBMA* 235).

While the placement of the head at the head of the Büchnerian corpus may thus be said to superimpose the human on the textual, Woyzeck's description of a bodiless head as a full-bodied hedgehog invites us to consider how the human intersects with the animal as well. Indeed, if it is quite literally a question here of intersection, it is because a cut human head and a cutting animal body are brought together. Made to intersect in this way, the two cut a new figure, the pointedly double-edged image of a rolling head that is at once cut and cutting at every point, at each and every turn of its spherical structure. As such, it reminds us of the title character's own trenchant gait. "Woyzeck," the person known only as Captain (*Hauptmann*) tells him, "you rush through the world like an open razor, you'll cut us all to ribbons . . ." (Er läuft ja wie ein offnes Rasiermesser durch die Welt, man schneidt sich an Ihm . . .) (*CPLOW* 9: 123 trans. mod.; *WBMA* 244).

Given all these heads that ironically and indecisively cut both ways, that are left hanging between the activity of cutting and the passivity of being cut in the grammatical suspension of the middle voice that plays such a crucial role in the Büchnerian corpus, it is important to recall that the fish Büchner dissects in his anatomical studies is one that not only has no neck that would indicate where exactly the head begins, but, as Müller-Sievers observes, "has in contrast to Lenz, the ability to walk on its head, thus eliminating the horizon in which its up-down direction could be stabilized."[13]

While questions of orientation are often explicitly thematized in Büchner's scientific and literary works, nowhere are they more implicit or of greater structural significance than in his unfinished play *Woyzeck*. As John Reddick points out, "the first thing to be said about this most famous and influential of Büchner's plays is that, strictly speaking, it does not exist. Any supposedly 'complete' version . . . is necessarily a makeshift, a patchwork assembled . . . by its particular editor, since Büchner left nothing but incomplete manuscripts when he died so unexpectedly in February 1837."[14] Given the absence of a definitive version of the drama, the editorial reshuffling to which its scenes have been subjected is certainly understandable. Yet, I would suggest that this perpetual re-ordering of the text may also bear witness to the insistence of something static and unassimilable within it. It is as though there were some kind of fatal impulse already at work in the play, something that kept it moving in place and that kept repeating itself from place to place.

I have tried to suggest some of the ways in which this compulsion to repeat is associated with the moment of the meridian. In turning now to the end of the play—if we may still speak at this point in such linear terms—I want to examine how the modes of suspension we have come to associate with this eternal instant transform a seemingly straightforward scene in which Woyzeck appears to do nothing more than toss a knife in a pond into a hallucinatory scene of traumatic repetition. Woyzeck goes to the pond in order to dispose of the weapon he has just used to murder his lover, Marie. Standing at the water's edge, he cries:

> Here it goes! [He throws the knife in the water.] It's sinking in the dark water like a stone! The moon's like a bloody knife! Is the whole world going to give me away? No, it's too close in, when they go swimming—[he enters the pool and throws the knife further out]. There! But how about the summer when they dive for mussels?—but no, it'll rust. Someone might recognize it.—Wish I'd broken it in pieces! Is there blood on me still? I need to wash myself. There's a stain! And there's another!
> (CPLOW 26: 137; WBMA 254–55)

Thrusting the bloody knife into this dark body of water, Woyzeck pierces its smooth surface as though stabbing Marie yet again. There where his knife parts the water, phantom lips appear to open.[15] Hearing their cry, Woyzeck abruptly shifts from the exclamatory to the interrogatory mode and asks, "Is the whole world going to give me away?" Not only do the violently parted lips, opened by the very gesture of burying the knife in silence, threaten to betray Woyzeck's deed to the world but, bleeding into the pond, they also turn it literally into a bloodbath. Wading into the pool, Woyzeck seems at once to immerse himself in the blood and to cleanse himself with the water. Unable to do either the one or the other, he can only repeat the initial gesture of throwing away the knife. Thrusting it yet again, this time more deeply into the body of water, Woyzeck cannot help but incise yet another pair of lips in the pond, lips which now appear as the mussels people will be diving for in the summer months ahead. If the association of lips with mussels implies that the violence still to be wrought upon the latter in prying them open has already been done to the former, more generally it suggests that the entire scene be read in the repetitive temporal framework of the future anterior. The particular use of the term *Muscheln* also suggests that these lips, which will have been prized open like bivalves, are themselves organs that, in parting, disclose other organs—in this case ears, or *Ohrmuscheln*, that are penetrated in their turn by piercing cries resounding in the depths.[16] As Woyzeck immerses himself more deeply in the pond, in this sea of severed organs, the contours of his own body begin to dissolve. If he feels the need to wash himself so compulsively, finding ever more bloodstains on his own skin, it is no doubt because the stabbing wounds repeatedly inflicted on the spectral body of his lover have now begun to open like stigmata on his own. What is reenacted here is not only the scene of Marie's violent murder but also another, less easily identifiable trauma—one that hovers more massively and hauntingly over Büchner's text and that we have come to associate with the eternal instant of the meridian.[17]

We encounter this moment again in *Danton's Death* in a scene carefully timed to culminate at the stroke of midnight. As it opens, we find Danton standing by the window, having just been awoken by a terrifying scream.

> Danton: Is it never going to stop? Will the glare never pale, the roar never die? Will it never be dark and still, so we're no longer forced to see and hear our horrible sins?—September!—
>
> [. . .]
>
> Julie [enters]: Why are you shouting?
>
> Danton: Shouting? Was I shouting?
>
> Julie: You called out something about "horrible sins," and then you moaned "September"!
>
> Danton: Me, me? It wasn't me that spoke, scarcely me that even thought such secret, silent thoughts.
>
> Julie: You're shaking, Danton.
>
> Danton: Aren't I right to shake, when even the walls begin to talk? When my body's so broken that my thoughts escape and scatter and speak with lips of stone? It's all so strange. [. . .] I don't want to think at all any more if it's going to mean these voices. Julie, there are thoughts that no ear should hear. It's a terrible thing if they holler and scream like babies the moment they're born, a terrible thing. [. . .] The scream was "September": isn't that what you said?
>
> Julie: Yes, Danton, I heard it ringing through every room.
>
> Danton: When I got to the window—[he looks out] the city's quiet, the light's all out . . .
>
> [. . .]
>
> Danton: When I got to the window, a single word howled and screamed through all the streets: "September!"
>
> Julie: Be strong, Danton: you were dreaming, that's all.
>
> (*CPLOW* 2.5: 37–38; *WBMA* 98–99)

Standing by the window as the scene opens, Danton does not know whether the piercing cry he hears has come from inside or out. Without origin and without end, it rings through his shaking body and reverberates from room to room, speaking through the walls of the house and echoing through all the neighboring streets. This wandering cry, Danton says, itself gives voice to "unsteady, errant thoughts" (Gedanken, unstät, umirrend) (*CPLOW* 2.5: 37 trans. mod; *WBMA* 98), thoughts that take him back to the September days of 1792 when, in the general hysteria stirred up by the threat from the Austrian and Prussian armies, the prisons of Paris were invaded and at least 1,400 inmates—more than half the total prison population—were systematically butchered (*CPLOW* 223, n. 25). While Danton, serving as Minister of Justice at the time, did not instigate these massacres, he did know they were due to happen, refused to prevent them, and, once they had begun, allegedly justified them as an "indispensable sacrifice."

"September" is thus a date that minds Danton to the point of obsession, a date he cannot help but remain mindful of. As noted in Chapter 2, it is this double sense of "minding" that is evoked in Celan's *Meridian* address when he uses the term *eingedenk bleiben* to characterize the novelty of poems written today: "daß hier am deutlichsten versucht wird, solcher Daten eingedenk zu bleiben" (*CP* 47; *GW* 3:196). For Celan, "attempting to remain mindful of such dates" means being doubly bound to them as their captivated keepers. Thus, when he asks, "Aber schreiben wir uns nicht alle von solchen Daten her? Und welchen Daten schreiben wir uns zu?" (*GW* 3:196), it is not merely a question of actively "writing ourselves from and toward such dates" but also, at the same time, of being passively written by them—of having such dates ascribed to us, inscribed and incised upon us.

"September" is in this sense the circular itinerary written on Danton, the one he is compelled to trace as he is summoned to return time and again to the meridian where time will have stood still for him. It is this traumatic puncture wound, this abyssal point in time, from which he will never have emerged except in the most superficial way. "September" is a date that inhabits him, keeping him as he keeps it lodged in the labyrinth of the ear. Incapable of being either removed or assimilated, this wandering cry remains stuck and suspended there like a thought too painful to hear as such. "There are thoughts," he tells Julie, "which no ear should hear."

Like the nightmare of the September days, the scene in which those days are re-dreamt carries over beyond its own apparent end. Danton is about to be arrested. As a mob gathers outside his house, one of its leaders, a theater prompter named Simon, asks, "How far into the night are we?" "How *what*?" a citizen replies.

> Simon: How far's the night?
> 1st Citizen: About as far as from dusk to dawn, I reckon [So weit als zwischen Sonnenuntergang und Sonnenaufgang].
> Simon: Bugger you, what's the time?
> 1st Citizen: Try looking at your watch. It's the time when all those stiff little pendulums stop swinging beneath the bed sheets [es ist die Zeit, wo die Perpendikel unter den Bettdecken ausschlagen].
> Simon: Let's go and get him! Come on, you lot! Dead or alive, or it's curtains for us.
>
> (*CPLOW* 2.6: 39; *WBMA* 100)

Reaching its belated climax at the stroke of the nocturnal meridian, the scene within the house carries over into the one set just outside. Made to overlap in this way, the two scenes mark the moment when time again comes to a standstill, when the stiff little pendulums beating under the sheets stand straight up and down. This point of temporal disjunction is marked in spatial terms as an interval between inside and out. While the interior scene opens with Danton standing absently at the window, the one taking place just outside closes with the assembled citizens forcing their way into the house to arrest Danton on orders from Robespierre. In a sense this arrest does little more than literalize Danton's own sense of being suspended at a point where time not only stands still for him but also does so precisely to the extent that it moves forwards and backwards at once; that is, it moves back to the executions of September and ahead to Danton's own beheading, ahead to the guillotine as the belated repetition of an unassimilable past, back to the date in which the future beheading was already *eingeschrieben*, inscribed in the belated temporality of the future anterior.

"September" is at once the date that wakes him and the date to which he is condemned to awaken, a past returning as though from the future, a trauma he is condemned to relive in every waking moment. The trauma of these September days may well have resonated in Büchner's obsessive preoccupation with the fate of Friedrich Ludwig Weidig, with whom he wrote *The Hessian Messenger*. Describing Büchner's "delirious ravings" on his Zurich deathbed in 1837, Reinhold Grimm speaks of how

> he is haunted by hallucinations of being arrested and extradited to his homeland; he is obsessed with the ghastly lot of his fellow conspirators imprisoned there, such as Friedrich Ludwig Weidig, the co-author of that subversive pamphlet . . . which brought about Büchner's flight from his native country and Weidig's close confinement in a dungeon. In point of fact, this Lutheran minister and upright democrat, having been tortured for two years, both physically and mentally, will die in Hesse (murdered, as some maintain, or, in any case, systematically driven to suicide) only fours days after the political refugee expires in Swiss exile.[18]

Poetic Interventions

Like so many of Büchner's works, Celan's own speech, to which I now turn in conclusion, circles obsessively around the moment of the meridian. Yet, as we shall see, his particular way of intervening in the closed circle of traumatic fixation and compulsive repetition we have come to associate with this moment is to pay special attention to all the dead ends one encounters in Büchner. Celan reads these endings meridianally—that is, as potentially double-edged moments of closure and opening, of, to use his terms, *Wiederkunft* and *Zwischenkunft*.

As noted in Chapter 1, *Wiederkunft*—a movement of circular repetition, vicious cycling, and compulsive return to and of the same—is associated from the very beginning of *The Meridian* with the movement of "art." "Die Kunst," Celan observes in the first line of the second paragraph, "kommt wieder." This movement of artistic recurrence is directly contrasted with another mode of coming described in the preceding sentence. Here it is "coming" in the sense of an intervention, intercession, or interruption: "Es kommt etwas dazwischen." The temporality of this "coming in the meantime," of that which never comes as itself and which never presents itself as such (precisely the temporality of "the majesty of the absurd" and the coming of that which "has no definitive name" but which Celan believes "is . . . poetry"), is what will concern us in what follows in conjunction with the topos of the uncanny and with regard to Celan's discussion of the poem as "desperate conversation."

One begins to get a sense of the way Celan poetically intervenes in the closed circles of compulsive repetition and traumatic fixation with which he finds himself confronted in the Büchnerian corpus in his discussion of the prose fragment *Lenz*. Starting with its famous last lines, "His existence was a necessary burden for him.—Thus he lived on . . ." and adding, "Here the narrative breaks off," Celan draws attention to the way the text founders on the point of an existential impasse, remaining stuck at a moment associated with the protagonist's separation from the pastor Oberlin and his reluctant return to his widowed father and forsaken *Vaterstadt*. Like Lucille's suicidal cry of "Long live the king!" in *Danton's Death*, the mention here of Lenz's living death in the phrase "So lebte er hin . . ." stops the narrative dead in its tracks.[19]

In order to move the fragment beyond this existential and narrative impasse, Celan suggests that it is necessary not just to return to the beginning of the text but also to begin again at the very place where an impossible desire for another kind of gait, for a way of moving that might itself pioneer new paths, is expressed for the first and only time in the text: ". . . only it sometimes bothered him that he could not walk on his head." For Celan, this return to a path not taken, to a path that might itself only be opened by the preposterous gait of a character walking on his head, has the structure of a "step."

Such a step—which, as Celan notes, Büchner's Lenz might have taken on the twentieth of January—is associated with the possibility of beginning again, of beginning to move in a necessarily circular and belated manner beyond the living death at the text's end.[20] It is also associated, more generally, with a way of opening a stagnating movement in place to "something" that, in Celan's words, "dazwischen kommt." What "comes between," "comes in the meantime," in the time-space of an interval, comes in the context of Celan's *Meridian* as an intervention of the Other. It comes as an interruption that may reorient a fatally closed circle of repetition, respacing and rearticulating a closed, exclusive, and painfully isolating ring of circular return.[21] This is why Celan lays such stress on a peculiar textual event that befalls the Büchnerian corpus, one that intervenes in it in an uncanny way, coming neither simply from within nor without. I am referring to that moment in his speech when he discusses the belated advent of the word "coming" in the *First Critical and Complete Edition of Georg Büchner's Works and Posthumous Writings*, edited by Celan's fellow countryman, Karl Emil Franzos, and published by Sauerländer in 1879.

In a seemingly irrelevant philological aside, Celan draws our attention to an error made by Franzos in his edition of Büchner's 1836 comedy, *Leonce and Lena*. Franzos, he notes, mistakenly rendered the play's last words, which should have read "eine commode Religion," as "eine kommende," as a "coming" rather than a "comfortable religion." As though to highlight the importance of the moment, Celan dramatically slows the pace of his speech at this point, multiplying signs of caution as he approaches it. "And here," he says, "with the last two words of this work, I have to be careful. I have to be careful not to misread, as Karl Emil Franzos . . . did—I have to be careful not to misread *das Commode* as *ein Kommendes*" (*CP* 53–4 trans. mod.; *GW* 3:190).

It is not immediately apparent what hidden perils Celan senses here or why it should be so difficult *not* to make the same mistake Franzos did. Whatever the dangers may be, the poet's curious show of vigilance seems intended to narrow the audience's own focus at this point, to sharpen its attention literally to a point, giving it what he earlier refers to as "the acute accent of the present" (den Akut des Heutigen) (*CP* 40; *GW* 3:190). It is as though Celan were inviting his listeners not just to zero in on the last two words of Büchner's play or to take seriously the threat of misreading them but also and perhaps above all to attune themselves to what the Franzos mistake lets slip. This shift from error to opportunity is reflected in the *Und doch* with which the following sentence opens: "And yet [Und doch]: is *Leonce and Lena* not full of words which seem to smile through invisible quotation marks, which we should perhaps not call *Gänsefüßchen*, or goose feet, but rather rabbit's ears, that is, something that listens, not without fear, for something beyond itself, beyond words?" (*CP* 54; *GW* 3:202).

In order to gauge the significance of this abrupt shift and tease out its implications for a reading of the Franzos parapraxis, one might begin by considering the various versions this passage went through in the composition of *The Meridian*. In one such version Celan writes, "Franzos took seriously the quotation marks which are so visible to us and which smile so earnestly at us in the $\frac{Kommode}{Kommende}$ religion" (*M* 168, trans. mod). In another he writes about "hermetics today," asserting that "it is necessary to turn away from received and compromised notions of the beautiful in order to open it [hermetics] to the possibility of a coming—rather than a comfortable—truth; I plan to speak here about hope [Hoffnung]; the poem 'listens attentively' [verhofft] like a hunted animal."[22]

Common to all of Celan's reflections on the Franzos error is an interest in the various openings it will have made: first and most obviously, the opening of Büchner's play at its very end, an opening that will have kept *Leonce and Lena* from drawing comfortably to a close; second, the opening of one word to the chance "coming" of another, an accident which effectively turns the word *commode* into a pair of smiling quotation marks (*Gänsefüßchen*) as another word is cited to appear in its place; third, the opening of these citational "goose feet" to the "rabbit ears" they disclose, to little ears (*Hasenöhrchen*) attuned to small things, to the belittled and the insignificant, to that which never speaks for itself or in its own voice, "speaking" only to the extent that it *misspeaks* itself; fourth, the opening of a "comfortable religion" to the possibility of a "coming" one. As Celan's subsequent remarks on *das Verbindende*, on "the connective," suggest, it is less a question here of a positive religion yet to come than of *Religion* understood in its etymological sense of *religare*—that is, as a certain ligature and mode of linkage, to which we will return below. This is perhaps why Celan speaks in a related note not of Judaism *per se* but, more generally, of "Jewish tradition." "Im Jüdischen," he observes, "God is conceived not as the One who Has Come [der Gekommene] or the One who Will Come Again [der Wiederkommende], but rather as the Coming One [der Kommende]; here time is determinitive and co-determining; where God is near, time is at an end."[23]

One begins to get a sense here of how seriously Celan took the editorial error Franzos made. As the foregoing analysis has sought to demonstrate, it has for him the status of a textual event whose impact and repercussions register at different levels of *The Meridian* and at various stages of its composition. Up to this point, I have tended to accentuate only the accidental, unwitting character of this parapraxis, treating it as though it came simply from Franzos and supervened in the Büchnerian corpus from without, as though the text subjected to this violent—if unintended—misreading were itself already complete and its meaning otherwise intact.

Celan's focus on the citational character of this textual event forces us, however, to question such assumptions. Indeed, when he notes that *Leonce and Lena* is "full of words which seem to smile through quotation marks," he reminds us that it is a play composed as a montage of citations drawn from a wide range of works. So extensive are these borrowings and so constitutive is their role in the composition of the play that this practice of literary citation has come to be recognized by Büchner scholarship as *the* decisive aesthetic principle underlying the construction of the text.[24]

Aware of this aesthetic *Bauprinzip*, Celan appears to take it a step further, suggesting that the moment marked by the Franzos slip is one in which the text effectively *cites itself*. He suggests, in short, that the "coming" word, which intervenes at the end of the play and which keeps it from coming simply to an end, is one that will have come back from somewhere within the text itself. What Celan is suggesting, in other words, is that the citational principle already at work within the play is raised to a higher power of ironic reflection in the moment of *self-citation* marked by the editorial slip. What then is being cited at this moment and how does this textual dynamic alter our understanding of the editor's role in the play?

Let us begin with the second question. Like the fool Valerio—who claims that he is perhaps the third and oddest of the automata assembled at the play's end, that he knows nothing of what he says, and that he is "simply being *made* to speak like this" (daß man mich nur so reden l ä ß t)—Franzos is cast in Celan's reading as yet another automaton. Like Valerio, he makes an uncanny appearance at the play's end, giving voice to what he does not know. As the fourth and most outlandish of the play's automata, Franzos mechanically recites a "coming" word whose significance he does not fully grasp, letting himself be ventriloquized by something that quotes and repeats itself in this most citationally constructed of Büchner's plays. Being made to perform in this way, Franzos rehearses his own captivation by and unwitting implication in the text he edits. Yet, it is precisely by means of this performance, Celan suggests, that the automaton makes contact with something powerfully at work within the text, something that could not have been approached in any more direct or conscious manner, something that the editorial slip literally acts out and to which it uncannily bears witness. It is perhaps for this reason that Celan approaches the Franzos misreading with such caution.

What the parapraxis makes contact with is a kind of nerve center in the text. Indeed, as we trace the quoted word "coming" back to its apparent source in the first act of the play, we find that a number of crucial questions come together there. First among them is the question of the prince's own origins. Consider then the following exchange between Leonce and Valerio in Act I, Scene 3. Exasperated by Valerio's incessant wordplay, the prince exclaims, "Good heavens, man, you're nothing but a walking pun, and a bad one to boot. You're nothing but the fruit of libidinous vowels, not ordinary mortals." Not to be outdone, the fool retorts: "And you, dear Prince, are a book without letters, full of nothing but dashes" (Und Sie, Prinz, sind ein Buch ohne Buchstaben, mit nichts als Gedankenstrichen) (*CPLOW* 1.3: 89; *WBMA* 171). Valerio, however, does not stop there, and it is no doubt the way he goes on that was of particular interest to Celan. Turning from the prince to address members of the privy council assembled in the royal chambers, Valerio continues,

> Come now, gentlemen, there's something very sad about the word 'come': if it's income you want, you have to steal; to come up in the world you have to be hanged; the ultimate outcome is when you are buried; but when it comes down to it you can rely on your wits when you've run out of words, like me right now—or you even before you have opened your mouth. There, gentlemen, you've had your come-uppance, so seek—I beseech you—a comely departure.
>
> (Kommen Sie jetzt meine Herren! Es ist eine traurige Sache um das Wort zu kommen, will man ein Einkommen, so muß stehlen, an ein Aufkommen ist nicht zu denken, als wenn man sich hängen läßt, ein Unterkommen findet man erst, wenn man begraben wird, und ein Auskommen hat man jeden Augenblick mit seinem Witz, wenn man nichts mehr zu sagen weiß, wie ich zum Beispiel eben, und Sie, ehe Sie noch etwas gesagt haben. Ihr Abkommen haben Sie gefunden und Ihr Fortkommen werden Sie jetzt zu suchen ersucht.)
>
> (*CPLOW* 1.3: 89–90; *WBMA* 171)

While the question of beginnings initially broached by Leonce and Valerio is effectively held open by the fool's seemingly endless plays on the infinitive "to come," it is given a further twist a moment later when the prince asserts that "everything begins *a posteriori*" (*CPLOW* 1.3: 90; *WBMA* 172). Franzos's belated postscript to *Leonce and Lena* brilliantly confirms this assertion. Not only does it keep the play open at its close, allowing textual energies concentrated within it to carry over and play themselves out after the fact, but it also does so precisely by returning us to the very moment in which there appears to be no end and no beginning to the coming, no way of harnessing its boundless energies in any determinate, finite form, no way of tethering it to any particular verbal prefix, no way, in short, of capturing its elusive ambiguity in any fixed, stable, or comforting sense.

The moment is of more than local importance. Indeed, it performs what is perhaps the most characteristic gesture of Büchner's play. For just as there is something unwieldy and elusive about the infinitive "to come" in Valerio's speech, something that allows it to slip the hold of anyone or anything that might attach itself to it, that might try to bind it in a particular way and give it some stable sense and direction, so too does the phrasing of the characters' speeches in general tend repeatedly to turn back on itself and mutate into ever-revised formulations. Consider, for example, Leonce's response to a question posed by Rosetta in the first act of the play:

> Rosetta: So you love me out of boredom?
> Leonce: No, I'm bored because I love you. But I love my boredom as much as you. You're one and the same. . . . Come, dear boredom, your kisses are a lascivious yawn, your every step a delicate hiatus. [Nein, ich habe Langeweile, weil ich dich liebe. Aber ich liebe meine Langeweile wie dich. Ihr seid eins. . . . Komm, liebe Langeweile, deine Küsse sind ein wohllüstiges Gähnen und deine Schritte sind ein zierlicher Hiatus.]
> (CPLOW 1.3: 84; WBMA 166)

Given Celan's privileging of a language of paths and steps throughout *The Meridian*, it is important to observe the "delicate hiatus" traced by Rosetta's step. Such an opening is a figure for the temporal movement—or rather for the lack thereof—in the play. It is not just that time ceases to flow here, continuing a long tradition in which temporal stagnation is linked to *taedium vitae* and melancholia, but rather that it is also lovingly distended and delicately swollen at each and every pregnant moment. What holds the moment open, stretching it as wide as the lascivious yawn of which Leonce speaks, are the competing assertions allowed to accumulate and coexist within it. Far from canceling each other out, these assertions are, as Leonce tells his beloved, "one and the same."

Coming back now to the end of the play, we recognize that the Franzos parapraxis, far from being an aberrant misreading of *Leonce and Lena*, uncannily acts out a certain logic of belatedness already at work within it, providing striking evidence of the prince's majestically absurd claim that everything begins *a posteriori*. For everything—including the play itself—to begin in this way, the end has to be open to other surprise endings, to that which may overtake it from without, adding something like a postscript on to it. Yet, what appears to come from without in the form of an editorial revision made some forty years after the fact is itself the very mutation the play will have called for, the belated beginning it will have awaited, the coming it will have prepared and in the end will have been able to accommodate.

It is no doubt telling in this regard that the moment to which Franzos's "coming" word returns us in *Leonce and Lena* is not simply a moment *in* the text but one in which the textual, personal, and corporeal come together as Valerio, having just been told that he is "the fruit of libidinous vowels, not ordinary mortals," tells Leonce that he himself is "a book without letters, full of nothing but dashes [Gedankenstrichen]" (*CPLOW* 1:3: 89; *WBMA* 171). Celan's reading of Büchner focuses on just this passage opened among seemingly independent and sovereign realms, letting itself be guided by the way verbal, textual, and human bodies come together in exuberant flashes of wit, in connections unwittingly forged by an unsuspecting editor, and in the uncanny interventions of words "coming" in place of others.

Or to be more precise, "das Kommende," for Celan, is ultimately less a word than a dash, a Büchnerian *Gedankenstrich*, and it is this "thought stroke" that is left hanging in suspense at the open end of *Leonce and Lena*.[25] Recalling the tiny line of the "*Gedankenstrichel* between yes and no" in *Woyzeck* on which the title character imagines someone wanting to hang himself, it also functions in Celan's *Meridian* as a hyphen or *Bindestrich*, as the *re-ligare* of the coming *Religion*, as that which belatedly and surprisingly reconnects the poet and his fellow countrymen, Reinhold Lenz and Karl Emil Franzos, to the question of their own beginnings and place of origin.[26] "I find," he says, "the connective [das Verbindende] which, like the poem, leads to encounters" (*CP* 54; *GW* 3:202).

Yet, the encounter to which Celan is led at this moment by the binding link of "the coming" is not with a once-familiar place, not with "the region from which" he and the others are said "to come," but rather with the very topos of the unlocatable, the *Utopie* (*CP* 54; *GW* 3:202) or no-place of the uncanny. It is at this point of *failed* homecoming—"None of these places," he says, "is to be found. They do not exist" (*CP* 54; *GW* 3:202)—that he also fails to meet up with himself, or rather that he suddenly and surprisingly *encounters himself as another*, as a doppelgänger of Büchner's Prince Leonce.

This uncanny way of coming upon himself as another, upon another who is in turn but "a book without letters, full of nothing but dashes," is made possible through the dash (*das Verbindende*) of a "coming" word, the very word that itself will have come via an editorial slip in place of another, in place, that is, of a word so closely resembling it in appearance that the one is mistaken for the other.[27] Just as Franzos's slip lets *Leonce and Lena* open again at the very point and with the very last words on which it was supposed to close, so too does Celan's speech come upon another just as it itself is about to come full circle. "I am again at my point of departure," he says, "searching for the place from which I come. I am looking for all this with my imprecise, because nervous, finger on a map—a child's map, I must admit. None of the places is to be found. They do not exist. But I know where they ought to exist, especially now, and ... I find something else!" (*CP* 54 trans. mod.; *GW* 3:202).

In lieu of the missing point of return, Celan, to his own apparent, even staged, surprise finds something unexpected, something that "consoles [him] a bit for having walked this impossible path [diesen unmöglichen Weg] in your presence, this path of the impossible [diesen Weg des Unmöglichen]" (*CP* 54 trans. mod.; *GW* 3:202). What comes in the meantime, in the timeframe of an interval marked by the ellipsis in the exclamation "and ... I find something else!" not only takes him unawares, but, even more surprisingly, reorients the very trajectory of his homecoming, turning a failure to find what he had come in search of into a more fractured, accidental, and seemingly "impossible way" of turning back. In lieu of returning to and as himself, what repeatedly intervenes in *The Meridian* is another in place of the self.[28] Moreover, in lieu of coming back to a place that cannot be found, a place that does not exist, such a revenant in turn finds something else, finds him- or itself *somewhere* else. It finds the circularly self-reflexive path it had heretofore been traveling—"this impossible path, this path of the impossible"—turning in another, more *heteroreflexive way*, from, through, and toward the Other. This self-altering movement is aptly summarized by Levinas who describes *The Meridian* as an "elliptic, allusive text, constantly interrupting itself in order to let through, in the interruptions, his other voice, as if two or more discourses were on top of one other, with a strange coherence, not that of a dialogue, but woven in a counterpoint that constitutes—despite their immediate melodic unity—the texture of his poems" (Levinas, "Paul Celan," 41).

Altered in this way, the poet "himself" comes to be seen as a suspensive *Gedankenstrich*: not just as a princely "book without letters full of nothing but dashes" but also as a poem precariously holding out on the edge of itself, as an existence tenuously suspended on the very brink of survival. "The poem," Celan says in *The Meridian*, "the poem today, clearly shows a strong tendency towards silence. The poem maintains itself [behauptet sich]—if you will permit me yet another extreme formulation—the poem keeps itself, holds out at the edge of itself [am Rande seiner selbst]; it ceaselessly calls and hauls itself back from its 'already-no-longer' into its 'yet-still' in order to go on [es ruft und holt sich, um bestehen zu können, unausgesetzt aus seinem Schon-nicht-mehr in sein Immer-noch zurück]" (*CP* 48–49; *GW* 3:197).

The meticulous attention Celan devotes to the word that comes via Franzos's slip at the very edge of Büchner's text is no doubt meant to sensitize his audience to the "coming" words of his own speech—most importantly, to the contrast he draws at the very beginning between two modes of coming. The one, as was noted earlier, is connected with a movement of artistic recurrence. "Die Kunst," he says, "kommt wieder." The other is associated with something that has no proper movement or time of its own, that "comes" only to the extent that it intervenes in the meantime. Celan does not name it, but says only "Es kommt etwas dazwischen," "something comes between." His reticence here reminds us of that other moment in his speech, the one with which we ourselves began, when he speaks of the majesty of the absurd. "This," he says, "has no definitive name, but I believe that it is ... poetry" (*CP* 40; *GW* 3:190). Although Celan never makes such a connection explicit, I would venture to say that "poetry" in the context of *The Meridian* stands in the same relation to "art" as "coming between" does to "coming again"—which is to say that the one is not easily distinguished from the other, that the one comes as a revenant of the other. Indeed, as Celan notes at many points in his speech, poetry must travel the same paths as art; it has no way of its own, no proper course.[29] Indeed, what is important to him, what requires a different kind of attunement and small rabbit ears to hear is the particular way "art" and "poetry" come together and pulse through one another in the cycles of repetition that are at the heart of the Büchnerian text and his own *Meridian* address.

For Celan, repetition is not a single, unitary force but a double and divided *com*-pulsion, an unconscious movement impelled to travel in two different ways at once: primarily back toward the sameness of an open wound in time but also "secondarily" *and along the same paths* toward the possibility of what is yet to come. It is in attuning ourselves to the surprisingly openended and double-edged nature of Büchner's work—to those instants I have analyzed as moments of absolute sovereignty, of stasis and traumatic fixation, but also of an uncertain opening toward what may possibly intervene in the meantime—that we may begin to understand why it was so important for Celan to speak in *The Meridian* about the relationship between *Hoffnung* and *verhoffen*, between "hope" and "the anxious attentiveness" of the persecuted creature.

In privileging the moment in *The Meridian* when an obvious editorial slip is treated as an unwitting point of connection linking the excessive energies at work in Büchner's text with that which never speaks for itself or on its own behalf in Celan, I have tried in my own way to circle around the Celanian notion of the poem as "desperate conversation" and to ask what kind of conversation between the poet and playwright takes place in *The Meridian*. "Only in the space of this conversation," Celan says, "does that which is addressed [das Angesprochene] take form and gather around [versammelt es sich] the I who is addressing and naming it. But the one who has been addressed [das Angesprochene] and who, by virtue of having been named, has, as it were, become a Thou [zum Du gewordene] also brings its otherness along [bringt . . . auch sein Anderssein mit] into the present, into this present [in diese Gegenwart]. Only in the here and now of the poem is it still possible—the poem itself, after all, has only this one, unique, punctual present—only in this immediacy and proximity does it let the Other's ownmost quality speak: its time [noch in dieser Unmittelbarkeit und Nähe läßt es das ihm, dem Anderen, eigenste mitsprechen: dessen Zeit]" (*CP* 50 trans. mod.; *GW* 3:198–9).[30]

Like the editorial slip Celan lets stand, the poem that is his *Meridian* lets the other speak. And if it is a question here of *mitsprechen*, it is the prefix *mit*- that deserves the accent, "the acute of the present." For, as Derrida has noted, this speaking is originally, *a priori*, a speaking with the other or to the other, even prior to speaking alone. What the poem lets speak with it, lets share in its speech, what it lets colloquize and con-voke, what it lets speak is the time of the other.[31] This time, I believe, is for Celan associated with that which only comes in the meantime, *pendant, dazwischen*. As he says at the beginning of *The Meridian*, at a beginning to which he will repeatedly circle back,[32] "es kommt etwas dazwischen."

FOUR

On the Stroke of Circumcision I: Derrida, Celan, and the Covenant of the Word

> *Die Toten—sie betteln noch, Franz.*
> (The dead—they still go begging, Francis.)
> —PAUL CELAN, "Assisi"

Derrida's "Shibboleth: For Paul Celan" is the revised text of a lecture he delivered in Seattle on October 14, 1984. Divided into seven sections marked by roman numerals, it begins: "Only one time [Une seule fois]: circumcision takes place only once [n'a lieu qu'une fois]."[1] Broaching the topic of circumcision and with it the related questions of its place and taking place in the very first line of the text, Derrida will nevertheless wait until the seventh section to address the "circumcision of the word" invoked in Celan's 1963 poem from the collection *The No-one's Rose* (*Die Niemandsrose*), "TO ONE WHO STOOD BEFORE THE DOOR" ("EINEM, DER VOR DER TÜR STAND"). At the opening of that section, he says, "An event seems to inaugurate the legitimate belonging of the Jew to his community, at the moment of the right of entrance or the rite of passage, and it takes place, we were saying at the outset, only once, at an absolutely set date: the circumcision. Such is, at least, the appearance" (*S* 53; *SPC* 97).

According to Jewish tradition, the circumcision of a male child is to be performed on the eighth day after birth. This, it appears, is the "absolutely

63

set date" to which Derrida refers. Yet, in dividing "Shibboleth" into sections corresponding to the seven days of the week, he suggests that his own appointment with the topic of circumcision will itself have been deferred to a time and place just beyond the threshold of his text.[2] Like the one who will have stood before the door in Celan's Kafkaesque poem, Derrida's own text thus appears to stand like a doorkeeper or supplicant at the threshold of another.

The questions implicitly raised through the structure of Derrida's text are thus: How will he, in the guise of postponing one kind of circumcision, the kind that appears to take place but once, have prepared the advent of another? How is this other scene of circumcision incised, inscribed, and perhaps even performed at the threshold of "Shibboleth"? What, precisely, is the relationship between this cutting movement of preparatory deferral circling about a scene that is never performed as such and the sense of "precision" underscored by Celan in his 1958 reply to a questionnaire from the Flinker Bookstore? In that response Celan writes:

> German poetry is going in a very different direction from French poetry. No matter how alive its traditions, with most sinister events in its memory, most questionable developments around it, it can no longer speak the language which many willing ears seem to expect. Its language has become more sober, more factual. It distrusts 'the beautiful,' it tries to be truthful. If I may search for a visual analogy while keeping in mind the polychrome of apparent actuality: it is a 'greyer' language, a language which wants to locate even its 'musicality' in such a way that it has nothing in common with the 'euphony' which more or less blithely continued to sound alongside the greatest horror.
>
> The concern of this language is in all the irreducible polyvalence of the term: precision [geht es, bei aller unabdingbaren Vielstelligkeit des Ausdrucks um Präzision]. It does not transfigure or render 'poetical': it names, it posits, it tries to measure the area of the given and of the possible. True, this is never the working of language itself, language as such, but always of an I who speaks from the particular angle of inclination which is his existence and who is concerned with outlines [Kontur] and orientation. Reality is not simply there, it must be searched for and won.
>
> (*CP* 16; *GW* 3: 167–8)

Emphasizing the *Vielstelligkeit* of the term "precision" (*Präzision*), Celan suggests it be understood not only in the more conventional sense of exactitude but, more literally, as an act of precutting related to what is described in the same paragraph as the speaker's concern with outlines (*Kontur*) and orientation.³ Like its English cognate, the German *Kontur* suggests a particular kind of outline, one that turns around a curving or irregular figure.⁴ The "precision" Celan speaks of should thus also be read as an act of circumcision, of tracing out the contours of a reality that "is not simply there," but that instead "must be searched for and won." It is this other scene of circumcision that Derrida's own text seeks to circumscribe, to trace out like the lineaments of the absolute poem that, as Celan exclaims in *The Meridian*, "does not and cannot exist!" (*CP* 51; *GW* 3:199) Derrida's "Shibboleth" would in this sense itself be the password, the word passed in the silence of a handshake at the threshold of a text, that gives access to this other scene. "Only truthful hands write true poems," Celan wrote to Hans Bender. "I cannot see any basic difference between a handshake and a poem" (*CP* 26; *GW* 3: 177).

How, then, does Derrida's text perform this handshake? What is the other scene of circumcision that it, in closing, opens onto?

The Tropic of Circumcision

Circumcision, Derrida observes, is not merely a cut to be read or even a wound that is legible. It is also and above all a kind of reading-wound, a wound inflicted by and on reading.

"Sie setzt/Wundgelesenes über" (it carries/the wound-read across). These lines from "DEIN VOM WACHEN" ("YOUR WAKING'S") (ctd in *S* 53–4, trans. mod.) speak, in Derrida's words, "of a passing beyond, over that which is *read* to the quick, to the point of bleeding, to the point of wounding, reaching the place where the cipher is painfully inscribed on the body itself" (*S* 54; *SPC* 97). Yet on whose body? On what body? Here Derrida relocates the circularity of circumcision's ring-shaped cut in a space that is opened in what gives itself to be read, to be deciphered like a cryptic code whose cracking would give way only to other crypts yet to be unsealed in a structure of infinite regress. That which offers itself to be read, which beckons the reader to penetrate ever more deeply into its hidden recesses, is thereby opened like a wound "to the point of bleeding." If such wounds may be said to be illegible, they are so not merely in the sense of being resistant to reading but in the way they inexhaustibly demand it. Giving themselves to be read "to the quick," these unreadable wounds also, as Derrida says, wear out reading "to the very marrow" (*S* 54; *SPC* 98). One might say, then, that it is at the very limit of legibility that the "experience of reading" first begins.[5]

Such an experience for Derrida is of necessity double-edged: a question at once of wounds inflicted by reading and upon it. What concerns him is not so much the literality of the word circumcision—which appears rarely in Celan, with the notable exception of the poem "TO ONE WHO STOOD BEFORE THE DOOR"—but rather its tropic. This "*tropic* of circumcision" (*S* 54; *SPC* 98) is itself to be distinguished from *trope* in the latter's sense of a figurative extension of the meaning of a word beyond the sense of a cut into the flesh, a movement of "spiritualization" or "interiorization," which, as Derrida says, "does not date from Saint Paul" (*S* 55; *SPC* 99). The turning of this tropic instead has more to do with the elliptical paths traced by the various gatherings of a poem such as "IN ONE" ("IN EINS"), where, as we saw in Chapter 2, each gathering "center" of the text will have been but a point of suspension, an elliptical mark defined less by what and where it is than by the place it holds open in relation to others. "The poem is the place," Celan asserts in *The Meridian*, "where all tropes, all tropics [alle Tropen], . . . want to be led *ad absurdum*" (*CP* 51; *GW* 3: 199; trans. mod.).

It is the elliptical turning of this tropic of circumcision that one must follow in Derrida's reading of the phrase "all poets are Jews," which Celan, in the epigraph of "AND WITH THE BOOK FROM TARUSSA" ("UND MIT DEM BUCH AUS TARUSSA"), quotes in Russian from a poem by Marina Tsvetaeva. Rather than making one of the two nominal centers of the phrase "all poets are Jews" revolve around the other, an orbit that would effectively turn Jews into poets or poets into Jews, Derrida traces the elliptical path of the one about the other. It is this mutually decentering movement that tropically annuls whatever definitional or ontological fixity each of these "conturning" points might have had. The question is thus no longer, What are the attributes or properties of a Jew (or a poet)? Instead it is, How must one question differently after Auschwitz? How must one ask in a way that does not necessarily accede to the essentializing, racializing, and nominalizing demand implicit in the question, What is? How, in other words, can a certain tropic of circumcision begin "to displace the literality of belonging to Judaism, if one can still speak of belonging to a community to which, as 'Gespräch im Gebirg' ['Conversation in the Mountains'] reminds us, nothing properly belongs" (*S* 55; *SPC* 100)?⁶

> To say 'all poets are Jews' is to state something which marks *and* annuls the marks of a circumcision. It is tropic. All those who deal with or inhabit language as poets are Jews—but in a tropic sense. And the one who says this, consequently, speaking as a poet and according to a trope, never presents himself literally as a Jew. He asks: What is literality in this case?
>
> What the trope ... comes down to, then, is locating the Jew not only *as* a poet but also in every man circumcised by language or led to circumcise a language.
>
> (*S* 54; *SPC* 98–9)

It is at this point that Derrida turns from the double-edged experience of reading to what he calls "a certain concise experience of circumcision" (*S* 55; *SPC* 100). Those who have that experience—those who are at once circumcised and circumcisers—are, he says,

> Jews ... in all the senses of this word, the circumcised and the circumcisers. Anyone or no one may be a Jew. Jew, no one's name, the only one. No one's circumcision. If all poets are Jews, they are all, the poets, circumcised or circumcisers. This opens up, in Celan's text, a tropic of circumcision that turns from ciphered sores to reading wounds, all cut words ..."
>
> (*S* 55; *SPC* 100)

The Covenant of the Word

How, then, does the circumcision performed in "TO ONE WHO STOOD BEFORE THE DOOR"—this circumcision *of the word*—mark at once the becoming-poetic of the word and its becoming-Jewish?

> EINEM, DER VOR DER TÜR STAND, EINES
> Abends:
> ihm
> tat ich mein Wort auf—: zum
> Kielkropf sah ich ihn trotten, zum
> halb-

schürigen, dem
im kotigen Stiefel des Kriegsknechts
geborenen Bruder, dem
mit dem blutigen
Gottes-
gemächt, dem
schilpenden Menschlein.

Rabbi, knirschte ich, Rabbi
Löw:

diesem
beschneide das Wort,
diesem
schreib das lebendige
Nichts ins Gemüt,
Diesem
spreize die zwei
Krüppelfinger zum heil-
bringenden Spruch.
Diesem.
. . . .
Wirf auch die Abendtür zu, Rabbi.
. . . .
Reiß die Morgentür auf, Ra- — —

TO ONE WHO STOOD BEFORE THE DOOR, ONE
evening:
to him
I opened my word—: toward the
misbegotten I saw him trot, toward
the half-
shorn,
the
brother born in the
mercenary's dung-caked boot, the one
with the bloody
God-
member, the
chittering manikin.

> Rabbi, I gnashed, Rabbi
> Löw:
>
> For this one
> circumcise the word,
> for this one
> write the living
> Nothing in the heart,
> for this one
> spread the two
> cripplefingers in the hal-
> lowing sentence.
> For this one.
> . . . .
> Slam also the evening door shut, Rabbi.
> . . . .
> Fling the morning door open, Ra- —[7]

While the poem begins in the past tense, it shifts in the second strophe to a present in the past, directly addressing Rabbi Löw for the first time with the words: "For this one / circumcise the word." The circular movement of the poem—and, indeed, of the rounding cut of circumcision—is already evident in the connection between the first and last of the poem's addresses to the rabbi. Whereas in the first the rabbi is effectively positioned as a circumciser, or *Mohel*, in the last it is the agent of circumcision who is himself acted upon. That is, at the moment the poem breaks off, it is the rabbinic *Mohel*, the one initially asked to perform a circumcision of the word, who has his own body—the body of the word "Rabbi"—cut. Not only does the verbal body *Ra-* now bear the trace of an ironic operation that appears to cut both ways, turning back on the *Mohel* and circumcising the circumciser, but the circumcised word left open and wounded at the poem's equally open end itself never quite leaves the mouth of the one who had been addressing the rabbi, the one whose own speech act is interrupted literally in the midst of pronouncing the *Ra-*'s name.

At this overdetermined moment of textual, verbal, and corporeal interruption—the very moment in which these seemingly discrete spaces not only come together but intersect, literally cutting into and through one another—the speaker's own lips are in their turn circumcised. Cut open in this way, they part not so much in order to speak but rather to mark an opening at the very threshold of speech and silence, an opening marked in the poem by the hyphen appended to the truncated body of the *Ra-*. This trace of a silent cut, this all too literal sign of the covenant or *Bund* inscribed in the body of the word *Ra-*, is ultimately less the mark of an enduring or renewed bond to the God of the patriarchs than the stigma of a poetic double bind—which is why the poem breaks off not merely with the circumcised body *Ra-* but also with the trace of a double incision (Ra- —). Not only is the poem suspended at the very threshold of speech and silence, but, leaving itself open at this limit, at a limit marked by the spacing of the second dash, it also relocates itself at this very edge, at what is at once the uttermost and innermost limit of its existence. "The poem," Celan observes in his *Meridian* address, "clearly shows a strong tendency towards silence. The poem maintains itself [behauptet sich]—if you will permit me yet another extreme formulation—the poem maintains itself, keeps itself, holds out [behauptet sich] at the edge of itself [am Rande seiner selbst]; it ceaselessly calls and hauls itself back from its 'already-no-longer' into its 'yet-still' in order to go on [es ruft und holt sich, um bestehen zu können, unausgesetzt aus seinem Schon-nicht-mehr in sein Immer-noch zurück]" (*CP* 48–9; *GW* 3: 197; trans. mod.).

What is left hanging at the very limit of speech and silence is a kind of poetic stutter. Whereas such stammering is usually viewed merely as a kind of speech impediment, in Celan's poetry it has a more liminally equivocal and eccentrically central status. Its repetitions mark the lost edge of speech, the point at which it is contaminated by the silence toward which it tends and out of which it emerges. It "speaks," in the words of Celan's 1955 poem, "The Vintagers," "through the silence" (durchs Stumme hindurchspricht) (*SPP* 82–3; trans. mod.), enacting in this thoroughgoing passage a struggle at the poem's own edge ("am Rande seiner selbst"). The perseverations and faltering cadences that audibly scan Celan's poetological addresses and that palpably syncopate the rhythm of so many of his poems play out a struggle waged at this unstable, fluctuating, and permeable threshold, enacting an existential struggle (waged not only by the poem) to maintain itself, to keep itself at the very limit of survival, to hold out on the untenable edge of the "already-no-longer" and the "yet-still."

Is there a name, Celan seems to ask, for one left so abysmally hanging in suspense, for such an existence caught perpetually on the verge of survival, at the very edge (*Rand*) of itself? This is perhaps why the poem breaks off in the midst of an act of appellation, "Fling the morning door open, *Ra- —*." Not only is the *Ra-*'s name left incomplete here, but the very act of naming—interrupted and left in suspense at this point—is itself indefinitely prolonged by the interruption, becoming in its turn an interminably open-ended performative. The act of naming, it should be recalled, is an essential part of the Jewish ritual of circumcision. Not only does this ceremony traditionally involve the inscription of the sign of the covenant upon the flesh of a Jewish male but also the giving of a name at this moment of legitimate entry into the community. Since what is in question in Celan's poem is precisely the status of poets and Jews—of poets as Jews—it is not surprising that the act of naming should be suspended at the very moment when the circumciser is himself cut and the poem and its speaking are, in their turn, abruptly cut off. The intersection of these various cuts leads one to ask when, precisely, the circumcision being performed in the poem will have been completed. Has it already been carried out by the end or has its performance been interrupted before coming to an end, before coming, as it were, full circle?

In view of all of the cuts marking the interruption of the poem, of its address to the rabbi, and of the circumcision being performed by and upon him, it is perhaps more pertinent to ask at this point how these revolving incisions will have begun to circumscribe or pre-cise the contours of what Derrida refers to as an interminable "tropic of circumcision." Here it is a question not merely of the object of circumcision, of the body of a word being substituted for the flesh of a Jewish male. As was noted above, such a spiritualizing, metaphorizing displacement would merely repeat a turn already advocated by Saint Paul when he called for a new covenant of the heart, for a less literal and more spiritual testament inscribed *in* the heart. Instead, what is in question is another *practice*, a practice that is at once poetic and Jewish—or, to be more precise, that would no longer be simply poetic or simply Jewish—one that would inaugurate a different, more elliptical, and mutually decentering bond between bodies and words. Furthermore, if Jewish difference is indeed in question here, what this practice seeks to inscribe is another way of marking it. It seeks, in other words, to reopen the closed ring of the circular cut—decisive sign of membership in and exclusion from the Jewish community, sign of the proper and the improper, sign of the clean and the impure.

In its very decisiveness such a cut is itself painfully double-edged. For it raises not only the question of Jewish exclusiveness, but also the specter of the murderously exclusionary practices aimed precisely at those who, without their consent, were defined by the Nuremberg Laws *as* Jews. What is at stake for Celan in the turning cut of a movement repeatedly kept from closing, from ever coming completely full circle, is thus the vexed question of a community's relationship to the Other, the question of Jewish "exclusion" in both the active and passive senses of the term, a question addressed by Derrida, following Celan, no longer in terms of Jewish identity—in terms, that is, of a community's self-definition or of its definition by others—but rather in terms of Jewish "difference."

Implicit in what Derrida refers to as a "tropic of circumcision" is thus also the question of a different covenantal relationship, the question of how such a bond might be inaugurated in the very performance of Celan's writing. Derrida's plays on the term *alliance* throughout the French version of *Schibboleth* are therefore anything but gratuitous since what concerns him is precisely the way in which Celan's poem transforms the traditional *alliance*—the closed ring (*alliance*) and reciprocal obligation of the covenant (*alliance*) whose privileged sign is the circular cut—into a bond of solidarity with the Other, into the kind of alliances forged in a poem such as "In One." The uncanny doubling of the term *alliance* suggests less a *transformation* of the Jewish covenant—less a metaphorizing, spiritualizing supersession of it in the Pauline sense of a "new testament"—than a process of inner alteration. "Circumcision" would in this sense have always already been a trope—more specifically, a catachresis—a practice not simply extended at some determinate point from its literal meaning and proper place of inscription to other senses and different parts of the body, but instead a practice whose site is from the first multiple and divided, whose senses are already in the Scriptures tropically dispersed. "Before Saint Paul," Derrida reminds us, "the Bible tells of the circumcision or uncircumcision of the lips, that is to say, in this tongue, of the tongue (Exod. 6:12, 30), of the ears (Jer. 6:10), and of the heart (Lev. 26:41)" (*S* 59; *SPC* 106).

Furthermore, what is at stake in Celan's poem is the related question of traumatic repetition. Here the closed ring etched by the encircling cut may be said to trace the contours of a movement in place, a movement of compulsive return to and of the same place. Yet, because it is a question not merely of the circular course of a rounding cut but the elliptical structure of a tropic of circumcision, what is also at stake in this tropical movement for which there is no longer or not yet a proper name is the performance of "another scene" of repetition, a scene in which the compulsion to return is, in a manner of speaking, doubled and divided at every turn by an equally insistent movement of re-petitioning, by an internally altering movement of self-interruption associated in Celan's *Meridian* address with the intervention, or *Zwischenkunft*, of "something" that, as he says, "comes between."

All this, I would suggest, is at stake in Celan's poem—which is why Derrida takes so long (almost a week) to work his way up to it and why he spends so much time directly and indirectly addressing it. Not only is it a question at this point of the turn—or of what may come to pass at each and every turn—but also of the turning cut, of the contour pre-cised by such a cut, of the relationship between tropes and cuts. "*Circumcise*," Derrida writes,

> the word appears only once, in the imperative mode: *beschneide*.
> But the grammar of the verb, the modality of the imperative, does not necessarily signify an imperious order. Injunction, appeal, desire, supplication, prayer—these also may be conveyed through the same grammar.
> For this word, this word of command—injunction or appeal, desire, supplication, or prayer—bears this time *upon the word*. The verb has the word as its object, it speaks about an operation to be performed on the word, in other words, on the verbum. The word says: circumcise the word. Its complement is the word or, rather, the Word: "beschneide das Wort."
>
> (S 56; SPC 101)

While the "word," according to Derrida, "says: circumcise the word," the apparent reflexivity of this gesture is interrupted and derailed by the word's address to another—to a rabbinic *Mohel* who is asked not only to act on its behalf, on behalf of the *speaking* word, but also on behalf of another who never speaks for itself or in its own cause in the poem. "For this one," it says, "circumcise the word." In a related passage in *The Meridian*, Celan initially concedes that it is no doubt true that the poem "speaks only on its own, its very own behalf," only to add: "But I think—and this will hardly surprise you—that the poem has always hoped, for this very reason, to speak also on behalf of the *strange*—no, I can no longer use this word here—*on behalf of the other*, who knows, perhaps, of *an altogether other*" (CP 48; GW 3: 196).

Similarly, in "To One Who Stood Before The Door" the injunction "For this one/circumcise the word" is addressed to the rabbi on behalf of another, on behalf of the mute or silenced one, the other who, by definition, never speaks for or as itself. It asks that a circumcision be performed on the word, on the German *Wort*. "This word to be circumcised," Derrida continues,

> this word to be circumcised for someone, this word of *someone's* to be circumcised, this word which must thus be given, and given *once* circumcised, we may understand it as an open word.
>
> Like a wound, you will say. Yes and no. Opened, first of all, like a door: opened to the stranger, to the other, to the neighbor, to the guest, to whomever. To whomever no doubt in the figure of the absolute to-come [de l'avenir absolu] (the one who will come, more precisely, who *would come*, for this to-come [car cet avenir, celui *à venir*], its coming must be neither assured nor calculable), thus in the figure of the monstrous creature. The absolute to-come can only announce itself in the form of monstrosity, beyond all forms and norms that could be anticipated, beyond all genres or kinds.
>
> (S 56–7; SPC 102)

If this *Wort*, once circumcised, may be understood as an open word, it now opens not only "like a wound," as one might initially expect, but also "like a door." In order to approach this opening, Derrida himself seems to have no choice but to speak about it in an indirect way, using approximative comparisons to describe it. Yet surprisingly, the second simile to which he has recourse comes no closer to an adequate understanding of the way this word is opened than the first. Indeed, his point is precisely that there is *no proper way* to understand this opening, no way to speak about it that would not already be tropical, no way to approach it that would not of necessity be circuitous. "Is it on such paths," Celan asks in *The Meridian*, "that poems take us when we think of them? And are these paths *only roundabout ways*, detours from you to you [nur Um-wege, Umwege von dir zu dir]?" (*CP* 53; *GW* 3: 201). Derrida, speaking in his turn in a roundabout way about the turning cut of circumcision, thereby draws attention not merely to its circular movement but also and above all to the way it may never come full circle. Just as the paths along which Celan is thinking in *The Meridian* are no longer *merely detours* in the route taken "from you to you," so, too, is the possibility of going astray here no longer external to the actual movement of the poem, no longer incidental to the turning movement of its rounding cuts.

Indeed, the chance of slipping off course is now viewed as an essential poetic possibility, as a possibility now inscribed in the poem as a double-edged movement of return. Cutting both ways at once, this movement is not only bisected or split in two, but is itself caught between two different ways of turning. As in Kafka's story "In the Penal Colony," in which the sixth hour marks the pivotal moment in a twelve-hour cycle that is at once a turning point and a point of no return, so too in Celan's poem is the circular movement of turning back now opened at every point—at each and every turn—to the essential possibility of being turned away from itself, of being troped, of being returned to and as another in place of the self. This hetero-reflexive movement is essential to the poem in another way; for it is precisely this movement that opens the possibility of encounter, the possibility of *inadvertently* coming upon someone else, *upon something other than a self*, en route from one person to another, "from you to you." It opens, in other words, the possibility of something happening along the way, the chance of *happening upon* the very otherness which the "you" in Celan's *Meridian* address is said to "bring along with it" into the space of conversation. "Only the space of this conversation," he says, "can establish the addressee [das Angesprochene], can gather it into a 'you' around the naming and speaking I. But this 'you,' come about by dint of being named and addressed, brings its otherness along with it [bringt . . . sein Anderssein . . . mit] into the present" (*CP* 50; *GW* 3: 198).

It is in this way that one should understand Derrida's claim that the circumcised word is opened "like a wound . . . like a door: opened to the stranger, to the other, to the neighbor, to the guest, to whomever." If in a first moment it was necessary to stress the ineluctably indirect and necessarily figurative way in which the word is opened in Celan's poem—the way it is opened more than once, no one way ever being the proper or definitive way—it is now necessary to ask who or what it is that may stand before the door of the opened word. Derrida's response is again elliptical, for he suggests that the one to whom the door is opened is not a stranger *per se* but a foreignness close at hand, an "other" as strangely familiar as an uncanny neighbor, as *unheimlich* as the parasitic guest the "you" bears with it [mitbringt] into the present.

The poem does not specify which word, once circumcised, is to be opened like a door to the other. Yet we may assume that it is one of the speaker's own, for the poem begins: "To One Who Stood Before The Door, one/evening: /to him/I opened *my* word." We may further assume that it is a German word since the closed-mouthed speaker who addresses the rabbi midway through the text, speaking to him through clenched jaws and gnashing teeth ("Rabbi, knirschte ich . . ."), grinds out the command "beschneide das Wort." If the word to be circumcised is the German *Wort*, the speaker's own, *mein Wort*, then the one to whom it is opened upon circumcision is perhaps not just another person but another's word for word. If it is a question of opening "*my* word"—this word of belonging, this *Wort* that belongs not only to the German-speaking "I" of the poem but also to the language itself—what it opens onto is in one sense a foreign word, the Hebrew word for *word*, *Milah*. It is just this word, at once foreign and close at hand, that hovers at the threshold of the poem, for in Hebrew the term for "circumcision" is *Brit Milah*—literally, "covenant of the word."

Yet if upon circumcision the German *Wort* is to be opened like a door to this Hebrew word associated with the poem's *Morgentür*, why then does the speaker ask that the evening door of the German language *be shut*? What is the relationship between the poem's two concluding addresses to the rabbi?

Wirf auch die Abentür zu, Rabbi.
. . . .
Reiß die Morgentür auf, Ra- —

Slam also the evening door shut, Rabbi.
. . . .
Fling the morning door open, Ra- —

The parallel constructions of these successive addresses and their locations on either side of a perforated line invite one to read them as two versions of the same demand, as two sides of an equivocal threshold. On the one hand, the body of the poem is drawn to a close and sealed as its German *Tür*, its language of the evening, is slammed shut. On the other hand, that same body is torn asunder as its morning door is not only "flung open," as the English translation would have it, but *aufgerissen* (ripped apart). If, in a first approach to the poem, Derrida notes that the word that is "given *once* circumcised" may be understood "as an opened word"—stressing that it is opened not merely, as "you will say," "like a wound" but "first of all, like a door" (*S* 56; *SPC* 102)—at this point it is the doors themselves that are troped as opening and closing wounds, with the perforated line between them figuring in its turn the ambiguity of an opening or closing suture. The violence of the evening door's closure is thus to be read also as that of a prematurely stitched-up cut. It is no doubt telling in this regard that the verbal body of the *Rabbi*, the very one asked to perform a circumcision of the word, appears intact and uncircumcised in the unbroken line of the complete sentence: "Slam also the evening door shut, Rabbi." This is the only place in the poem where a sentence begins and ends on the same line. Yet the extraordinary formal closure of this line, coextensive with a sentence that itself expresses a demand for closure, ironically leaves open the following painfully double-edged question: Has the circumcision of the Rabbi's own word—of his verbal body—yet to be performed, or have the traces of circumcising violence already been undone? As Derrida notes, violence is associated with both the opening and the closing of the door *qua* wound. In the latter case, however, it is the immaculate violence of (self-)effacement that is in question, the violence of an undoing that will have been so complete, so thorough in its erasure of all traces of erasure, that the body of the *Rabbi* would appear to be as intact, unscarred, and "uncircumcised" as the complete line that the body itself brings to a close.

As though in anticipation of this moment, Derrida notes, toward the beginning of the seventh section of "Shibboleth," how "a tropic of circumcision . . . turns from ciphered sores toward reading-wounds, all cut words, notably in 'Engführung,' where a thread [fil] can be followed that passes through 'points of suture' [Nahtstellen], closed up tears or scars, words to be cut off that were not cut off, membranes stitched back together, and so on" (*S* 55; *SPC* 100). Taking up this thread in his discussion of "TO ONE WHO STOOD BEFORE THE DOOR," he reminds us that *aufreißen*, the verb associated with the opening of the *Morgentür*—of the door *qua* wound— means not just "to open brusquely, rapidly and wide" but also "to break or sometimes to *tear* in one stroke" (*S* 58; *SPC* 104).

The last, incomplete line of the poem ("Fling the morning door open, Ra- —") undoes the closure of the preceding one (if one may still speak at this point in terms of before and after). Its abrupt interruption marks a threefold (re-)opening (the parentheses, however inelegant, being unavoidable given the uncertain status of the "uncircumcised"). This *vielstellige* (re)opening onto, into, and through one another—"dans un seul coup," as Derrida puts it, in a single circumcising stroke, at one and the same time—is that of the line, the sentence, the morning door, the verbal body of the *Ra-*, and the bodily limit of the poem *qua* textual threshold. While the intersection of these various openings may keep the poem's evening door from slamming shut "as though flung in someone's direction" (*S* 58; *SPC* 104), the *Abendtür* may in its turn be said to impress its own poetic signature upon this opening, to seal it in its own occidental idiom, with the initials *R.a.* of the sundered verb *Reiß . . . auf* framing the morning door in the line: "Reiß die Morgentür auf, Ra- —"

The openings, however, do not simply end here. For if, as Derrida suggests, *Ra-* "is perhaps the Egyptian God as well, the sun or light, at the opening of the 'morning door'" (*S* 58; *SPC* 105), then it is not just the Hebrew word *Milah* associated with the Jewish practice of circumcision onto which the door finally opens. Read as a metonymic troping of the *Brit Milah*, this oriental word is itself a morning door that is opened in its turn in the direction of an excluded other. That other—the Egyptian operation from which the Jewish practice is said to derive (*S* 55; *SPC* 100)—is shut out precisely to the extent that the archeological chain is interrupted and the catachrestic movement of metaphorical displacement is brought to rest at a proper sense, at a properly Jewish point of origin. It is, therefore, ultimately less a question in the poem of an *Egyptian* proper name—or even of the sun or light with which the God Ra is associated—than of the way one eclipsed tradition may be said to hover like the penumbra of a repressed subtext at the threshold or morning door of another.

The last interrupted line of Celan's poem may thus be said to mark a particularly congested intersection, one in which a number of differentially articulated cuts are made to pass into and through one another in such a way as to leave the body of the text open and wounded at its close. Yet the more general question raised at this point is whether one can still treat this wound, which is no longer simply poetic or corporeal, as though it were localizable, as if this caesura were a determinate cut in an otherwise homogeneous, continuous, and integral space. The poem's repeated self-interruptions and heteroreflexive turns not only keep the movement of circular reappropriation from ever coming to a close but also, in doing so, keep "To One Who Stood Before The Door" perpetually suspended at its very edge. The tropic of circumcision is precisely what maintains the poem at this edge of its existence, leaving it to hover on that precarious threshold of survival that is repeatedly marked and effaced in its ceaseless movement back and forth between its "already no longer" and its "yet still."

It is at this limit that the tropic of circumcision should in its turn be situated. Already no longer continuous with the traditional Jewish practice of *Brit Milah*, it still (*immer noch*) does not decisively break with it. Instead, it opens in this precariously uncertain space of intervention the possibility of a different covenantal relationship. Such a relationship is tropically redefined in the poem's singular circumcision of the divine Word. As we have seen, the circumcision of the word in "To One Who Stood Before The Door" entails a practice of differential articulation, a way of passing doors, wounds, and words into and through one another, of "pre-cising" them in such a way as to open each to the intersecting mark of the other. It is in this way that the "carnal mark," as Derrida puts it, is "written, spaced, and inscribed in a network of other marks, . . . at once both endowed with and deprived of singularity" (*S* 54; *SPC* 98). Not only does this practice keep the rounding cut of circumcision from ever coming full circle, but it also keeps the very tropic of circumcision from closing back upon itself. In doing so, it articulates this circumcision with yet another Jewish practice, the one associated in Celan's poem with the name "Rabbi Löw." It is the elliptical articulation of these two practices to which we now turn.

FIVE

On the Stroke of Circumcision II: Celan, Kafka, and the Wound in the Name

The name "Rabbi Löw" is associated in Jewish tradition with a creative practice based on a certain performance of the divine Name. Invoking this practice, Celan's poem no doubt draws attention to its own creation. Yet if "To One Who Stood Before The Door" is a poem about poetry, about its own singular performance, it is poetry no longer viewed as *poesis*—that is, as a making or fashioning. Indeed, Celan conjures the mystical tradition of golemic creation that is associated with the name Rabbi Löw only to alter it from within, basing his own practice no longer on the properness of an unpronounceable Name but rather on a wound that will have opened in its place. If, as we have seen, the poem breaks off in the midst of an appeal to the "Ra-," it does so in order to hold open the very place of the proper name, in order to draw itself in this interminable act of appellation around a wounding and unstillable silence that will have gathered in its place.

Curiously, Derrida begins his discussion of "To One Who Stood Before The Door" *in medias res*, skipping over precisely those lines in the first strophe in which the figure of the Golem makes an uncanny appearance. As Derrida himself says, "I am passing over here what the sudden appearance of Rabbi Löw may recall for us of the Golem, the inventor of the monster: the narrative is given over in the poem to a transmutation, a transfigurative translation [traduction], meticulous in its letter and detail—yet another stone in the Prague cemetery—but totally emancipated. The transfer [translation] is beholden to the narrative, but absolved from and having no relationship to its literality" (*S* 57; *SPC* 102). In taking up the question of how exactly the narrative is given over to this "transfigurative translation," it is necessary to examine not only the relevance of the tradition of golemic creation to the poem but also the way such a tradition is itself reworked in being articulated with the tropic of circumcision traced thus far.

Rabbi Löw and the Performance of the Name

By way of introduction, it should be recalled how the term "precision" (*Präzision*) in Celan's work implies not just exactness or even a way of tracing the contours of a *future* (*zuküftigen*) reality. Its "pre-" is not merely preparatory in this sense. Its timing is instead, as we have seen, associated with various modes of intervention and intercession, with the *Zwischenkunft* of that which comes between and in the meantime, with the tropicality and uncanny otherness of that which never "comes" as itself. "Precision" should in this way be understood as the split temporal framework of unconscious repetition—which is why Celan, toward the end of his *Meridian* address, treats Franzos' editorial slip as an unwitting gift that inadvertently opens the way to an uncanny locus of encounter. As noted in Chapter 3, Celan does not simply correct Franzos's mistaken rendering of the play's last words—which should read "a comfortable religion" (eine commode Religion) rather than "a coming religion" (eine kommende Religion)—but instead allows this "coming" word to "come between," to intervene in such a way as to keep both Büchner's play and his own *Meridian* address from drawing neatly to a close. In short, rather than rectifying the editorial error and censoriously cutting off this discourse of the Other, Celan lets it speak.

In the poem "Engführung," whose relevance to "To One Who Stood Before The Door" has already been noted, it said of a stone that "it/was hospitable, it/did not cut in" (er/war gastlich, er/fiel nicht ins Wort) (*GW* 1: 201).[1] Like this stone—which, as Derrida suggests, is "that of the threshold, perhaps, or of the path, or of the first circumcisers" (*S* 62; *SPC* 109)[2]—Celan's texts repeatedly give way to the other. They let it pass precisely to the extent that they treat editorial and other kinds of "slips" as unwittingly proffered shibboleths, as frontier words imparted at carefully patrolled border crossings, as the very otherness of a discourse one would not know how to pronounce even if one knew in advance exactly how it was supposed to be spoken. It is for this reason that both the circumcision of the word and the passing of the shibboleth are to be understood as matters relating not to the body in general but to bodies cultivated in a particular way, in a particular manner of speaking. "The circumcision of the word," Derrida contends,

> must . . . be understood as an event of the body. There is an essential analogy between this event, on the one hand, and the diacritical difference between *shibboleth* and *sibboleth*, on the other. It is in the body, by reason of a certain impotence *coming over* [advenue] their vocal organs, but an impotence of the body *proper*, of the already cultivated body, limited by a barrier neither organic nor natural, that the Ephraimites experienced their inaptitude to pronounce what they nonetheless knew ought to be pronounced *shibboleth*—and not *sibboleth*.
>
> An "unpronounceable name" for some, *shibboleth* is a circumcised word.
>
> (*S* 59; *SPC* 106)

If it is therefore also a question in "To One Who Stood Before The Door" of the divine Word, of the unpronounceable *shem*, it is a matter at this point less of its correct articulation, less of knowing how this Proper Name ought properly to be pronounced, than of its necessarily improper and ineluctably tropical performance. In other words, it is less a matter of consciously performed speech acts than of unconscious *actes manqués*—which is why the *Mohel* asked to perform a circumcision of the Word in Celan's poem is none other than Rabbi Löw, legendary creator of the Golem.

Creation and the Name

It is through the figure of the Golem, associated with the name of this famous Prague rabbi, that Celan alludes to a mystical tradition that has sought, in its own performance of the unpronounceable Name of God, to create in a properly divine manner, to reperform the very act of divine Creation. As Gershom Scholem notes, *gōlem* is a Hebrew word that occurs only once in the Bible, in Psalm 139:16, the Psalm Jewish tradition puts into the mouth of Adam himself.[3] Here probably, and certainly in the later sources, *gōlem* means the unformed, the amorphous. In the philosophical literature of the Middle Ages it is used as a Hebrew term for matter, or formless *hylé*. The formation of the Golem is traditionally modeled on the divine Creation of Adam, who, according to the Aggadah, was the best share taken from the dough of the earth—that is, from the center of the world on Mount Zion, from the place where the altar would stand. "This Adam," Scholem explains, "was taken from the center and navel of the earth, but all the elements were combined in his creation. From everywhere God gathered the dust from which Adam was to be made, and etymologies interpreting the word *Adam* as an abbreviation of his elements, or of the names of the four cardinal points from which he was taken, gained wide currency" (*IG* 160–1).

These elements of creation, however, may also be the letters of the alphabet—"and how much more," Scholem adds, "those of the divine name or of the entire Torah, which was God's instrument of Creation." The initiate knows how to make use of the secret, magical power of these letters. Thus, it is said of Bezazel, who built the Tabernacle, that he "knew the combinations of letters with which heaven and earth were made" (*IG* 166–7). The *Sefer Yetsirah*, or *Book of Creation*, written by a Jewish Neo-Pythagorean sometime between the third and the sixth centuries, played a particularly important role in the development of the golem concept. Significant in the Golem's creation were the names of God and the letters that are the signatures of all creation. "These letters," Scholem explains, "are the structural elements, the *stones* from which the edifice of Creation was built. The Hebrew term employed by the author in speaking of the consonants as 'elementary letters' undoubtedly reflects the ambivalence of the Greek word *stoicheia*, which means both letters and elements" (*IG* 168, my emphasis). The second chapter of the *Book of Creation* speaks of "Twenty-two letter-elements: He outlined them, hewed them out, weighed them, combined them, and exchanged them [transformed them in accordance with certain laws], and through them created the soul of all creation and everything else that was ever to be created." Of particular relevance to Celan's poem—in which doors, words, and wounds are made to circulate in such a way as to pass tropically into, through, and for one another—is the section that describes the manner in which these letter-elements were combined, weighed, and exchanged:

> A [which in Hebrew is a consonant] with all [other consonants] and all with A, B with all and all with B, G with all and all with G, and they all return in a circle to the beginning through two hundred thirty-one gates—the number of the pairs that can be formed from the twenty-two elements—and thus it results that everything created and everything spoken *issue from one name*.
> (*IG* 168; emphasis added)

What is meant by this name from which all things issue is the unpronounceable Name of God. Thus, Scholem explains, "at every 'gate' in the circle formed by the letters of the alphabet there stands a combination of two consonants, which in line with the author's grammatical notions correspond to the two-letter roots of the Hebrew language, and through these gates the creative power goes out into the universe. This universe as a whole is sealed on all six sides with the six permutations of the name YHWH, but every thing or being in it exists through one of these combinations, which are the true 'signatures' of all being" (*IG* 168).

The version of the legend most closely associated with the name of Rabbi Löw involves the fashioning of a golem who did all manner of work for his master during the week. But because all creatures are required to rest on the Sabbath, Rabbi Löw turned his golem back into clay every Friday evening by taking away the name of God (or, in another version, by removing the letter *aleph* from the word *emeth* [truth] written on its forehead, thereby spelling its death in the word *meth*, meaning death). "Once, however, the rabbi forgot to remove the *shem* [name]. The congregation was assembled for services in the synagogue and had already recited the ninety-second Psalm, when the mighty golem ran amuck, shaking houses, and threatening to destroy everything. Rabbi Löw was summoned; it was still dusk and the Sabbath had not really begun. He rushed at the raging golem and tore away the *shem*, whereupon the golem crumbled into dust" (*IG* 202–3).

Dans un seul coup

In Celan's "To One Who Stood Before The Door," the Golem is most directly associated with the figure of the

misbegotten . . .
the half-
shorn,
the
brother born in the
mercenary's dung-caked boot, the one
with the bloody
God-
member, the
chittering manikin

Kielkropf . . .
halb-
schürigen, dem
im kotigen Stiefel des Kriegsknechts
geborenen Bruder, dem
mit dem blutigen
Gottes-
gemächt, dem
schilpenden Menschlein.

Yet, surprisingly, the name inscribed in this deformed, mutilated, and misbegotten *Kielkropf* is no longer that of God or even that of his animating word, *emeth*. Instead, it is the name Kafka, and it is here that the "transfigurative translation, meticulous in its letter and detail" of which Derrida speaks is to be located. In "passing over . . . what the sudden appearance [l'apparition] of Rabbi Löw may recall . . . of the Golem," Derrida leaves open a place in his own reading for the intervention of another. Indeed, what appears in the guise of Rabbi Löw, what haunts his own "apparition" is not merely the related story of the Golem but also the way in which one creation narrative involving the performance of a proper name—of indeed *the* Proper Name—is shadowed by another.

What is conjured here is the well-known story of Kafka's own creative practice, the way so many creatures and characters in his texts are brought to life as transfigurative translations of his own notoriously improper proper name. It is just this specter that appears to hover about the lines quoted above, the only lines Derrida does not quote in his discussion of the poem. While the name *Kafka* figures prominently in his reading of "To One Who Stood Before The Door," Derrida only explicitly mentions the parable

"Before the Law." Yet if it is indeed a question of apparitions here, one might ask in turn: What other Kafka texts may be said to haunt the thresholds of Celan's poem? What other associations does the apparition of the *Kielkropf* in the poem's fifth line conjure with regard to the performance of Kafka's name? What is the relationship between this "transfigurative translation" of the name *Kafka* in the author's works and the performance of the unpronounceable divine Name in the tradition of golemic creation? In taking up these questions, we are reminded of the way Derrida begins his discussion of this poem, which speaks of a misbegotten creature's "bloody / God / member," by asking: "does one ever circumcise without circumcising a word? a name? And how can one circumcise a name without touching upon the body? First, upon the body of the name, which finds itself recalled by the wound to its condition as word, then as carnal mark, written, spaced, and inscribed in a network of other marks?" (*S* 54; *SPC* 98)

As has often been noted, the name *Kafka* awakens no more than onomatopoetic associations in German. Yet in Czech, which was the language Kafka used in his business and daily affairs throughout almost his entire life, the meaning of his name is immediately recognizable: *kavka* means "jackdaw," a kind of crow, and just such a bird served as the company emblem on the stationery of Kafka's father.[4] It is in this way that the name Kafka, translated into "jackdaw," is related to the ravens, crows, blackbirds, vultures, and storks of the writer's stories as well as to proper names such as Eduard Raban and the hunter Gracchus. Of particular relevance to Celan's poem is an entry in Kafka's diary that speaks about the name he received on the day of his circumcision: "In Hebrew my name is *Amschel*, like my mother's maternal grandfather" (*Diaries* 197; *Tagebücher* 318). As Hamacher comments, "not only does the *Amsel* (blackbird), a paronomasia of *Amschel*, belong to the family of the jackdaw—or the *kavka* family—and thereby anticipate the ornithonym in the maternal lineage; the name *Amschel* also contains the anagram *Lamm* (lamb), just as Kafka's mother's maiden name, Löwy, leads with a slight shift to *Löwe* (lion) and then to the generic name 'cat.'" The relevance of these transformations becomes apparent in Kafka's story "A Crossbreed," which tells of a cross between a lamb and a cat. "Whatever else it may be," Hamacher notes, "the catlamb is also the literalization of the fatal crossbreeding of Kafka's metamorphosed family names" (*Premises* 312).

Celan's lifelong preoccupation with Kafka's name and work is well documented. While in Bucharest between 1945 and 1947, he translated four of Kafka's short stories into Romanian. After completing a *licence ès lettres* in July 1950 in Paris, Celan did extensive research on the author in 1951–2 at the Bibliothèque nationale in preparation for a *diplôme d'études supérieures* that was never completed. Not only was the poet keenly attentive to Kafka's ornithonymic translation of his Hebrew name, evoking it in the first words of his 1965 poem "Vom Anblick der Amseln" ("From Beholding the Blackbirds")[5] but, as Bertrand Badiou notes, he was also particularly invested in the etymological connection linking his own patronym, *Antschel*, to Kafka's *Amschel-Amsel*, a connection he noted in a July 7, 1962, letter to the Kafka scholar Klaus Wagenbach and mentioned again in a diary entry of May 18, 1965 (Celan and Celan-Lestrange 222).

As was already noted, the most obvious allusion to Kafka in Celan's poem is contained in its opening line (also its title), which echoes the title and opening words of the famous parable "Before the Law." Such allusions draw attention to the legal parameters of Kafka's text, to the threshold of the law in the text as well to as its legal status as a text—that is, as a body of work over which its author may exercise certain proprietary rights. Yet one of the questions implicitly raised in Celan's poem is, what is it that belongs properly to "Kafka"? At issue in this question is not only the legal status of the proper name but—particularly for a poem published in a collection entitled *The No-one's Rose*—also the philosophical, existential, and poetic significance of its loss.[6] "When it goes as far as the death of the name," Derrida writes, "as far as the extinction of the proper name that a date, bereaved commemoration, still remains, loss cannot be worse" (*S* 52–3; *SPC* 95).

How then might Celan's poem be said to commemorate the lost property and properness of Kafka's name and, through it, other unnamable losses? A passage from Kafka's undelivered "Letter to His Father" enables one to gauge the stakes of this loss. "But since there was nothing at all I was certain of, since I needed to be provided at every instant with a new confirmation of my existence, since nothing was in my very own undoubted sole possession [eindeutig bestimmten Besitz], determined unequivocally only by me—in sober truth a disinherited son—naturally I became unsure even of the thing nearest to me, my own body."[7] This sense of radical dispossession, this visceral sense of self-estrangement and profound uncertainty with regard to the things nearest to him, is painfully enacted in Kafka's seemingly gratuitous plays on the body of his name. Disinherited and orphaned,[8] the name *Kafka* is but a misnomer, an uncircumcised "no name," a disembodied name and a nameless body, a no-one's body, a nothing and nobody.

Antonomasia is the rhetorical term for Kafka's disidentifying practice of translating his name into a common noun. Not only does antonomasia wipe away the singular traits marked by a name but it also takes away the transparency of the concept that is supposed to correspond to this name in the translation, rendering this concept useless as the instrument of a clear and distinct denotation. I quote again from Hamacher's Kafka essay:

> Wherever names and nouns, singular and general terms, can be generated from one another through antonomasia, critical distinctions in the domain of concept are no longer possible without qualification. And the same can be said of the production of concepts, the transparency of the particular within the general, and the subsumption of an individual under a universal law—all of which are demanded by conceptual thought. Virtually all words, not only nouns, construct a gloomy court around themselves by means of antonomasia, a court that becomes impenetrable once antonomasia spins out an entire story.
>
> (*Premises* 310)

While antonomasia clouds the transparency of the particular within the general and impedes the subsumption of an individual under a universal law, it also keeps the name from functioning as a unifying title or collective heading under which an otherwise diffuse corpus or anxiously dissolving body might be gathered together and held intact. What gathers by means of antonomasia in place of a discrete body, in place of the thing nearest to Kafka and still not exactly or entirely his own, is something hazy and spectral, a "gloomy court," as Hamacher writes, but also something Kafka would refer to as "the wound." It is this wound—gathering in the name of Kafka, gathering in a cloudy region somewhere between a proper name and a common noun, gathering as a "turbulent and ever-moving . . . mass" *in place of* a name or a body—that Celan reads in the Kafkan text. Like the poem "YOUR WAKING'S" discussed earlier, "TO ONE WHO STOOD BEFORE THE DOOR" "carries/the wound-read, the wound-gathered across" (setzt/Wundgelesenes über) (ctd in S 53–4; trans. mod.). Indeed, it is no exaggeration to say that it is around this wound that Celan's poem gathers itself together.

Shortly after coughing up blood on the night of August 4, 1917, and being diagnosed a month later with pulmonary tuberculosis, Kafka wrote the following to his friend Max Brod:

> there is still the wound of which the lesions in the lungs are only the symbol. You misunderstand it, Max, . . . but perhaps I also misunderstand it and there is no understanding these things . . . because there is no seeing it whole, so turbulent and ever-moving is the gigantic mass which yet at the same time never ceases to grow [weil es keinen Überblick gibt, so verwühlt und immer in Bewegung ist die riesige, im Wachstum nicht aufhörend Masse]. Misery, misery, but what is it but our own natures? And if the misery were ultimately to be disentangled (perhaps only women can do such work), you and I would fall apart.
>
> In any case my attitude toward the tuberculosis today resembles that of a child clinging to the pleats of its mother's skirts. If the disease came from my mother, the image fits even better, and my mother in her infinite solicitude, which far surpasses her understanding of the matter, has done me this service also. I am constantly seeking an explanation for this disease, for I did not seek it. Sometimes it seems to me that my brain and lungs came to an agreement without my knowledge. "Things can't go on this way," said the brain, and after five years the lungs said they were ready to help.[9]

The reference here is to Kafka's tempestuous five-year relationship with Felice Bauer. Stymied in his repeated attempts to break it off, he viewed the blood that flowed from his throat ("das Quellen aus der Kehle")[10] for ten minutes or longer in the night as an unconscious outburst. Speaking through his body, through a tacit agreement reached between his brain and his lungs without his knowledge, Kafka's unconscious now erupted in a bloody outpouring, giving voice to what he himself—*he as himself*—had been unable to put into words.[11] Later the same month, he wrote again to Brod: "Should I give thanks that I have not been able to marry? I would then have become all at once what I am now gradually becoming: mad. With shorter and shorter intermissions—during which not I but It gathers strength" (*Letters to Friends* 142). In a letter of the same month marking the beginning of the end of their gloomy courtship conducted largely through an extensive correspondence,[12] Kafka tells Felice of the events of early August and of his subsequent diagnosis, concluding the letter with a description of his tuberculosis as "a knife that stabs not only forward but one that wheels around and stabs back as well [es kreist und sticht auch zurück]" (*Letters to Felice* 544, trans. mod.; *Briefe an Felice* 754).[13]

If the rounding cut of circumcision delineates one crux of "To ONE WHO STOOD BEFORE THE DOOR," the wheeling knife of Kafka's tuberculosis marks the other. While the one is associated in Jewish and other traditions with life's beginnings—with the giving of Kafka's Hebrew name of matrilineal descent and, through Rabbi Löw, with the mystical tradition of golemic creation—the other is clearly associated with life's end. Perhaps nowhere in Celan's work is this wounding intersection of the thresholds of birth and death more painfully marked than in the 1953 poem he wrote in memory of another Franz. That poem, "Epitaph for François," was written in commemoration of the tragic loss of his first-born son, who died shortly after birth on October 8, 1953. In the poem life's beginning and end are figured as "both doors of the world," as doors that "stand open: / opened by you / in the twinight." As in Celan's epitaph for his French son—the *französichen Franz*, whose given name seemed to carry the promise of repatriation and naturalization the displaced poet so desperately sought at this time—the violently opening and shutting doors of "To ONE WHO STOOD BEFORE THE DOOR" stand together at the poem's swollen thresholds, each one beating through, each one striking at, the heart of the other.[14]

"To ONE WHO STOOD BEFORE THE DOOR" draws these two thresholds—each of which is opened to and by the circularly revolving, doubled-edged cut of the other—into the singular site of a multiple gathering, into the spreading mass of a mutating wound. "There is no seeing it whole," Kafka writes of this wound of which the lesions in his lungs are but a symbol, "so turbulent and ever-moving is the gigantic mass which yet at the same time never ceases to grow."[15] Gathered into Celan's text, this wound continues to grow, amassing all the incised words and cutting marks of the poem around it, drawing the poem itself into the vortex of a throttling silence.

This silence is most obviously associated with the figure of the Golem. "Rabbi Löw's homonculus," John Felstiner reminds us, "cannot speak" ("Kafka and the Golem" 175). Celan's *Kielkropf*, however, is not simply mute. It is a "schilpende[s] Menschlein," a chirping, cheeping, twittering, chittering manikin. While these birdlike sounds evoke Kafka's various ornithonyms and the Hebrew name given him upon circumcision, another letter to Brod of mid-September 1917 suggests a more specific reference. Characterizing himself as a vulture at the beginning of this letter, Kafka proceeds to describe the writing he and Brod do as "the same knife against whose blade our throats, our poor pigeons' throats, one here, one there, are cut," before recasting himself as a "reincarnation" of his uncle, "the country doctor."[16] "I sometimes call [him] the Twitterer, because he has such an inhumanly thin old-bachelor's birdlike wit that squeaks out of a constricted throat and never deserts him" (*Letters to Friends* 140). While the avuncular Twitterer may resonate in Celan's "chittering manikin," the narrows of his constricted glottis, out of which squeaks a birdlike wit, is linked to the other, even more unusual word, *Kielkropf*, used by Celan to refer to the golem.

It should be noted that the term *Kielkropf* had particular resonances for Celan, as the preliminary drafts of his 1960 *Meridian* address demonstrate. There he writes, "Only once you have been with your innermost pain among the crooked-nosed and Jew-speaking and misbegotten, goitery dead of Auschwitz and Treblinka and elsewhere [Erst wenn du mit deinem allereigentsten Schmerz bei den krummnasigen und mauschelnden und kielkröpfigen Toten von Auschwitz und Treblinka und anderswo gewesen bist], do you encounter the eye and its almond" (*M* 127; trans. mod.). *Kielkropf*, Felstiner notes, is a dialect term meaning changeling, abortion, monster, or, colloquially, dolt. The editors of the *Tübinger Ausgabe* of *Die Niemandsrose* define it as a misshapen child, a satanically inserted changeling ("von Satan untergeschobenes, mißgestaltetes Kind").[17] The creature's malformation, its aborted, unfinished *af*formation, certainly link it to the Hebrew sense of the term *gōlem* appearing in Psalm 139:16, where it means the unformed, the amorphous. Yet, insofar as this figure is a misshapen changeling, it stands also as the very figure of disfiguring substitution, as a figure for the rhetorical figure of paronomasia privileged by Celan in his poetry. The relevance of this figure to the ensuing argument is such that I quote Hamacher's comprehensive discussion of it at length.

> In explicit instances of paronomasia—as when *"Zangen"* [forceps] is placed alongside *"Zungen der Sehensucht"* [tongues of longing], the *"Verbrante"* [incinerated] alongside the *"Verbannten"* [exiled], *"Schläfe"* [temples] alongside *"schlaflos"* [sleepless], *"Erzväter"* [patriarchs] alongside *"Erzflitter"* [the glitter

of ore], and *"das blutende Ohr"* [bloody ear] alongside *"blühselige Botschaft"* [blessed tidings]—the phonetic proximity of the words whereby one affects the other with its semantic potential sets a verbal unity into oscillation . . . In implicit instances of paronomasia, a minimal alteration of the phonetic or graphic form of a word that does not itself appear produces another word, and this other word acts as a distorted echo of the first: *"rauchdünn"* [smoke-thin] thus replaces *"hauchdünn"* [filmy] (1: 288); *"Morgen-Lot"* [morning plumb line] stands in for *"Morgenrot"* [dawn]; *"Ferse"* [heels] for *"Verse"* [verses] (2: 25); *"Pestlaken"* [plague shroud] for *"Bettlaken"* [bed sheet] (2: 153); and *"Datteln"* [the dates one eats] for *"Daten"* [the dates of a calendar] (2: 134). If in explicit paronomasia the alteration is manifest and the semantic destabilization is confined to the localized zone of the word as it appears in the text, the corresponding word in implicit paronomasia remains latent, its shape uncertain, and so it exposes every word in the text to the possibility of being an alteration of some lost paradigm, which stubbornly withdraws from rational or divinatory reconstruction. Each of these words presents itself—if not exclusively then at least primarily—as the disfiguration of what has gone silent, *a limine*, as the translation of what does not give rise to voice, as the carrying over of everything muted.

(*Premises* 355–7)

In "To One Who Stood Before The Door," the word *Kielkropf* is not only the figure of this figure but also itself an implicit paronomasia of the German term *Kehlkopf*, or "larynx." As Celan well knew, Kafka suffered and eventually died from the tubercular infection that, by 1924, had spread from his lungs to his larynx. Toward the end of his life, the pain in his throat had become so acute that Kafka was prevented from eating, drinking, or even speaking. "Frankfurt, September," the second poem of *Fadensonnen* (*Threadsuns*) published in 1968, alludes in its last lines to this fatal condition, linking it to the squeaking or *piepsen* of Kafka's last story, "Josefine, the Singer, or the Mouse People," written at a time when the author had first begun to notice the symptoms of the disease of the larynx. As a friend of Kafka's last days, Robert Klopstock notes, "one evening when he had finished the last page of the story he said to me: 'I think I began to investigate that animal squeaking at the right time'" (*Letters to Friends* 495). The *Kielkropf* of "To One Who Stood Before The Door" presents itself then as the disfiguration of what has gone silent, as the carrying across of Kafka's muted *Kehl-*

kopf, as the translation of what gives rise not to voice but instead only to a certain twittering.

Read as an implicit paronomasia of *Kehlkopf*, Celan's *Kielkropf* links the twittering of the golemic manikin to the squeaking of Kafka's tubercular larynx. It also at the same time draws attention to the goiterous neck (*kropfigen Hals*) of the changeling, or *Wechselbalg*, as it is depicted in fairy tales and sagas of the nineteenth century, during which time the term *Kielkropf* was still very much in use. Commenting on Celan's own use of the term, Elke Günzel observes that the "word itself onomatopoetically stages the figure's distortion. Like the keel of a ship, the goiterous swelling juts out of the throat [Wie ein Schiffskiel beult sich der Kropf aus dem Hals]" (208, my trans.). In the context of all the cut words, marks, and lines of the poem—among which "Ra- —," "halb-/schürigen," and "Gottes-/gemächt" are only the most explicit examples—it should be noted that the term *Kielkropf* is itself composed of two cutting instruments. *Kiel*, as Günzel notes, is the keel of a boat as well as a quill or stylus and the keel-shaped anatomical part, ridge, or process known in English as a carina. Similarly, *Kropf* can mean not only goiter, but also the crop, craw, or maw of a bird, the bow of a ship, or a projecting part.

While Celan probably did not know Kafka's letters to Felice—which were purchased by Schocken Books in 1955 but not published until 1967, at the time when "To One Who Stood Before The Door" was written—and may therefore not have read Kafka's particular description of his tuberculosis as a wheeling knife, the resemblance between this knife and the term in Celan's poem most closely associated with Kafka's tubercular *Kehlkopf* is nonetheless striking. If Kafka's tuberculosis is a double-edged illness and itself related to the knife of writing, against whose blade two "poor pigeons' throats [armer Taubenhälse] ... are cut,"[18] Celan's *Kielkropf* is a monstrously deformed figure misbegotten as the intersection of two cutting edges, as the wounded and wounding pairing of a *Kiel* and a *Kropf*. Insofar as this *Kielkropf* is also a changeling substituted by means of paronomasia for a *Kehlkopf*, the quills, keels, craws, maws, and bows it carries may themselves be resituated in the narrows of Kafka's closing throat. Taking the place of Kafka's silenced *Kehlkopf* in the poem, Celan's *Kielkropf* stands at the very intersection of body and text. This edge on which the poem maintains itself marks the point at which the body of a word gathers like scar tissue around an acute and throttled pain only to have the seam along which it is stitched together, the syllabic break within the word *Kielkropf*, torn asunder. Parting into a *Kiel* and a *Kropf*, the two sides of the word are reopened as the cut and cutting edges of a resurfacing wound.[19]

In "Frankfurt, September," this unmutable mass of ever-moving silence suffers another disfiguring mutation, resurfacing at the poem's conclusion as a singular occlusion, as a *Kehlkopfverschlusslaut*, or glottal stop that sings.[20] I cite in its entirety this poem woven like a *Traumschrift* both from Kafka's diaries and stories and from fragments excerpted from Freud's *Interpretation of Dreams*.

> Blind, light-
> bearded display wall. '
> A maybeetle dream
> illuminates it.
> Behind it, lamentation-screened,
> Freud's forehead opens up,
> the tear
> hard-silenced outside
> shoots up with the phrase:
> "For the last
> time psycho-
> logy."
> The simili-
> jackdaw
> breakfasts.
> The glottal stop
> sings.[21]

> Blinde, licht-
> bärtige Stellwand.
> Ein Maikäfertraum
> leuchtet sie aus.
> Dahinter, klagegerastert,
> tut sich Freuds Stirn auf,
> die draußen
> hartgeschwiegene Träne
> schießt an mit dem Satz:
> "Zum letzten-
> mal Psycho-

logie."
Die Simili-
Dohle
frühstückt.
Der Kehlkopfverschlußlaut
singt.

(GW 2: 114)

The last word, "sings," associated with Josefine's squeaking and Kafka's own stopped-up glottis, occupies the same place in the poem as the "Ra- —" of "To One Who Stood Before The Door." If, in a first moment, this "Ra- —" was viewed in relation to the scene of circumcision staged in the poem as a cut ironically incised in the body of the circumciser, in the body of the name Rabbi Löw, it now must also be read, with regard to the wound gathered in Kafka's disease-ridden larynx, as the insistence of an unstillable silence, as the mute outpouring of an unconscious body, as the disowned voice of an unconscious that twitters unwittingly in the name of Kafka. Celan's poem gathers itself about this unconscious opening like the mouse folk around Josefine, gathering itself toward it as the *Rachenlaut*, or guttural sound, of the *Ra-* left to resonate in its own occluded end.[22] It is in this way that the singular cut of circumcision, the belated temporality of what is repeatedly enacted in one double and divided stroke—"dans un seul coup"—is displaced by the wheeling knife of Kafka's tuberculosis and silently reinscribed in one throat, "dans un seul cou."

In the Place of Kafka's Throat

"I think I began to investigate that animal squeaking at the right time," Kafka said upon the completion of "Josefine." Celan's poetic reading of Kafka's last story, a reading that, in the words of "Your Waking's," carries the wound-read across, raises questions that resonate with—and ultimately stand as open as—the wounds of which they treat. On the one hand, "Frankfurt, September" suggests that the silent assemblies once occasioned by Josefine's squeaking now find another gathering place, a new—perhaps even an "old-new"—"synagogue" in the constricted narrows of Kafka's tubercular larynx.²³ It further implies that it is here that the memory of her actual squeaking, of a squeaking that even in her lifetime had already been nothing more than a memory, is kept. On the other hand, the poem suggests that what "sings" in "Josefine" is but the turbulently catachrestic, ever-moving mass of the wound growing in Kafka's throat. Rather than choosing between these two hands, Celan's hauntingly resonant sentence "The glottal stop/sings" presses them together and, in doing so, reminds us that for him there is no "basic difference between a handshake [einem Händedruck] and a poem."

Like the body of the poem "To One Who Stood Before The Door," which is drawn around the throttled *râle* of the " Ra- —" it draws toward,²⁴ "Frankfurt, September" contracts around a narrow opening at its end, an *Engführung* in which the singing of Kafka's last story and the straitened glottis of his last days pass anxiously into and through one another. It is into the narrows of this tightly compressed passageway that the "wound-read, the wound gathered"— the gathering wound Celan never stopped reading in the name of Kafka—is carried. Ostensibly an act of translation and transmission, an act of *Übersetzung*, this process of carrying the wound across becomes for Celan a way of opening his language and poetry to the untranslatable violence of an unspeakable and irrepressible pain stuck in the throat, a pain that cannot simply be silenced or voiced. As though suspended at the very threshold of speech and silence, this unassimilable excess is left to perseverate there, simultaneously calling for and resisting translation.

Like the *après coup* of the singular stroke of circumcision in Derrida's "Shibboleth," Kafka's throat for Celan is never *un seul cou*. It is instead the singular site of a multiple gathering. Indeed, what gathers in the place of Kafka's throat, in the place of mouse-like stillness held open in the midst of the people by Josefine's singing, is the traumatic memory of yet another unforgettable loss—that of Celan's own beloved mother, Fredericke. Deported from Czernowitz to a German camp in the Ukraine, she was murdered by the SS in 1942. According to the most reliable reports, the cause of death was a gunshot wound to the neck.²⁵

SIX

Poetry's Demands and Abrahamic Sacrifice:
Celan's Poems for Eric

In the spring and summer of 1968 Paul Celan addressed a number of poems to his son Eric, the second of his sons and the only one still alive. His first, François, had died shortly after birth in October 1953 and, as noted in Chapter 4, his passing is commemorated in the poem "Grabschrift für François" ("Epitaph for François"), which was published in the 1955 collection *Von Schwelle zu Schwelle* (*From Threshold to Threshold*). Celan and his wife, the artist Gisèle Celan-Lestrange, were deeply marked by the loss of their first child. We know from their correspondence that the child's name had been agreed upon very early on in their courtship.[1] Indeed, for the poet described by his future wife's family as "un juif . . . apatride . . . de langue allemande" (a stateless . . . German-speaking . . . Jew) (*CCL* II: 72), the name *François* seemed to carry a promise of repatriation associated with the naturalization papers he filed at this time along with a request to have his surname, *Antschel, francisé* as Celan.[2] In the name *François* he thus seems to have imagined his own translation into a French citizen with an officially recognized French name.

97

Yet, as a poet Celan remained deeply attached to the German language. A brilliantly accomplished translator of poems from French, Slavic, and Anglo-American traditions, Celan always insisted that his own poems be written in German—even if, as he put it, these poems could no longer "speak the language which many willing ears seem to expect" (*CP* 15); even if, one might add, these poems sometimes bore French titles or were arranged as multi-lingual citational compositions.

There was, however, one poem Celan wrote entirely in French, a poem addressed to his thirteen-year-old son, Eric, in the summer of 1968. Unlike the two written in German shortly beforehand, both of which bear the dedicatory title "Für Eric" ("For Eric") and are included in the collection *Schneepart* (*Snow Part*), this French poem remained untitled and unpublished during Celan's lifetime.[3] Appearing only in a posthumous edition of his work, the poem is accompanied there by a photograph of the page—or rather the *feuille*—on which it was written (Celan, *Die Gedichte* 327).

As noted above, all three poems were written in the late spring and summer of 1968. Among the questions to be explored in what follows are, Why at this time was Celan writing poems to his son? What was his relationship to poetry and to Eric at this time? In what ways are these poems *about* time—or more specifically about "this time"? To what does the deictic "this time" (*ce temps*) that appears in the French poem point? What is the relationship between this temporal index and the figure of the "arrowing hand" with which the first of the two German poems closes? Why, finally, was the only poem Celan ever wrote entirely in French addressed to his son?

These are fairly specific questions about poems that until now have received little critical attention. Yet in posing them I want to begin to approach a much larger and more troubling issue. Throughout the 1960s Celan suffered from increasingly debilitating mental breakdowns often associated with violent acts committed by him or that he feared were going to be committed against his loved ones. These acts included an attempt to kill his wife with a knife in the night of November 23–24, 1965, after which he was taken to a hospital and placed in a straightjacket (*CCL* II: 264). In a letter of December 9, 1965, written from the clinic to which he had been confined, he confided to Gisèle that he found himself faced with a terrible alternative, the precise nature of which he did not specify at that time.[4] However, in an letter dated January 14, 1970, and addressed to his wife, from whom he was now forced to live apart because of his unstable mental condition and the potential danger he posed to her and their son, he returned to this alternative, noting, "The 'kilodrama' has taken place. Faced with the alternative between my poems and our son I have chosen: our son. He is entrusted to you, help him" (Le 'kilodrame' s'est produit. Devant l'alternative entre mes poèmes et notre fils, j'ai choisi: notre fils. Il t'est confié, aide-le) (*CCL* I: 687).[5] To this letter the following note is added by Bertrand Badiou, editor of the couple's correspondence: "According to oral testimony given by Gisèle . . . and reported by André du Bouchet, Celan would express this alternative in explicit terms during moments of delirium, saying that poetry was demanding of him that he re-perform 'the sacrifice of Abraham'" (en disant que la poésie exigeait de lui qu'il refasse "le sacrifice d'Abraham") (*CCL* II: 449). The phrase "sacrifice of Abraham" is of course terribly ambiguous; for it suggests not only that the sacrifice demanded by poetry be performed by the father on his beloved son but also, at least grammatically, that the father himself be the sacrificial victim. The genitive construction thus compels us to consider a possible identification of father and son, a sacrifice of the one as the other.

Celan's fears about the safety and well-being of his son were at times so acute in the late 1960s that on one occasion he became delirious and attacked a neighbor living on his floor at the rue Tournefort who he imagined was in the process of hurting Eric.[6] Immediately afterward, Celan was taken to a psychiatric infirmary where, according to Badiou, he remained in a state of total silence ("dans un mutisme total") interrupted only by murmurs of "je suis français" (I am French) and "j'ai été opéré d'un poumon" (*CCL* II: 427), the latter an allusion the lung operation performed on him following his January 30, 1967, suicide attempt in which he tried to stab himself in the heart.[7]

While I see no direct connection between the events just described or the remarks cited and the poems Celan addressed to his son in 1968, and while I will not read these poems exclusively or even primarily as playing out in some way the "terrible alternative" with which Celan saw himself faced at times—and perhaps on some level at all times—I do think it is important to have a sense of the very fraught, complex, and ultimately undelimitable context in which these poems were written.

The remarks I have cited do suggest that Celan at times conceived of his relationship to poetry and to his son in terms of "the sacrifice of Abraham" and that, in these terms, he experienced poetry's address—its calling, vocation, demands, and exactions—in a manner not unlike Abraham when he felt himself addressed by Yahweh. That said, the topos of Abrahamic sacrifice can in no way be confined to this context—especially not in the work of Celan, where it is enmeshed throughout his oeuvre in a network of relations involving burnt offerings, holocausts, sacrificial victims, animal substitutes, scapegoats, and rams' horns. Derrida's reading of the poem "GROSSE, GLÜHENDE WÖLBUNG" ("VAST GLOWING VAULT") in his essay "Rams" focuses on just this network of relations, doing so with exemplary sensitivity and rigor (Derrida, *Sovereignties* 135).

Written in the Stars

Bearing all these caveats, contexts and questions in mind, let us turn now to the first of the three poems Celan wrote to his son, Eric.

> FÜR ERIC
>
> Erleuchtet
> rammt ein Gewissen
> die hüben und drüben
> gepestete Gleichung,
>
> später als früh: früher
> hält die Zeit sich die jähe
> rebellische Waage,
>
> ganz wie du, Sohn,
> meine mit dir pfeilende
> Hand.
>   (*GW* 2: 372)

> FOR ERIC
>
> A conscience
> enlightened, rams
> the equation plagued
> on both sides,
>
> later than soon: time
> sooner holds its sheer
> rebellious balance,

just as you, son,
my hand that arrows
with you.
    (*Snow* Part 82)

    Beginning with the layout of the words on the page, it should be noted how, in contrast to Farley's translation, the first and last words of the original poem, *Erleuchtet* and *Hand*, are given their own lines. Set off at the beginning and end in the only two single-word lines of the poem, they illustrate the theme of symmetry that runs throughout. It should further be noted that the first word *Erleuchtet* ("enlightened" or "illuminated") stands alone at the head of the poem. All lit up, as it were, it stands over the text, standing overhead like a luminous word in the heavens, like a glowing star or astral cluster to which a word or name has been assigned. Indeed, what the first word, *Erleuchtet*, gives us to see are the clusters of word-stars, the verbal-astral constellations, and signs of the zodiac arrayed across the three stanzas of the poem. Each stanza is associated with a different astrological sign: the first with Aries or *Widder*; the second with Libra or *Waage*; and the third with Sagittarius or *Schütze*. Since the three stanzas are all part of a single sentence, we may assume that the sign associated with each stands in some relation to the others, an assumption reinforced by the commas placed at the end of the first two stanzas. Setting them off as independent units, the commas also join each of these stanzas to the one or ones that follow. In doing so, they arrange the poem into a cluster of zodiac signs, into a constellation of constellations that have to be read not only in terms of their own static pattern, their own location in the heavens or the time of year with which they are associated, but also and above all in relation to one another.

    It is not by chance in this regard that the first two signs, Aries and Libra, are connected with times of transition, with particular turning points in the zodiac calendar. Beginning on March 21, Aries is associated with the vernal equinox, while Libra, beginning around September 23, coincides with its autumnal counterpart. At these two times of the year, known in German as *Tagundnachtgleiche*, day and night are not only of equal length but also in effect of equal weight. Balancing each other out, they hold time in the balance—which is to say that they hold it open and in suspense.

    Allusions to these astrological signs and the meridianal moments associated with them—moments, that is, when time seems momentarily to pause, gape, and come to a standstill—are legible in the first two stanzas of the poem. In the first stanza, the sign of Aries, or *Widder*—and the vernal equinox with which it coincides—is most closely associated with the verb *rammt* (rams) in line two, the ram, and in particular its horns, being the sign's visual symbol. The equal length of day and night at the time of the vernal equinox is suggested not only by the symmetry, rhyme, and meaning of the phrase *hüben und drüben* (on both sides) in the third line but also in the word *Gleichung* (equation) at the end of the fourth. That this equation is the object of the verb *rammt* and is itself modified by the adjective *gepestete* (plagued) suggests not only that the precarious equation of day and night is being rammed and upset on both sides at once but also that such equinoctial equivalences have from the very first been plagued by a certain instability, the very instability that moves this otherwise self-contained stanza beyond itself, tipping it over into the next.[8]

The second stanza does not so much follow from the first as repeat it in displaced form, just as the autumnal equinox—associated with the sign of Libra, or *Waage*, which is mentioned by name in this stanza—marks the same day-night equivalence as its vernal counterpart. The difference or displacement in the repetition is reflected in a shift between stanzas from the language of mathematics and equations to that of weights and balances as well as in a shift from the sphere of conscience to that of justice and its scales. The temporal equipoise associated with the autumnal equinox is reflected in the rhetorical equilibrium of the terms *früher* and *später* ("earlier" and "later"), which are placed like scales at each end of the second stanza's first line, and is reinforced by the assertion that "time holds its ... balance." Yet at the same time that such an assertion is made, a destabilizing force seems once again to be at work, unsettling the balance from within. This force is associated not only with the imbalance of the phrase *später als früh* (later than soon) but also with the adjective "rebellious," which suggests an internecine struggle and perhaps even a renewal of hostilities after a tense standoff or temporary truce.

Once again, it is this element of internal conflict, this imbalance of forces within a seemingly stable, well-balanced, and evenly matched situation, that moves the stanza beyond itself, carrying its unresolved tensions over into the next. These tensions are perhaps most closely and literally associated with the tensed bow held in what is referred to as the poet's own "arrowing hand." This self-characterization of the poet as archer is doubly motivated; for it not only places the final stanza under the sign of Sagittarius, or *Schütze*—which is traditionally associated with the image of a centaur holding a drawn bow—but it also draws attention to the fact that this sign was Celan's own. It is perhaps for this reason that the poet, born on November 23, speaks at this point of *"my* . . . arrowing/hand."

As the unresolved tensions of the preceding stanzas carry over into the third, so too does a language of equations and scales heretofore associated with those equinoctial moments when day and night are of equal length and time itself seems to hold its balance. Such language is taken up most obviously and immediately in the opening words of the stanza: "ganz wie du, Sohn" (exactly like you, son). Just as time holds out against itself, holding itself open and in suspense, so, too, do you, son, hold my arrowing hand. Holding it back, you hold it poised to shoot. Yet this poise, this careful weighing, must also hold itself in the balance, hold itself against itself in exquisite equipoise, hold itself—and the arrow it holds tightly in its hand—delicately balanced on the point of being shot.

That the hand held at the point of utmost tension between father, son, string, and arrow is placed on a separate line at the very end of the poem is telling. For its placement seems to focus all our attention on that hand, on the energies gathering within its grip, and on the arrow it holds but never quite lets fly. Held at the point of release, the conjoined arrow and hand, the "arrowing/hand," as Celan calls it, holds on to its potential, holds on and holds out as sheer potential.[9]

Yet, well aimed, it nevertheless points, tracing a virtual trajectory we can follow beyond the poem's end, a trajectory that will lead us *später als früh* (later than soon) from the hand to a certain heart. Indeed, if we look to the heavens and follow the archer's aim, we see that the arrow of Sagittarius points directly at the star Antares, also known as the "Heart of the Scorpion." Like the unreleased arrow of its concluding stanza, the poem itself points beyond the *Punkt* or period on which it ends. Like that arrow, it points without ever striking, instead only tracing a visual trajectory we can follow. This sightline is in a sense the virtual last line of the poem, the line never committed to paper whose traces are nevertheless legible in the heavens.

Yet, once again, it is not only the sheer potential of the final stanza that carries over into this last line—if indeed it is one—but also the element of unresolved conflict. As we have seen, an inherent instability associated with adjectives like "plagued" in the first stanza and "rebellious" in the second repeatedly spills over from one strophe to the next, setting not only the poem but time itself back in motion. As the poem is now made to move again—moving this time from a seemingly well-defined, symmetrically balanced verbal corpus to a brightly glowing astral body—the elements warring within it move as well. Nowhere is this more apparent than in the name of the luminous red star sighted at the end of the poem's last line. For the name *Antares*, meaning "against or opposed to Ares," refers to the star's age-old rivalry with Ares' Roman counterpart, the planet Mars, that other bright red body shining in the heavens. At war with Mars, Antares carries that rivalry within its own doubly martial name.

There are, however, moments when the star manages to outshine its rival. Indeed, at no time during the year does Antares, the bloody red "Heart of the Scorpion," shine brighter than on May 31, the date on which the poem was written. Pointing beyond its end, the poem thus in a sense points back to its beginning. Yet, in doing so, it also locates itself among all those luminous points in the heavens, all those constellations and zodiac signs it will have traversed in its own poetic movement. It pursues this course, the title suggests, for the sake of Eric.

In pointing to his son, addressing him directly within the poem and dedicating the poem itself to him, does Celan thereby include him in it? And what would it mean to be included in this poem written in the stars? Composed a week before Eric's thirteenth birthday, the poem is perhaps a blessing, one that may in its own way repeat the blessing of Abraham. For, as will be recalled, it is immediately after the interruption of the sacrifice that Yahweh tells Abraham that he will make his descendants as numerous as the stars of heaven (Gen. 22:17), that his seed will multiply like the stars. Have we moved then from the "sacrifice of Abraham," with which we began and which caused Celan such terrible anguish, to the equally equivocal "blessing of Abraham," to which the poem seems to allude and which the poet himself appears even to perform? Are the sacrifice and blessing in fact so different or, are they, as Derrida has suggested, but two aspects of one and the same scene, two sides of the same interruption?[10] It might be recalled in this regard that it is on both sides, *hüben und drüben*, that the ramming of the opening stanza occurs.

Poetry in Translation

Celan's second poem dedicated to his son was composed two days after the first, on June 2, 1968. In contrast to the first poem, which seems to have been written in the stars, the second appears firmly grounded in the events of May 1968, many of which took place near the poet's home on the rue Tournefort and his place of work, the École normale supérieure on the rue d'Ulm. It is necessary to read the poem in the context of these events but also to follow a linguistic thread spun out in the movement of its single sentence across four stanzas of alternating two- and one-line lengths. It is this thread, I will argue, that ties the two German poems Celan wrote for Eric to the one he composed entirely in French a number of weeks later.

FÜR ERIC

In der Flüstertüte
buddelt Geschichte,

in den Vororten raupen die Tanks,

unser Glas
füllt sich mit Seide,

wir stehen.

(*GW* 2: 376)

FOR ERIC

In the megaphone,
history is grubbing away,

in the suburbs tanks creep like caterpillars,

our glass
fills itself with silk,

we stand.

(Celan, *Last* 127)

The megaphone with which the poem opens and in which history is said to be "grubbing away" certainly locates the text in the volatile atmosphere of the student uprising and the demonstrations in which Celan and his son participated. As Felstiner notes, Celan was living apart from his family at the time, and when his son Eric, just turning thirteen, visited him, they walked through the streets, Celan singing the Internationale and other revolutionary songs in Russian, Yiddish, and French. Eric felt proud of his father. At the same time Celan bridled when students mimicked the Hitler salute or proclaimed "We are all Jews," or when wall posters equated Paris security police with the SS or De Gaulle's logo with the swastika. "It's not all that simple," he was heard to say. And he saw in Paris the dangers of revolutionary fanaticism.

(Felstiner, *Paul Celan*, 258)[11]

There is thus something equivocal about the megaphone mentioned in the poem's opening line. For while it no doubt expresses Celan's solidarity with the demonstrators, it also at the same time indicates a certain wariness of demagogic posturing—precisely the kind of posturing with which he had already taken issue in the first poem of the 1967 collection *Atemwende* (*Breathturn*) and to which he would return in the opening lines of the French poem addressed to his son a few weeks later.[12] Echoing the opening of "Für Eric," that poem begins with the admonition "Ô les hableurs / n'en sois pas" (O the braggarts / don't be one of them).

Not only does "Für Eric" appear to take aim at the figure of the *Maulheld*—the boaster, braggart, or loudmouth—but, curiously enough, it seems to focus less on the sounds that come out of the megaphone, less on the voice amplified and projected by it, than on what goes on within it: "In der Flüstertüte / buddelt Geschichte" (In the megaphone / history is grubbing away). The importance of this location and the digging or grubbing that goes on inside it is emphasized by the parallel construction of the following phrase which begins "in den Vororten" (in the suburbs). To understand what is going on inside this megaphone, it is necessary to look more closely at the word *Flüstertüte*, which Celan uses in place of the more common nouns *Megaphon* or *Sprachrohr*.

The source of the term is apparently an article published in the weekend issue of the *Frankfurter Allgemeine Zeitung*, June 1–2, 1968, entitled "Revolutionäre Frühling" ("Revolutionary Spring"). Celan closely followed coverage of current events in the German press, seeking not only to gauge foreign reactions to the Paris student uprising and the French government's often brutal response to it but also to keep abreast of the development of modern colloquial German, to which he otherwise had access only through occasional trips to Germany and Switzerland and correspondence with friends, like the poet Franz Wurm. The *FAZ* article on which he draws describes the *Flüstertüte* as a transitorized megaphone that, in the course of the Paris demonstrations, had become something of a "tactical weapon" (*taktische Waffe*).[13] Its use by the student leader Daniel Cohn-Bendit, in whom Celan had taken a strong personal interest because of the controversies surrounding his national citizenship and his expulsion to Germany on May 22, receives special mention in the article: "Kühl, hell und klar klingt seine Stimme aus der Flüstertüte" (His voice rang out coolly, brightly and clearly from the megaphone).[14] Here the emphasis is on the speaker and the quality of his mechanically augmented voice, whereas in Celan's poem it is more a question of what goes on within the apparatus itself. Indeed, Celan's use of the highly unusual and colloquial term *Flüstertüte*, literally meaning "whisper bag," suggests that there is something else quietly at work in the sound system, something gently whispering amid all the loud noise. Not only does this whisper speak with and through the more audible voice of the poem but, as we shall see, it also burrows, digs, and grubs its way through it.

To explore this burrowing and the historical animal implicitly associated with it in a poem composed in the potentially revolutionary context of May 1968, it is necessary to turn briefly to Marx's *Eighteenth Brumaire*. An analysis of the 1851 coup d'état of Louis Napoleon, Marx's text not only describes revolutionary movements in pointedly theatrical terms but also cites a key moment in Shakespeare's *Hamlet* in which the ghost in the cellarage is addressed as an "old mole." Describing the revolution as "thoroughgoing" (*gründlich*), "still journeying through purgatory," and doing "its work methodically," Marx predicts that when it has completed the second half of its "preliminary work, Europe will leap from her seat and exultantly exclaim: "Brav gewühlt, alter Maulwurf!" (Well grubbed, old mole!).[15] As has often been noted, the accent here is on the mole's burrowing and digging, just as Hegel's discussion of *Hamlet* in his *Lectures on the Philosophy of History* focuses on the animal's subterranean labor: "Brav gearbeitet, wackerer Maulwurf" (Well done, intrepid mole).[16] Anxious to emphasize the labor of the negative, the silent underground work of preparation, and the "purgatorial" activities of mining and undermining in which the Revolution and or the Spirit are engaged, both Marx and Hegel leave out the first words of the passage in *Hamlet* to which they refer. The omission is all the more significant given the fact that the passage in question concerns not only the relationship between speech and silence but also the performance of words as deeds.

Having just concluded a solitary meeting with the ghost of his father in Act 1, Hamlet is joined on stage by Horatio and Marcellus, of whom he begs, "Never make known what you have seen tonight" (1.5: 144).[17] When the Danish prince asks his friends to swear on his sword to be silent, the ghost of his father echoes this demand from its position under the stage, in the so-called cellarage, the scenic metaphor for Purgatory.[18] To this Hamlet quickly responds, "Well said, old mole, canst work in the ground so fast? / A worthy pioneer" (1.5.162–3).[19]

Like Hamlet's speech, the first two lines of Celan's poem bring together the act of saying with that of grubbing, as though the one were from the very first at work in the other, pioneering underways into and through the other, opening speaking to the silent labor of digging, excavating within speech a literary-historical echo chamber, and cellaring within it haunting citations that in their very multiplicity resonate with and are amplified by their relations to others. If *Geschichte* (history) is the grammatical subject and literal agent of the first stanza, it is a revolutionary subject that grubs away in the megaphone only to the extent that its digging makes way for something else. Self-undermining, it leaves its voice open to the whispering of others, to a colloquy of citations reverberating through the burrows of history, to citations that speak in underground ways about history's own underground ways.[20]

Obviously, there is no explicit mention of any speaking or pioneering animal in the opening lines of the poem—such are, perhaps, its underground ways. The animal's presence, however, is retroactively suggested by the strangely out-of-place appearance of a caterpillar, or *Raupe*, in the very next line: "in den Vororten raupen die Tanks" (in the suburbs tanks creep like caterpillars). Celan coins the verb *raupen* on the model of the noun *Raupe* (meaning "caterpillar," "grub," or "worm") and the adjectival prefix *Raupen-*, which appears in terms like *Raupenhelm* and *Raupenkette*, both of which are relevant to the poem. *Raupenhelm* denotes a helmet with a caterpillar-shaped decoration worn by nineteenth-century German cavalry regiments and is to be found in an earlier draft of the text[21]; *Raupenkette* is a technical term referring to the crawler or rotating track over and by means of which a tank moves, and it appears in the final version of the poem as the verb *raupen*, itself a metonym of *Raupenkette*. The term no doubt alludes to the movement of the tanks deployed by the government to the outskirts of Paris in late May 1968. Yet however motivated the military allusion may be, what still remains to be explained is why the martial and the animal, the *Raupenhelm*, *Raupenkette*, and *Raupe*, are brought together here.

To begin to address this question, it is worth recalling that the phrase in which the verb *raupen* (to creep like a caterpillar) appears begins like the one preceding it, with an "in the" construction. The formal similarity of the two phrases, however, serves only to underscore their symmetrical opposition; that is, the action in the one occurs within and below, while the other takes place without and above.[22] To put it in less formal terms, the historical and grammatical subject of the first stanza, *Geschichte*—a relative perhaps of Marx's revolutionary mole—seems to work and whisper in underground ways (and perhaps even, like the student protestors, to travel the Parisian underground, emerging with mole-like unpredictability at particular Métro stations and secretly whispered rallying points),[23] while the caterpillar-like tanks of the second move above ground in the suburbs, laying the very tracks upon which they creep and threatening to crush whatever stands in their way.

These relationships change in the third stanza, where yet another animal appears—or rather appears to appear—on the scene. In contrast to the revolutionary and counterrevolutionary animals of the first two stanzas, both of whom are introduced by "in the" constructions and each of whom is positioned as a mirror-like inversion of the other, the animal appearing here is much harder to locate. No longer held in place by parallel constructions and symmetrical inversions, it is associated instead with the between-space of glass mentioned in the pivotal phrase "unser Glas / füllt sich mit Seide" (our glass / fills itself with silk). To explain why this glass should be seen less as a transparent container and more as a translucent between-space, it is necessary to note first how a change in spatial relations in this stanza is closely related to a shift in the status of subjects and verbs. Whereas the third-person subjects of the two preceding stanzas—*Geschichte* (history) and *Tanks* (tanks)—were accompanied respectively by transitive and intransitive verbs—*buddelt* (grubs away) and *raupen* (creep)—in this stanza a first-person subject—*unser Glas* (our glass)—has as its predicate a reflexive verb—*füllt sich* (fills itself).

Returning now to the new animal that appears to appear in this stanza, it should be noted how, as the glass fills itself with *Seide* (silk), the *Raupe* (caterpillar) of the previous stanza seems to metamorphose into a *Seidenraupe* (silkworm), doing so, it would appear, on the glassy surface of language itself. Yet precisely because language is in this transitional moment the very locus of metamorphosis, it can no longer be considered glassy—at least not insofar as glassiness is traditionally associated with a certain transparency and self-effacement of the linguistic medium.

Moreover, as the medium draws attention to itself as a locus of transformation, as an inter-space in which caterpillars metamorphose into silkworms, so too does the language of the poem itself undergo a metamorphosis. Yet rather than changing immediately into another language, rather than shifting tongues in a clear and obvious way, it remains indefinitely suspended between languages, tarrying in the inter-medium of translation. This inter-medium, the poem suggests, is an inter-state, a state of incomplete metamorphosis, a silky, semitransparent cocoon-like state of suspension, a state in which translation and transformation are themselves suspended in each other.[24]

To put it another way, translation and transformation pass for each other here, passing into and through one another without the one ever being fully transformed into or translated by the other.

In such a between-state, the glass that fills itself with silk is no longer simply a container but a translucent medium, a glass that does not efface itself as we look through it—or that *only* effaces itself to the extent that what we see in looking through it is yet another glass. It is a question here of "another glass" because *unser Glas*, our German glass, is at this moment of increasing fullness being translated and transformed. We thus see through the German *Glas* the French *verre* and through this *verre* filling with silk *un ver à soie*. Through this French silkworm, we see the German *Raupe*, the armored caterpillar creeping through the second stanza, metamorphose into the *Seidenraupe* of the third. Through this *ver à soie* we see the poem itself turn into a *vers à soie*, a silken, single-sentence verse spun out across four stanzas.

Through all these translations and transformations we see *unser Glas* (our glass) as a new way of seeing or rather of *seeing through*.[25] Like the megaphone held up to the mouth not just to amplify the voice but also to let something else whisper through it, this glass held up to our eye only brings distant objects closer to the extent that it estranges the familiar. It is perhaps for this reason that Celan appended a quote regarding vision to an earlier draft of the poem. According to Valéry, "Toute vue des choses qui n'est pas étrange est fausse" (Any view of things that is not strange is false).[26]

In the midst of all these translations, transformations, and perspectival revisionings a new subject takes shape, appearing even to take a stand in the concluding line of the poem. With the assertion *wir stehen* (we stand) a metamorphosis of the poem's own voice now seems complete, accomplishing a gradual process of transformation from the third to the first person with a transition through the possessive pronoun *unser* (our) in the middle. This movement also involves a shift from a single voice speaking through a megaphone to a collective voice speaking and standing up for itself. This is perhaps the voice of the demonstrators responding to the *Maulheld* or the speaking stance of those who, standing fast, stand up to the tanks.[27]

The question of where and with whom this "we" stands is complicated, however, by its position in the poem. On the one hand, it stands apart from the rest; that is, it is given a stanza all to itself and is the only complete, self-contained, grammatically free-standing unit in the poem: a subject and a verb, period. On the other hand, it stands with the rest as the completion of a long, carefully punctuated sentence; the final unraveling of a single silken thread into which the poem will have been transformed; the culmination of a movement of self-assertion traced in the progression from third person to first; and the coming together of the son addressed in the title and the poet-father with whom he stands in the end.

On the one hand, on the other—this oscillation seems to hold open the very space of the inter-medium, the between-space in which translation, transformation, and perspectival revisioning occur. And it is in this oscillation between German and French, human and animal, text and textile, that we stand. The poem Celan dedicates to his son may thus be said to speak from a place between the two languages they share. Addressing Eric from that place, the poet also summons him to it, inviting him to stand in this oscillation between languages, to stand there together and apart.

Your father, your pauls

It is this tenuous space of translation, transformation, and oscillation that seems to close in the summer of 1968 when Celan addresses a third poem to his son, the only one he would ever compose entirely in French.

Ô les hableurs
n'en sois pas.
Ô les cableurs
n'en sois pas.
L'heure, minutée, te seconde
Eric. Il faut gravir ce temps.
Ton père
t'épaule.
    (Celan, *Die Gedichte* 229)

O the braggers
don't be one of them.
O the cablers
don't be one of them.
The hour, minuted, seconds you
Eric. One has to scale this time.
Your father
shoulders you.
    (trans. mine)

As noted earlier, this last poem's opening admonitions recall the beginning of the second poem written for Eric. They require little additional comment, and it is therefore with the two central lines that we begin: "The hour, minuted, seconds you / Eric. One has to scale this time."[28] Combining "climbing" and "timing," the lines figure the minutes carved into the hour and the seconds scored into the minutes as little notches, as small hand- and footholds by which one might get a grip.[29] Digging into these little cuts dug into the stony, implacable face of time, one might be able, if not to scale "this time," at least to get a footing, to make it in some way one's own. As the concluding lines suggest, one is not alone in such an endeavor. "The hour, minuted, seconds you / Eric," the poet writes. "Your father / shoulders you."

Like the units of time that in the course of the poem turn from nouns into verbs as the nicks in time become smaller and smaller, so too does the proper name, Paul, the name of the father, lose its fixity and monolithic solidity. The paternal name, the poet seems to say, is not a burden but a support. "Your father / shoulders you" (Ton père / t'épaule). Whereas the solitary noun "hour" becomes at once passive and active when cut into smaller units, becoming both an object that is minuted and a subject that seconds, the single name *Paul*, implicit in the signature *ton père*, is at once divided and multiplied when turned into a verb. For the verb *t'épaule* must also be read as the plural *tes pauls*. "Your father/shoulders you" should thus also be viewed as the double and divided signature "Your father/your pauls."

While Celan played with his name throughout his work, always with great ingenuity and often with obvious delight, there appears to be something more desperate being performed in this particular play on his name. Whereas the mutability of the name may be associated with an urge to reinvent and transform oneself, it can also bear witness to an unstable, unsettled sense of identity, to a life lived in perpetual translation as a radically uprooted and displaced person—as a *juif apatride de langue allemande*, as the Lestrange family once put it, as a traumatized survivor who never felt at home in the world.[30] Amid all the losses, Celan never quite got the bearings he so desperately sought through language. An eloquent and highly accomplished translator, he lived in a kind of suspended animation among a number of different tongues, no one of which ever seemed to be his own—especially German.

Indeed, it was only through the birth of his two French sons that he was eventually naturalized and granted French citizenship. Perhaps the plays on his first name, *Paul*, in a poem addressed to his one surviving son, assuring him of his support and placing him on his shoulders, are quite literally an attempt to translate himself into French, to find through his son the home that he had lost and had in many ways never been able to provide. As was noted earlier, the Celan family was itself living apart at this time because Celan's severe psychological crises made him a danger to his wife, himself, and others. That Celan would translate himself into French in this way is perhaps the sign of a desire to take root in this language, to disseminate his name like the scattering of so many seeds, nicking and notching time in order to find a place in it, in order, if not to scale this time, perhaps at least to get a foothold, a handhold, a grip.

Yet where exactly are these nicks, notches, and cuts in time to be located? While they are certainly associated in the poem with a division of the hour into minutes and minutes into seconds, none of these divisions functions simply as a positive unit of time. On the contrary, each is divided from itself and made to hover between different parts of speech in the equivocal phrase "L'heure, minutée, te seconde/Eric" (The hour, minuted, seconds you/Eric). As was noted above, the noun "hour" is both a passive object that is "minuted" and an active subject that "seconds." Grammatically, the terms "minuted" and "seconds" function as verbs. Yet, when read in the sequence—"hour," "minute," "second"—they mark ever-smaller divisions in time. There is thus a tension between grammar and rhetoric, between subject–verb agreement and metonymic juxtaposition, and it is this tension, this pull between competing forces simultaneously at work, that once again seems to hold time open.

Neither exactly the act of seconding nor a discrete unit of time, this *seconde* can only be located in an equivocal beating back and forth between verbal and nominal functions. Indeed, it is this equivocation that holds the second open from the very first, allowing it to function as a slight opening, as perhaps even a narrow gateway, that *kleine Pforte*, through which, according to Benjamin, the Messiah might come. Were this *seconde* of Celan's poem the site of such a coming, it would no doubt be a coming without arrival, a coming in the *meantime* through the strait gate of linguistic equivocation, a coming through a second held open through its irreducible oscillation between nominal and verbal forms. Here one might recall Benjamin's remark about the coming of the Messiah in "Franz Kafka: On the Tenth Anniversary of his Death," a text Celan knew well and from which he often quoted.[31] There Benjamin, himself quoting a "great rabbi," notes that the Messiah "will not wish to change the world by force but will merely make a slight adjustment in it" (dass er nicht mit Gewalt die Welt verändern wolle, sondern nur um ein Geringes sie zurechtstellen werde) (*SW* 2: 811; *GS* 2.2: 432). Does the equivocation of the Celanian *seconde* constitute just such an adjustment?

Slight is the adjustment the Messiah may make, strait is the gate through which he might enter. These motifs of the seemingly minor alteration and the narrow passage that Benjamin associates with the coming of the Messiah are developed in an equally small, equally subtle way by Celan in his critical reworking of the very notion of coming in his 1960 *Meridian* address. As noted in Chapter 3, he makes a distinction there between two related ways of coming: *Wiederkommen* or "coming again," which is associated with the return of art (*die Kunst kommt wieder*) (*GW* 3:187); and *Dazwischenkommen* or "coming between," which is associated with a very particular mode of intervention and counter-rhythmic interruption (*Es kommt etwas dazwischen*) (*GW* 3:187).[32] The latter way of coming intervenes in the former in such a way as to alter it from within, interrupting and rearticulating its movement of repetition and return, its circular way of coming back to itself. It is via these interventions that one may begin to glimpse a very different way of coming, a way that might help us in turn understand why Benjamin concludes his theses with the famous sentence "For every second was the small gateway through which the Messiah might enter" (*SW* 4: 397; *GS* 1.2: 704). Reading Benjamin through Celan—and vice versa—one comes to see this second not only as a narrow entryway but also as an internally divided moment of suspense, as a tension-filled, equivocally *split* second.[33]

In this regard it is important to recall how the term *seconde* in Celan's poem is itself split between two senses, functioning at once as a noun associated with a moment in time and as a verb connected with the act of seconding or supporting another. Even more important than these two positive definitions or functions is the way the word is redefined and redeployed in the course of the poem. Thus, as we have seen, the noun *seconde* no longer designates a particular unit of time but instead marks a suspensive opening in it. The verbal sense of the term moves in a similar direction. Emerging from its traditionally supportive role, it seconds in a way that challenges the authority of the first, the original, the parent, the precursor.

Such a challenge is played out in the last lines of the poem, which, as we have seen, end in a pointedly open-ended manner with a punning equivocation between *t'épaule* and *tes pauls*, between a verb whose direct object and sole addressee is "you," Eric, and a paternal name, *un nom propre*, that is not one. More and less than one, *tes pauls* is both irreducibly plural and pointedly improper. Positioned directly below the poetic signature, "Ton père," this pluralizing pun on the poet's first name appears merely to second and reinforce it in the same way that the admonition "Ô les cableurs/n'en sois pas" seems to do nothing more than repeat and amplify the plea voiced in the nearly identical preceding sentence "Ô les hableurs/n'en sois pas." Yet whereas the opening lines of the text emphasize through their acoustic harmony and grammatical fixity a very traditional notion of seconding—in which repetition is viewed as a relation between otherwise stable identities and is itself assumed logically *to come after* an original and mimetically *to take after* it—in the last lines repetition effectively *splits what it seconds*, doubling and dividing the signature of the father. Coming after "Ton père" and appearing merely to take after it, the pun *t'épaule/tes pauls* divides the paternal name from within. In doing so, it not only sounds out a plurality and equivocality at the heart of what is assumed to be the most proper, individual, and self-identical mark, the signature of the one who signs this poem like a letter or last testament addressed to his son, but it also splits the second from itself. Not only is this second no longer secondary with regard to any would-be predecessor, no longer in any sense a "faithful second," but it is, moreover, no longer even itself, no longer *a* second. Indicative of its new, irreducibly plural and internally split status is the difficulty one has in deciding where precisely to place the accent in the poem's last lines, "Ton père/t'épaule." Does one read them grammatically as "your father/shoulders you" or metonymically as the double and divided signature of "Your father/your pauls"?

The problem encountered here is the same as the one posed by the sentence "L'heure, minutée, te seconde/Eric," which can be read grammatically as "The hour, minuted, seconds you/Eric" or metonymically as a division of the hour into minutes and of these minutes into seconds. That the same problem crops up more than once suggests that it is difficult to locate as such. It suggests, in other words, that even when the term *seconde* appears as such in the fifth line, it is already split, already here and gone. Indeed, its splitting tends to run like a proliferating fault line through the poem, leaving its traces throughout the text without, however, being identified with any particular part of it. Split between grammar and rhetoric, the poem is held open and in suspense, and it is through such fissures—through the very failure of the text to be one, to be whole, together, complete, and not least of all publishable in the poet's name during his lifetime—that it leaves itself open to the coming of another.

Eric and the Errant Address

Whereas the coming to which the poem remains open may be that of an unspecified and unspecifiable messianic figure, that which might come between and in the meantime, coming in such a way that it will have split the second from the very first, is perhaps also the haunting specter of Celan's first-born son, François, who died shortly after birth.[34] What I am suggesting is that the second son may have been for his parents—and perhaps especially for his father—a replacement child. "In the narrowest sense," the psychoanalysts Leon Anisfeld and Arnold Richards write,

> a replacement child is a child born to parents who have had a child die
> and then conceive the second in order to fill the void left by the loss of the

first ... The psychological dynamics of the parents, who have themselves survived the trauma of the real or symbolic death of a child, mediate between the sick or deceased child and the sibling who is his or her surrogate.[35]

Elaborating on this definition, the critic and analyst Gabriele Schwab adds,

> The death of a child is always a wound and an outrage, an improper death, a death that haunts parents, siblings, or entire communities. Parents are not supposed to survive their children. This is why they are unconsciously compelled to try to undo for themselves and their affective life what should not be. Unconsciously taking in their parents' fantasies, replacement children grow up in confusion about their identity and sometimes about their gender. Supposed to live someone else's life, they never quite come into their own.[36]

That the status of the *seconde* is so equivocal, so fraught and overdetermined in Celan's poem—that it is neither simply a unit of time nor a supportive act; that it is split between grammar and rhetoric; that it challenges the authority of the first, the original, and the precursor; and that in its very splitting it holds open the poem (and indeed itself) to the coming of another—suggests that the identity of the text's addressee may be as irreducibly plural as that of its sender and signator. "Your father/your pauls" may, in other words, address himself/themselves not only to the son apostrophized in the poem, whose full name is in fact Claude François Eric Celan, but also through him to the deceased, yet still somehow undead François. While, as we saw earlier, the name *François* resonated strongly with the poet's wish in 1953 to be naturalized as a French citizen and to have his own surname, *Ancel*, anagrammatically rearranged and *francisé* as Celan, the name *Eric* is, according to at least one source, to be understood as an anagram of the French imperative *Écris!*.[37] Indeed, in three letters addressed by Celan to his son there is evidence of him beginning to write the name *Eric* only to correct himself and replace it with the imperative *Écris*.[38] How much more impossible then must the situation have been for the poet when he saw himself confronted with having to choose between writing and his son.

In this poem multiply signed by the father and addressed to one or more of his sons, to the one through the other, to the living as the already/not yet dead, how is one to read its most impersonal address, the imperative "Il faut gravir ce temps" (This time must be scaled)?[39] The place from which this order issues is telling, for it is voiced right after the son, *Eric*, and just before the father, *Ton père*, are named. Located in a mediate position between them, it no doubt says something about their relationship, about the ties, obligations, dictates, and aspirations that bind—and perhaps also separate—them. What kind of imperative is this? Is this yet another poetic exigency, another categorical demand? What is its tone? If it is a strongly felt wish expressed with the strength of paternal confidence, support, and determination, is it realizable? Or does the imperative perhaps give voice to a sense of despair, acknowledging in its very imperiousness a certain impossibility, a desperate need to accomplish what must and yet cannot be done? When the second is split and when it keeps on splitting, how is one to scale this time? Is it perhaps to the very fault lines that one must hold fast, getting a grip only in this repeatedly self-undermining and ungrounding movement, in this fall from abyss to abyss?

Failure in Translation

What would it mean to hold fast amid the spreading fault lines, the inevitable failures and incessant fallings? To begin to address to this question, it may be useful to consider Paul de Man's response to a related passage in Benjamin's "Task of the Translator" essay, in which de Man speaks about "Hölderlin in his constant falling." Describing "the enormous danger inherent in all translations," Benjamin writes, "the gates of a language thus expanded and modified may slam shut and enclose the translator in silence. Hölderlin's translations from Sophocles were his last work; in them meaning plunges from abyss to abyss until it threatens to become lost in the bottomless depths of language" (Benjamin *SW* 1: 262; *GS* 5.1: 21). There follows a sentence, "Aber es gibt ein Halten," which de Man cites first in German and about which he notes, "one tends to read this as saying, 'but there is a stop to this,' one can stop this if you go to the sacred text."[40] Working against this prevailing tendency, de Man offers a more prosaic translation. "You can also read it to mean, *'Aber es gibt ein Halten,'* in which you hold on to this obstinately, to this notion of *errance*, that you stay with it, in a sense. Then something occurs in the very act of your persisting in this, in this . . . that you don't give in to everything that would go in the other direction. At that moment, translation occurs. In Hölderlin, translation *occurs*" (de Man 104).

For Benjamin, Hölderlin would thus represent the exemplary case of a poet who succumbed to the dangers inherent in all translations, who came to be enclosed in silence, madness, and a kind of living death when the gates of a language were expanded by his daringly aberrant acts of translation.[41] If, as de Man suggests, these acts involve an obstinate holding on to a certain notion of *errance*, they should be viewed first and foremost as *actes manqués*—that is, as translational "failures" that inadvertently let slip another level of textual functioning, that unwittingly unleash a force of repetition silently at work in the original and that, in so doing, let something unforeseen occur.

For Celan, Benjamin was not only a critic able to describe the extreme dangers of translation with great precision, dangers he himself no doubt felt, but also and above all a Hölderlinian translator who succumbed to the very force of repetition about which he wrote, who experienced translation as a traumatic occurrence, as an uncanny *recurrence* of Hölderlin's own precipitous fall into silence at the gates of language.[42] In the summer of 1968 Celan wrote another poem, entitled "Port Bou—deutsch?" ("Port Bou—German?"), that remained unpublished during his lifetime.[43] As the title suggests, Celan saw the French-Spanish border town of Port Bou, in which Benjamin found himself trapped and in which he took his life in September 1940, not only as an impassable national or political border but also as a linguistic aporia, as a place where the gates of a language—of German at the frontier of French and Spanish—had once again been expanded and modified in such a way as to slam shut and enclose Benjamin, silencing him forever.[44] Whereas Benjamin saw the late Hölderlin as a poet-translator stranded and suspended in a dangerous crossing, in the expanded gateway and abyssally distended inter-space of translation, Celan saw in the figure of Benjamin, the critic-translator, a stateless political refugee, another *juif apatride de langue allemande*, a *confrère*.[45]

The poems that Celan wrote for Eric in the spring and summer of 1968 may themselves be read as a meditation on the equivocal *Aufgabe*—the "task" that is also the "giving up"—of the translator. Beginning in German, these poems move progressively into French, with the middle one, spun out like a silkworm's cocoon, figuring a metamorphic inter-state, a translational inter-space between the two languages. Dedicated to his one surviving son, yet haunted still by the death of the other, these poetic addresses may also be read as Celan's paternal legacy, as his blessing, his seconding, and his summons. Each of them speaks to Eric from the limit of itself, holding him in the tense equipoise of its arrowing hand, drawing him into the glassy surface of its interlingual verse, and setting him the futilely necessary task of scaling its split-second time.

As we have had occasion to note at various points, Celan wrote these poems at a time when he felt himself confronted with the "terrible alternative" of having to choose between poetry and his son. Faced with this choice, he, unlike the patriarch to whom he compared himself, chose not to choose, chose to write poems *for* his son, chose to write Eric (and, to some extent, his undead brother) into them. Addressing and dedicating these texts to his beloved child, Celan in effect made a place in them for the right not to choose. In asserting this right, he also made time, remaking it in such a way as to hold it open, in abeyance and in suspense, open to something other than divine intervention and the accompanying slaughter of a surrogate victim.

Choosing not to choose, Celan may thus have averted one possible reperformance of the "sacrifice of Abraham" that he at times believed poetry to be demanding of him. Yet, as was noted earlier, the ambiguity of the double genitive construction in which this demand was framed makes it impossible to specify who exactly the agent and the object of this sacrifice were to be. Contained in this ambiguity is thus also the doubly lethal possibility of a sacrifice of the son that would in effect be the death of the father, a (self-) sacrifice of the father that would mortally wound—or at the very least severely traumatize—the son.[46] Feeling himself called upon to reperform such a sacrifice, Celan was thus confronted with a number of terrifying scenarios, all of which included the contemplation of his death and another, of his death as that of another—the relation to the other being defined here not in terms of surrogacy but rather as a chain of multiple, repercussive, interimplicating fatalities. In writing a series of poems to his son—poems, I have argued, that must themselves be read in conjunction with the contemporaneously composed "Port Bou—deutsch?"—Celan was perhaps envisioning these interrelated deaths.

On Behalf of the Other

If, as I have suggested, we view these poems as a kind of paternal legacy, as a last will and perhaps even as a suicide note addressed to Eric, who then will have signed them in the end? As has already been observed, the last of these poems bears a double and divided signature, the multiple ambiguities of which I have sought to develop in the foregoing analysis. These ambiguities all work to hold open the place of the signature, letting the poetic address to Eric be cosigned not only by more than one paul but also by those whose fatal ends deeply marked Celan—in particular those translator doubles, Hölderlin and Benjamin, who were for him also in their own way *pauls*.[47] Beyond these determinate others, the place of the signature is also held open in the end to those who cannot sign in their own names, those for whom and on behalf of whom, Celan says, the poem speaks. "But the poem speaks!" he exclaims in his *Meridian* address.

> It is mindful of its dates, but it speaks. True, it speaks only on its own, its very own behalf.
> But I think—and this will hardly surprise you—that the poem has always hoped, for this very reason, to speak also on behalf of the *strange*—no, I can no longer use this word here—*on behalf of the other*, who knows, perhaps of an *altogether other*.
> (CP 48; GW 3: 196).[48]

Who knows? Does the poem only *hope* to speak on behalf of "an *altogether other*" or does it perhaps also speak in such a way as to leave itself open to hope, open to the possibility that such an other might, like Benjamin's Messiah or Eric's spectral sibling, come through the strait gate of its poetically split second?[49]

Remaining unpublished during his lifetime, Celan's poem will have left itself open to the impress of yet another signature. Set aside and stored in a dossier on top of a paulownia leaf that the poet had picked up, the page on which the poem was written eventually absorbed the lineaments of the leaf. As one *feuille* bled through another so, too, did the leaf, in whose name Celan recognized a version of his own, come to add another signature to the poem.[50] Here it is the material support of the *feuille de paulownia*, a support added after the fact but for which a place had in a sense already been made, that broadens the father's child-bearing shoulders by once again doubling and dividing his name. *Ton père / t'épaule.*

Ô les hâbleurs,
n'en sois pas,
ô les câbleurs,
n'en sois pas,
l'heure, minutée, te reconte,
Éric. Il faut passer ce temps.
Ton père
t'épaule.

Manuscript of "Ô les hableurs." (Courtesy of Suhrkamp Verlag.)

Paulownia Leaf Underlying Manuscript Page of "Ô les hableurs." (Courtesy of Deutsches Literaturarchiv Marbach.)

NOTES

1. A TIME TO COME: HUNCHBACKED THEOLOGY, POST-FREUDIAN PSYCHOANALYSIS, AND HISTORICAL MATERIALISM

1. Walter Benjamin, *Gesammelte Schriften*, eds. Rolf Tiedemann und Hermann Schweppenhäuser, vol. 1.3 (Frankfurt am Main: Suhrkamp, 1972), 1226. Translation mine. Henceforth, all references to the *Gesammelte Schriften* will appear in parentheses in the body of the text as *GS* followed by volume and page number

2. Walter Benjamin, *Selected Writings*, eds. Howard Eiland and Michael W. Jennings, trans. Edmund Jephcott et al., vol. 4 (Cambridge, MA: Harvard University Press, 2003), 389–90. Henceforth all references to the *Selected Writings* will appear in parentheses in the body of the text as *SW* followed by volume and page number.

3. Werner Hamacher, "'Now': Walter Benjamin and Historical Time" in *Walter Benjamin and History*, ed. Andrew Benjamin (London: Continuum, 2005), 40–1; originally published as "'Jetzt.' Benjamin zur historischen Zeit" in Benjamin Studien/Studies 1, eds. Helga Geyer-Ryan, Paul Koopman, and Klaas Yntema (Amsterdam: Rodopi, 2002), 150. References to and quotations of this essay will appear henceforth first in the English and then in the German.

4. ". . . an die Stelle eines vom Menschen mit Bewußtsein durchwirkten Raums ein unbewußt durchwirkter tritt . . ." (*GS* 2.1: 371).

5. In a sense to be developed below and further in Chapter 2, it is a "citable" moment, one *already* estranged from its surroundings. Calling for citation, it calls for another context in which it may speak, another context that will in its turn be estranged, unsettled, and made to speak otherwise by the citation inserted into it. Citability, as we shall see, is to be understood as a summoning together of mutually unsettling moments, calling them together in an instant of "Now-Time." See also Richard Sieburth, "Benjamin the Scrivener" in *Benjamin: Philosophy, Aesthetics, History*, ed. Gary Smith (Chicago: University of Chicago Press, 1989), 13–37, esp. 31;. Samuel Weber, *Benjamin's -abilities* (Cambridge: Harvard University Press, 2008), 95–115.

6. There is no doubt a strong affinity between Benjamin's notion of the optical unconscious—and, in particular, his contention that it is "another nature that speaks to the camera"—and the notion of a *punctum* developed by Barthes in *Camera Lucida*. The *punctum* is not so much a positive point as a notion whose value can only first be circumscribed through a comparison with that affect Barthes calls *studium*. This Latin term to which he has recourse should not itself be translated immediately by its cognate, "study," but should be understood more distantly and patiently as an "application to a thing, taste for someone, a kind of general, enthusiastic commitment." Roland Barthes, *Camera Lucida: Reflections on Photography*, trans. Richard Howard (New York: Farrar, Straus and Giroux, 1981), 26.

Punctum, in contrast, is that "second element" that breaks or punctuates the *studium*. "This time," he says,

> it is not I who seek it out (as I invest the field of the *studium* with my sovereign consciousness), it is this element which rises from the scene, shoots out of it like an arrow, and pierces me. A Latin word exists to designate this wound, this prick, this mark made by a pointed instrument: the word suits me all the better in that it also refers to the notion of punctuation, and because the photographs I am speaking of are in effect punctuated, sometimes even speckled with these sensitive points: precisely, these marks, these wounds are so many *points*. This second element which will disturb the *studium* I shall therefore call *punctum*; for *punctum* is also: sting, speck, cut, little hole—and also a cast of the dice. A photograph's *punctum* is the accident which pricks me (but also bruises me, is poignant to me.) [qui . . . me point, (mais aussi me meurtrit, me poigne).]
>
> (Barthes, 26–7; Barthes, *La chambre Claire: Note sur la photographie* [Paris: Éditions de l'Étoile, Gallimard, Le Seuil, 1980], 49)

As in Benjamin, the *punctum* that addresses Barthes as if by accident and is itself described by him as "the accident which pricks me" is not associated with any gaze directed at the viewer, nor is it part of the positive content of the photo. It is instead a point of rupture, a break in the visual field, a puncture wound in time that, like Benjamin's eloquently nesting future, speaks beyond its present moment. Yet in doing so as a point of grammar, it does not so much speak as repunctuate what is said, rearticulating relationships in such a way as to allow a certain unsaid to address us.

7. Benjamin, *Origin of the German Tragic Drama*, trans. John Osborne (London: Verso, 1985), 45 (trans. mod.).

8. When Hamacher speaks of a "hunchbacked time" he is not merely alluding to the famous first thesis in which theology, figured as a hunchbacked dwarf hidden inside a chess-playing apparatus, might, according to Benjamin, be "enlisted

in the service" of "the puppet called 'historical materialism'" in order to create a winning combination. He is also and above all dialectically reworking the relationship between hunchback and puppet, doing so in such a way that theology is no longer viewed one-sidedly in a position of servitude vis-à-vis materialism—that is, as a player whose *services might be enlisted* by it [wenn sie (die Puppe) die Theologie in ihren Dienst nimmt] (*SW* 4: 389; *GS* 1.2: 693, trans. mod.)—but instead two-sidedly in a relationship of mutually unsettling liberation.

This relationship depends in turn on a crucial reinterpretation of the Kantian assumption of a transcendental form of time. Thus, Hamacher writes with regard to Benjamin's twist on the Kantian "Copernican turn,"

> the turn Benjamin wants to bring about—analogous to Kant's—intended to indicate the conditions of synthesis under which that which until now appeared as a "fixed point" can only be brought to a "dialectical fixation." This fixing in the synthesis between what-has-been and the present that Benjamin called dialectic does not assume a definite past—in that respect it follows the Kantian turn; nor however, does it assume a fixed instrumentation of the cognitive apparatus that could pre-form its results—in that respect it goes beyond the Kantian assumption of a transcendental form of time.
>
> ("'Now,'" 45–6)

9. On the "leap" of the *Ur-sprung* and its suspension between the two poles of coming and going, past and future, see Samuel Weber, "Genealogy of Modernity: History, Myth and Allegory in Benjamin's *Origin of the German Mourning Play*," *MLN* 106, no. 3 (1991): 469. See also his *Benjamin's –abilities*, 88–89.

10. Strong in the sense of *Kraft* as agency or potency, in the sense of *in Kraft sein*, or "to be in force or effect."

11. The prefix *mit-* also plays a pivotal role in Celan's *Meridian* address, which is discussed at length in Chapter 3.

12. Paul Celan, *Collected Prose*, trans. Rosemarie Waldrop (New York: Sheep Meadow Press, 1986), 54; Paul Celan, *Gesammelte Werke*, eds. Beda Alleman and Stefan Reichert, vol. 3 (Frankfurt a. M.: Suhrkamp, 1986), 202. All subsequent references to Celan's *Meridian* address will appear in parentheses beginning with the English edition abbreviated as *CP* and followed by the German abbreviated as *GW*. Unless otherwise indicated, all translations follow this edition.

13. Derrida, "Shibboleth: For Paul Celan" in *Sovereignties in Question: The Poetics of Paul Celan*, trans. Thomas Dutoit and Outi Pasanen (NY: Fordham UP, 2005), 3; *Schibboleth pour Paul Celan* (Paris: Galilée, 1986), 11. Henceforth all references will appear in the body of the text in parentheses beginning with the English edition abbreviated as *S* and followed by the French abbreviated as *SPC*.

14. Paul Celan and Gisèle Celan-Lestrange, *Correspondance*, ed. Bertrand Badiou., vol. 1 (Paris: Seuil, 2001), 324. All references to the correspondence and

accompanying volume of commentary will henceforth appear in parentheses in the body of the text as CCL I (letters) and CCL II (commentary) and will be followed by the corresponding page number. All translations are my own.

2. THE DAY THE SUN STOOD STILL: BENJAMIN'S THESES, CELAN'S REALIGNMENTS, TRAUMA, AND THE EICHMANN TRIAL

1. In the German-speaking world, the text is generally referred to by the name Adorno gave it, *Über den Begriff der Geschichte*. When first published in English, it appeared in *Illuminations* under the title "Theses on the Philosophy of History." Upon its republication in volume 4 of *Walter Benjamin: Selected Writings*, it was renamed "On the Concept of History." For a detailed reconstruction of the composition and publication history of the theses, see Walter Benjamin, *Über den Begriff der Geschichte*, in *Walter Benjamin: Werke und Nachlaß Kritische Ausgabe*, ed. Gérard Raulet (Berlin: Suhrkamp, 2010). See especially pp. 166, 174–8.

2. See also influential studies of the theses by Astrid Deuber-Mankowsky, "'... das Bild von Glück, das wir hegen': Zur messianischen Kraft der Schwäche bei Herman Cohen, Walter Benjamin und Paulus" in *Die Entdeckung des Christentums in der Wissenschaft des Judentums*, ed. Görge K. Hasselhoff (Berlin: de Gruyter, 2010); Georgio Agamben, "The Messiah and the Sovereign: The Problem of Law in Walter Benjamin" in *Potentialities*, trans. Daniel Heller-Roazen (Stanford: Stanford University Press, 1999); Irving Wohlfarth, "On the Messianic Structure of Walter Benjamin's Last Reflections," *GLYPH: Johns Hopkins Textual Studies*, 3 (1978): 148–212; Susan Buck-Morss, *The Dialectics of Seeing: Walter Benjamin and the Arcades Project* (Cambridge: MIT Press, 1999).

3. Walter Benjamin, *The Arcades Project*, trans. Howard Eiland and Kevin McLaughlin (Cambridge, MA: Harvard University Press, 2002), 479; Walter Benjamin, *Das Passagen-Werk*, vol. V in *Gesammelte Schriften*, eds. Rolf Tiedemann und Hermann Schweppenhäuser (Frankfurt am Main: Suhrkamp, 1982), 600. All future references to this work will appear in the body of the text as *AP* for the English and *GS* for the German.

4. In a French translation of the text that Benjamin himself had prepared, he uses the phrase "L'idée de bonheur enferme celle de salut, inéluctablement" to render the German "Es schwingt [. . .] in der Vorstellung des Glücks unveräusserlich die der Erlösung mit" (GS 1.3: 1260). It should also be noted that the passages in question that use the subjunctive in German are translated into the French future perfect or subjunctive. Thus, the French reads, "Un bonheur susceptible d'être l'objet de notre envie n'existera que dans un air qui aura été respiré par nous; il n'existera qu'en compagnie de gens qui auraient pu nous adresser la parole à nous; il n'existera enfin que grâce à des femmes dont les faveurs nous auront combler, nous" (GS 1.3: 1260).

5. This series of open-ended questions posed with regard to that of redemption might be read in relation to the following: "Wer wissen wollte, in welcher Verfassung sich die 'erlöste Menschheit' befindet, welchen Bedingungen das Eintreten dieser Verfassung unterworfen ist und wann man mit ihm rechnen kann, der stellt Fragen, auf die es keine Antwort gibt" (*GS* 1.3: 1232).

6. Cf. Heidegger's discussion of possibility in section 53 of *Being and Time*, trans. John MacQuarrie and Edward Robinson (New York, NY: Harper & Row, 1962). As Samuel Weber notes, "his analysis of being-towards-death in terms of 'possibility' opens the way toward rethinking [this] category as something other than a subordinate, unfulfilled mode of reality qua actuality, which is how 'possibility' had been thought in the tradition emanating from Aristotle. Heidegger argues that being-towards-death can only be construed in terms of a possibility that cannot be measured in terms of realization or actualization" (*Benjamin's -abilities* 331, fn. 3).

7. Taking as his point of departure Werner Kraft's commentary on Kafka's story "A Fratricide," Benjamin writes, "Just as this bell, which is too loud for a doorbell, rings out toward heaven, the gestures of Kafka's figures are too powerful [zu durchschlagend] for our accustomed surroundings and break through into wider areas [und brechen in eine geräumigere ein]." Walter Benjamin, "Franz Kafka: On the Tenth Anniversary of his Death" (*SW* 2: 801; *GS* 2.2: 418).

8. Cf. *Amerika: The Missing Person*: "Just then a bell rang out twelve times in rapid succession, with each chime breaking into the previous one; Karl could feel a breeze on his cheek from the great movement of the bells. 'What was this village that had such bells!'" Franz Kafka, *Amerika: The Missing Person*, trans. Mark Harman (NY: Schocken, 2008), 80. On the accumulation of potential through pointedly open-ended questions see also *Amerika*, 144.

9. To this series of *mit-* verbs should be added *mitführen*, which is found in the notes Benjamin wrote in the context of his theses: "In Wirklichkeit gibt es nicht einen Augenblick, der s e i n e revolutionäre Chance nicht mit sich führte" (*GS* 1.3: 1231).

10. In a related context, to which Carol Jacobs draws our attention, Benjamin explicitly contrasts the static notion of star cluster (*Gestirnstand*) with the more dynamic, transitory, and fleeting notion of a constellation (*Gestirnkonstellation*). Thus, he writes in his 1921 essay "Doctrine of the Similar" that the "star cluster displays a characteristic unity and [it is] first in their operation in the star cluster that the characters of the individual planets are recognized" (*GS* 2.1: 206; Jacobs trans., 98). In contrast, the notion of a constellation involves a "perception [that] is in every case bound to an instantaneous flash. It flits by, can perhaps be won back, but cannot be held fast like other perceptions. It offers itself to the eye just as fleetingly, transitorily, as a constellation of stars. The perception of similarities thus appears bound to a moment in time. It is like the supervention [Dazukommmen] of the third, of the astrologer [who is explicitly not an

astronomer], to the conjunction of two stars that wishes to be grasped in the moment [Augenblick]." (*GS* 2.1: 206–07; Jacobs trans., 99). As Jacobs brilliantly notes, "Unlike the astronomer, the astrologer appears with no tools of observation and can expect no reward [. . .]. Rather, in this newly conceived moment of interpretation the reader-astrologer—this is what is so astonishing—both completes and is assimilated into the constellation in a flash, a constellation that is not one until the astrologer joins the two stars that otherwise form no figure at all." That this joining is less a moment of knowledge, of an intellectual grasp, than a moment that slips through one's fingers, that "cannot be held fast like other perceptions," and that involves, if anything, a certain lapse of consciousness to which we will return, is suggested by Jacobs when she notes that "If in the constellation of 'Doctrine of the Similar' it is just when the observer grasps (at) what she sees that she becomes part of its configuration, in 'Towards the Image of Proust' Benjamin gives us several formulations to mark this lapse" (101). Carol Jacobs, *In the Name of Walter Benjamin* (Baltimore: Johns Hopkins University Press, 1999).

11. While never mentioning Benjamin in this context, Derrida does use the noun "constellation" and the verb "to constellate" a number of times in his reading of "IN ONE." Drawing attention to its multiple gatherings (as well, I would suggest, as those associated with the Benjaminian notion of a constellation), he makes rather heavy-handed use of the prefixes *con-* and *col-*, speaking, for example, of the way a "multiplicity of languages may concelebrate, *all at once*, on the same date, the poetic and political anniversary of singular events, spread like stars over the map of Europe, and henceforth conjoined by a secret affinity." Jacques Derrida, *Sovereignties in Question: The Poetics of Paul Celan*, trans. Thomas Dutoit and Outi Pasanen (New York: Fordham University Press, 2005), 23–4; see also 20–6. Henceforth references will appear as *S* followed by page number. References to *Schibboleth pour Paul Celan* (Paris: Galilée, 1986) will appear as *SPC*. The above-cited passages may be found in the French pp. 46–47; 41–49.

12. *Selected Poems and Prose of Paul Celan*, trans. John Felstiner (New York: Norton, 2000), 188–89 (trans. mod.). Henceforth abbreviated as *SPP*. Paul Celan, *Gesammelte Werke*, vol. 1 (Frankfurt am Main: Suhrkamp, 1983), 270. Henceforth references to the German edition of Celan's works will be noted as *GW* followed by volume and page number.

13. While the translation is my own, it is based largely on those of Rosemarie Waldrop in Paul Celan, *Collected Prose*, 47 and John Felstiner in *SPP*, 408; *GW* 3: 196.

14. Shortly after his flight to Strasbourg in 1834, Büchner began research on *Danton's Death*, completing the play in February 1835. This was followed by work on *Lenz* in 1835, *Leonce and Lena* in 1836, and *Woyzeck* in 1837.

15. When Benjamin speaks of blasting moments out of a historical continuum, we might think of this act as an attempt to wrench citations out of their initial

context. Blasting or wrenching, the violence associated with these attempts at decontextualization and—via citation—with the dynamic realignment of these liberated fragments in a constellation saturated with tensions involves the use of a kind of historical dynamite, the very kind alluded to by Benjamin in the part of his Kraus essay devoted to the use of citation, where he speaks of the Austrian critics' strategic spacing out of the letters G r a n a t, silently transforming a pomegranate into a hand grenade. See also the mutating interrelationship of the signifiers: *heraussprengen, aufsprengen, springen, Ursprung, Tigersprung,* and *Sprengstoff* in the theses. Dynamically clustered about one another, these verbal fragments are charged and volatilized. Their explosive potential, never voiced as such, is instead conveyed only through a certain resonance, through the tension-saturated static of their linguistic interference.

16. See "[Reply to a Questionnaire from the Flinker Bookstore, Paris, 1958]" in Paul Celan, *CP,* 16; *GW* 3: 168.

17. As Benjamin observes in *Central Park,* "That which the allegorical intention has fixed upon is sundered from its customary context: it is at once shattered and preserved. Allegory holds fast to the ruins. It offers the image of petrified unrest. Baudelaire's destructive impulse is nowhere concerned with the abolition of what falls prey to it" (*SW* 4: 169).

18. In a related passage from *Central Park* Benjamin compares Baudelaire to Joshua, noting "To interrupt the course of the world—that was Baudelaire's deepest intention. The intention of Joshua. Not so much the prophetic one, for he gave no thought to any sort of reform" (Ibid., 170).

19. "What characterizes revolutionary classes at their moment of action," Benjamin writes, "is the awareness that they are about to make the continuum of history explode. The Great Revolution introduced a new calendar. The initial day of a calendar presents history in time-lapse mode. And basically it is this same day that keeps recurring in the guise of holidays, which are days of remembrance [Tage des Eingedenkens]. Thus, calendars do not measure time the way clocks do; they are monuments of a historical consciousness of which not the slightest trace has been apparent in Europe, it would seem, for the past hundred years" (*SW* 4: 395; *GS* 1.2: 701–2).

20. See in this context Benjamin's response to "A remark by Ernst Bloch apropos of *The Arcades Project*: 'History displays its Scotland Yard badge.'" He writes, "It was in the context of a conversation in which I was describing how this work—*comparable, in method, to the process of splitting the atom—liberates the enormous energies of history that are bound up in the 'once upon a time' of classical historiography*. The history that showed things 'as they really were' was the strongest narcotic of the century" (*AP* 463: *GS* 5.1: 578; emphasis added).

21. Consider here as well the movement in the Artwork essay from painting to film, a movement in which static, self-contained images (comparable to the eighteen theses and two appendices of "On the Concept of History") are set

in motion when projected at twenty-four frames per second. Associated with this high-speed intersection of formerly discrete and independent images is the explosion of the "prison-world" of the familiar via the medium of film. As Benjamin says, "Our bars and our city streets, our offices and furnished rooms, our railroad stations and our factories seemed to close relentlessly around us. Then came the film and exploded this prison-world with the dynamite of the split second, so that now we can set off calmly on journeys of adventure among its far-flung debris. With the close-up, space expands, with slow motion, movement is extended" (*SW* 4: 265).

22. *The Concise Oxford Dictionary of English Etymology*, ed. Terry F. Hoad (Oxford: Oxford University Press, 1996), s.v. "second," on encyclopedia.com, accessed February 27, 2013, http://www.encyclopedia.com/topic/second.aspx#4. For a thorough analysis of Celan's own divisions and recombinations of the German phrase *die Sekunde* see Werner Hamacher, "The Second of Inversion: Movements of a Figure through Celan's Poetry" in *Premises: Essays on Philosophy and Literature from Kant to Celan*, trans. Peter Fenves (Cambridge: Harvard University Press, 1996), 337–87.

23. "Redemption," Bejamin notes in *Central Park*, "depends on the tiny fissures in the continuous catastrophe" (*SW* 4: 185). "That things are 'status quo' *is* the catastrophe" [Dass es 'so weiter' geht, ist die Katastrophe] (*SW* 4: 184; *GS* 1.2: 683).

24. As Hamacher notes,

> By virtue of its 'historical index' each Now is marked as the Now of another Now, the 'Now of a particular recognizability.' It would be quite simply unrecognizable, unperceivable, it would not be what it is intended to be, if it lacked the complement of a second Now, a distinct one and yet one that is united with it, it would lack the chance to become encircled as the Now that it is. There is no Now that could qualify as being temporal or even historical if it lacked all tension to another, distinct Now. But neither would there be a Now if it were separated by an impermeable barrier from the other Now and were untouched by that other Now, in which it is supposed to be recognized. In order to be Now and one Now, it has to be one that takes itself apart into two. This is brought about by the critical point of movement at the inside of time. This 'critical point,' or, more precisely, the crisis of the Now-point, is what 'rescues' time and the historical phenomena in which it contracts itself: as Benjamin notes, phenomena 'are rescued through the exhibition of a leap within them.' Therefore this 'leap,' the discontinuous as such, that which creates clefts in the course of time, is at the same time the 'nucleus,' the time nucleus of the phenomenon, the time out of which the phenomenon forms itself [. . .]. Benjamin can therefore compare the process of determining this

medium [of the 'synchronistic' image] with 'the method of splitting the atom,' i.e. not just with the enclosure of the nucleus of time but with nuclear fission. If, however, only the fission of the time nucleus sets free its historical forces, then this nucleus with its forces, paradoxically, is situated in the fission.

("'Now'" 58–60)

25. I explore this relation between time and consciousness at greater length in my reading of Benjamin's essay "On Some Motifs in Baudelaire" in Michael G. Levine, *Writing Through Repression: Literature, Censorship, Psychoanalysis* (Baltimore: Johns Hopkins University Press, 1996), esp. 101–3.

26. "The nucleus of time," Hamacher stresses, "lies in the cleft that its crisis opens up. Splitting between fore- and after-history, this nucleus lies between object and cognition, and is that in which the two touch each other, not in a positive third, but in the gap between them" ("'Now'" 58).

27. For accounts of Benjamin's last days at the French–Spanish border see Michael Taussig, *Walter Benjamin's Grave* (Chicago: University of Chicago Press, 2006); Momme Brodersen, *Walter Benjamin: A Biography*, trans. Malcolm R. Green and Ingrida Ligers (New York: Verso, 1997) 259–61; Lisa Fittko, "The Story of Old Benjamin," in *AP*, 946–54; Hannah Arendt, *Men in Dark Times* (New York: Harcourt, Brace & World, 1968), 153–206; and Gershom Scholem, *Walter Benjamin: Story of a Friendship* (Philadelphia: Jewish Publication Society of America, 1981) 221–6.

28. Shoshana Felman, *The Juridical Unconscious* (Cambridge: Harvard University Press, 2002), 13, 18, 31, 32, 47, 49, 53. All references will henceforth appear in the body of the text as *JU*.

29. Shoshana Felman and Dori Laub, *Testimony: Crises of Witnessing in Literature, Psychoanalysis and History* (New York: Routledge, 1992), 21.

30. Scholem, *Walter Benjamin: Story of a Friendship*, 188.

31. It should be noted that Benjamin's wish that the papers of the brothers Fritz and Wolf Heinle find a final resting place in the manuscript department of the library of the Hebrew University of Jerusalem was never realized. Instead, as he writes in a letter of November 1, 1938, to Gretel Adorno, "As of now, the only thing yielded by my persistent effort to get some more of my books, but above all my papers, out of Berlin is the virtual certainty that the following things have been destroyed: the complete papers of the two Heinles, my irreplaceable archive on the history of the leftist bourgeois Youth Movement, and finally my youthful writings—among them the 1914 Hölderlin essay." *The Correspondence of Walter Benjamin 1910–1940*, eds. Gershom Scholem and Theodor W. Adorno, trans. Manfred R. Jacobson and Evelyn M. Jacobson (Chicago: University of Chicago Press, 1994), 578–9. While he was wrong about the Hölderlin essay, of which Scholem had a copy, the Heinle papers do indeed appear to have been destroyed, lost, as it were, in transmission.

32. Here one might recall Benjamin's discussion in *A Little History of Photography* of the picture of the photographer Dauthendey and his wife-to-be who would later commit suicide. See Chapter 1.

33. Peter Demetz, introduction to *Reflections*, by Walter Benjamin, trans. Edmund Jephcott (New York: Harcourt Brace Jovanovich, 1978), xv.

34. The story of double suicides, double friendships, and improper burials does not end here; for it now appears that the Jew, Benjamin, through whose hands the writings of two non-Jews were to pass, via Scholem, to their final resting place in the manuscript department of the library of the Hebrew University of Jerusalem was himself buried in a *Catholic cemetery* in Port Bou under the name *Benjamin Walter*. As Taussig explains, "upon his death Walter Benjamin entered the official records (supplied by the recently established Walter Benjamin Museum in Port Bou) not as a Jew but as a Roman Catholic with the name of [. . .] *Doctor* Benjamin Walter. . . . [H]e was buried in the cemetery reserved for Catholics and far from being nameless, he became a fake just like his grave, a fake Christian and a body with a fake name." Taussig, *Walter Benjamin's Grave*, 5. See also Brodersen, *Walter Benjamin: A Biography*, 259–61.

35. Here one might recall as well Celan's famous poem, "Deathfugue." Parroting with bitter irony the imperious voice of the "master from Germany," he writes, "You'll rise up as smoke in the air/then you'll have a grave in the clouds" [dann steigt ihr als Rauch in die Luft/dann habt ihr ein Grab in den Wolken] (*SPP*, 33; *GW* 1: 42).

36. Lawrence Douglas, *The Memory of Judgment: Making Law and History in the Trials of the Holocaust* (New Haven: Yale University Press, 2001). See especially Part 2, 97–182.

37. Hannah Arendt, *Eichmann in Jerusalem: A Report on the Banality of Evil* (New York: Penguin, 1963), 6. Henceforth cited as *EJ*.

38. "Our memory," writes Valéry, "repeats to us the discourse that we have not understood. Repetition is responding to incomprehension. It signifies to us that the act of language has not been accomplished" (cited in Felman, *JU*, 231, fn. 8). One might understand the address in question here, the address of a collective memory yet to be grasped, of an *automated call* ringing out repeatedly and in its very incomprehensibility as that "secret appointment" or "clandestine rendezvous" between past generations and our own of which Benjamin speaks.

39. While it is a question of looks rather than images here, it is just this *mise en abîme* structure of the endlessly, vertiginously exchanging look that enables one to grasp Benjamin's notion of the dialectical image. "It's not that what is past casts its light on what is present, or what is present its light on what is past; rather, image is that wherein what has been comes together in a flash with the now to form a constellation. In other words, image is dialectics at a standstill. For while the relation of the present to the past is purely a temporal, continuous one, the relation of what-has-been to the now is dialectical: is not progres-

sion but image, suddenly emergent. Only dialectical images are genuine images (that is, not archaic); and the place where one encounters them is language" (*AP* 462).

40. For other accounts and interpretations of this incident see Lawrence Douglas, *The Memory of Judgment*, 145–9, and Tom Segev, *The Seventh Million*, (New York: Henry Holt and co., 1991), 11.

3. PENDANT: CELAN, BÜCHNER, AND THE TERRIBLE VOICE OF THE MERIDIAN

1. Celan explicitly links the word *Meridian* to the time of day in question here in an early draft of his Darmstadt address. There it is immediately followed by the term *Mittags*—at noon. Paul Celan, *The Meridian: Final Version—Drafts—Materials*, trans. Pierre Joris (Stanford: Stanford University Press, 2011), 77; and Paul Celan, *Der Meridian: Endfassung—Entwürfe—Materialien*, eds. Berhard Böschenstein and Heino Schmull (Frankfurt a. M.: Suhrkamp, 1999), 77. Henceforth all references will be provided in the body of the text. Since the page numbers in both editions are the same they will only be given once preceded by the abbreviation *M*.

2. Georg Büchner, *Complete Plays, Lenz and Other Writings*, trans. John Reddick (New York: Penguin Books, 1993), 72; Georg Büchner, *Werke und Briefe, Münchner Ausgabe*, eds. Karl Pörnbacher, Gerhard Schaub, Hans-Jochen Simm, and Edda Ziegler (Munich: Carl Hanser, 1988), 132. All subsequent references will appear in parentheses as Act. Scene: Page Numbers. References will begin with the English edition, abbreviated as *CLPOW*, and will be followed by the German, abbreviated as *WBMA*.

3. The passage thus stands in ironic contrast to the pointedly reactionary words uttered by the President of the Land of Popo to King Peter at a critical moment in *Leonce and Lena*: "Let your Majesty take comfort from other Majesties" (Troste sich Eure Majestät mit andern Majestäten) (*CPLOW* 3.3: 104, *WBMA* 185). For further discussion of this passage in the context of the reactionary regimes of post-1815 Europe, see Gerhard P. Knapp, *Georg Büchner* (Stuttgart: Metzler, 2000), 172–3.

4. Noon is of course also the time when the sun is at its zenith, another sense of *Hochzeit*.

5. Such a position is summarized in the regal pronouncement: "I am I" (Ich bin ich) (*CPLOW* 1.2: 83; *WBMA* 165) and is associated throughout the play with certain *a priori* modes of thought. As Leonce comments early on: "*A priori*—that's something my venerable father could teach us" (*a priori*, das muß man bei meinem Herrn Vater lernen) (*CPLOW* 1.3: 90; *WBMA* 172). In the second scene of the play this mode of thought is staged as a parodic dressing down of the absolutist *Lever*: "King [while being dressed]: 'Man must think, and I must think for my subjects, for they never think at all, they never think at all.—

The essence is the in-itself, and that is I [Die Substanz ist das an sich, das bin ich].' [He runs around the room almost naked] 'Have you got that [Begriffen]? The in-itself is the in-itself, do you understand? Now it's the turn of my attributes, accidents, properties and modifications: where is my shirt, where are my trousers?'" (*CPLOW* 1.2: 82; *WBMA* 164). In contrast to this position, the play asks in effect what it would mean to begin *a posteriori*. It is precisely this question that Celan takes up toward the end of his *Meridian* address and to which we will return below.

6. Evidence of Celan's own sensitivity to such moments of natural doubling and organic pairing in Büchner is to be found in the preparatory notes for his *Meridian* address. In the convolute labeled "Encounter" (Begegnung) he cites a remark made by the prostitute, Marion, in Act I, Scene 3 of *Danton's Death*: "Danton, your lips have eyes" (Danton, deine Lippen haben Augen). Underlining the sentence and placing an additional mark next to it in the margin, he comments, "no metaphor" (keine Metapher) (*M* 134, 242 n. 439).

7. Such a moment evokes the traditional epithet of depression as "the demon of noontide." See Andrew Solomon, *The Noonday Demon: An Atlas of Depression* (New York: Scribner, 2001).

8. The moment of the meridian also seems to mark the midday of Celan's life. As Stéphane Mosès observes, "In retrospect, the *Meridian* speech appears both as the midpoint of Celan's poetic work and as the decisive turning point of his biography." Stéphane Mosès, "Celan Wins Büchner Prize" in *Yale Companion to Jewish Writing and Thought*, ed. Sander Gilman and Jack Zipes (New Haven: Yale UP, 1997), 716.

9. In another series of complex calculations, this time regarding the amount of time it will take for the new regional parliament (*Landtag*) to be born, Büchner notes in a letter of August 13, 1833 to Edouard Reuss that the normal lifespan of a person is sixty years: "Ein Mensch lebt 60 Jahr." Returning then to the long anticipated birth of the *Landtag*, he notes that it is still unclear "whether the child will see the light of day head or bottom first" (ob das Kind mit Kopf oder podex zuerst auf die Welt kommt) (*WBMA* 282, trans. mine). As was noted above, the question of what it might mean to be born head or bottom first is also addressed in *Leonce and Lena* in an exchange between the crown prince of the kingdom of Popo and the fool Valerio: "Leonce: 'Valerio! Valerio! We need to do something completely different. What's your advice?' Valerio: 'There's the world of learning, how about that? Let's become philosophers! *A priori*? Or *a posteriori*?' Leonce: '*A priori*—that's something my venerable father could teach us. *A posteriori*—that's how everything begins . . .'" (*CPLOW* 1.3: 90; *WBMA* 172).

10. In a related passage in *Danton's Death* Laflotte remarks, "And then—it's not death I'm afraid of, but pain. . . . They say it only lasts a moment, but pain has the subtlest sense of time: a fraction of a second can last an eternity" [Man

sagt zwar es sei nur ein Augenblick, aber der Schmerz hat ein feineres Zeitmaß, er zerlegt eine Tertie] (*CPLOW* 3.5: 53; *WBMA* 114).

11. In *Geschlossene und offene Form im Drama*, Volker Klotz describes Woyzeck as a "monagonist." In coining this term, he draws attention to a situation in which the hero's antagonist is no longer an identifiable individual or even a single agent; instead, the whole world, "in the plenitude of its discrete phenomena," has assumed an antagonistic function and presses on the protagonist: "Rushing upon him from all sides, it turns the hero into a 'monagonist' while subjecting the action . . . to an indeterminate circular movement. . . . The dominant principle of composition is that of a rotating variation." Cited in English translation in Reinhold Grimm, *Love, Lust, and Rebellion: New Approaches to Georg Büchner* (Madison: University of Wisconsin Press, 1985), 25.

12. Celan cites this passage in the convolute labeled *Aufzeichnungen zu Büchner* (*Notes on Büchner*), adding in parentheses, "actually I don't understand it" (eigentl. versteh ichs nicht) (*M* 177).

13. Helmut Müller-Sievers, *Desorientierung: Anatomie und Dichtung bei Georg Buchner* (Gottingen: Wallstein, 2003), 71 [trans. mine]. More generally, as Müller-Sievers observes, it is a question in the *Treatise* of orientation in both the transitive and intransitive sense—on the one hand, a question of how to establish the left-right, up-down, front-back orientation of the fish nerves and, on the other, of where exactly to place the fish brain in the history of vertebrate development. Of particular interest is Büchner's ultimate inability to reconcile these two related concerns, to coordinate the two poles of the study, to bridge the differences that emerge between anatomical classification on the one hand and "nature philosophical" (*naturphilosophischen*) classification on the other. It is this crisis of orientation, this unresolved conflict between description and interpretation, metonymy and metaphor that, according to Müller-Sievers, is dramatically played out on the "other scene" of Büchner's literary work. For an abridged English version of Müller-Sievers's fascinating argument, see "Of Fish and Men: The Importance of Georg Büchner's Anatomical Writings," *MLN* 118 (2003): 706.

14. Georg Büchner, *Complete Plays, Lenz and Other Writings*, trans. John Reddick (New York: Penguin Books, 1993), 247.

15. See Freud's famous reference to the scene in Tasso's *Gerusamme Liberata* in which Tancred, having wounded his beloved Clorinda in battle, unknowingly, seemingly by chance, wounds her again. This repeated wounding is described by Freud as follows: "He slashes with his sword at a tall tree; but blood streams from the cut and the voice of Clorinda, whose soul is imprisoned in the tree, is heard complaining that he has wounded his beloved once again." Sigmund Freud, *The Standard Edition of the Complete Psychological Works of Sigmund Freud*, trans. and eds. James Strachey, Anna Freud, Alix Strachey, and Alan Tyson, vol. 18, *Beyond the Pleasure Principle* (London: Hogarth, 1975), 22.

Of particular relevance to my reading of Woyzeck's repeated knife thrusts is Caruth's discussion of Freud's reference to Tasso. "I would like to suggest," she writes, "that the literary resonance of Freud's example goes beyond this dramatic illustration of repetition compulsion and exceeds, perhaps, the limits of Freud's conceptual or conscious theory of trauma. For what seems to me particularly striking in the example of Tasso is not just the unconscious act of the infliction of the injury and its inadvertent and unwished-for repetition, but the moving and sorrowful *voice* that cries out, a voice that is paradoxically released *through the wound* .... Tancred's story thus represents traumatic experience not only as the enigma of a human agent's repeated and unknowing acts but also as the enigma of the otherness of a human voice that cries out from the wound, a voice that witnesses a truth that Tancred himself cannot fully know." Cathy Caruth, *Unclaimed Experience: Trauma, Narrative, and History* (Baltimore: Johns Hopkins University Press, 1996), 6–7.

16. On the violence of "prizing open" directed at the secret recesses of a woman's body and consciousness, see Virginia Woolf's *The Lady in the Looking-Glass* (London: Penguin Classics, 2011). Also see the first lines of Buchner's first play in which Danton says, "Look at Madame over there—how sweetly she fingers her cards. She knows how, all right, they say her husband always gets the *coeur*, the others the *carreau*" (*CPLOW* 1.1: 5 trans. mod; *WBMA* 69).

17. See Müller-Sievers's analysis of the words *Immer zu* in *Woyzeck* where the perpetually (*immerzu*) repeated signifier *zu* is associated at once with the closure of the main character's linguistic cosmos (*Er ist für immer zu*), with the knife plunged repeatedly (*immer zustoßend*) into Marie's body, and more generally and phantasmatically, with the violence done to and by the verbal bodies of the text. Of particular importance here is the insistence of the double-edged signifier *zu*, whose verbal thrusts (*zu, zu, zu*) not only pierce the linguistic surface of the play but leave *zu*-shaped stigmata all over its wound-ridden body. So violent is the movement of repetition here, so viciously circular is its logic, that it appears to carry over and bleed into the body of the critical text. Thus, Müller-Sievers writes, "In Woyzecks Welt ist ihm alles immer zu ... —immer verschlossen, aber auch immer zu bedrohlich, zu verwirrend, zu viel, bis er dann, um Marie für den Versuch der Zucht von Tambourmajors, das heißt für ihre Unzucht, zu bestrafen, zustößt, bis Marie nicht mehr zuckt" (Müller-Sievers, *Desorientierung*, 146).

18. Reinhold Grimm, *Love, Lust, and Rebellion: New Approaches to Georg Büchner* (Madison: U of Wisconsin Press, 1985) 8–9. Grimm's account is based on the testimony of Wilhelm Schulz as quoted by Walter Grab, "Der hessische Demokrat Wilhelm Schulz und seine Schriften über Georg Büchner und Friedrich Ludwig Weidig," *Georg Büchner Jahrbuch* 2 (1982): 227–48.

19. As Richard Sieburth remarks in the "Translator's Afterword" to his exquisite *Lenz* translation, "The last, laconic sentence of the novella merely informs us: 'So lebte er hin' (And so he lived on). Not happily ever after, as in a fairy-tale,

but numbed out, resigned to fate, condemned (like Beckett's characters) simply to endure that 'living on' . . ." Georg Büchner, *Lenz*, trans. Richard Sieburth (New York: Archipelago Books, 2004), 170.

20. As noted in Chapter 2, January 20 also had special significance for Celan as the date of the 1942 Wannsee Conference to which he alludes in such poems as "Huhediblu." In the context of Büchner's other works, it marks the eve of the execution of Louis XVI on January 21, 1793 and is mentioned in this connection in *Danton's Death* (*CPLOW* 3.4: 51; *WBMA* 112). In contrast, the belatedness of the circular movement associated with that which "comes between" is related to Prince Leonce's claim, "*A posteriori*—that's how everything begins," to which we will return below.

21. As noted in Chapter 1, Celan's notion of *Zwischenkunft* bears a certain affinity to the Hölderlinian notion of caesura developed in his commentaries on Sophocles. There he defines "caesura" as a "counter-rhythmic rupture" in which the crucial moment of tragic reversal takes place. On the pertinence of this notion to Celan's poetics, see Philippe Lacoue-Labarthe, *Poetry as Experience*, trans. Andrea Tarnowski (Stanford: Stanford University Press, 1999). Of particular relevance is his reading of *The Meridian* in the chapter entitled "Catastrophe," where he writes,

> The interruption of language, the suspension of language, the caesura ('counter-rhythmic rupture,' said Hölderlin)—that is poetry, then. '[Robbed] . . . of breath and speech,' the 'turn' of breath, the 'turn at the end of inspiration.' Poetry occurs where language, contrary to all expectations, gives way. Precisely at inspiration's failing—and this can be understood in at least two senses. Or, even more precisely, at retained expiration, the breath-holding: when speaking (discoursing) is about to continue, and *someone*, suddenly free, forbids what was to be said. When a word occurs in the pure suspension of speech. Poetry is the spasm or syncope of language. Hölderlin called the caesura 'the pure word.'"
>
> (Lacoue-Labarthe, 49)

22. "Hermetik heute: sich dem überkommenen, kompromitierten Schönen verschließen um sie einem vielleicht Kommenden—nicht 'Kommoden'—Wahren aufzutun; Ich würde hier von Hoffnung sprechen; das Gedicht 'verhofft' wie die gejagte Kreatur." *M* 149, trans. mod.

23. "Im Jüdischen: Gott nicht als der Gekommene und Wiederkommende, sondern als der Kommende; damit ist die Zeit bestimmend, mitbestimmend; wo Gott nah ist, geht die Zeit zu Ende." *M* 131, trans. mod.

24. "Das literarische Zitat ist . . . das entscheidende ästhetische Bauprinzip," writes Walter Hinderer in *Büchner Kommentar zum dichterischen Werk* (Munich: Winkler, 1977), 133, further noting that *Leonce and Lena* draws on texts by Shakespeare, Sterne, Musset, Goethe, Holberg, Tieck, Brentano, Jean Paul,

Friedrich Schegel, and Bonaventura as well as the tradition of the *Commedia dell'arte*.

25. Here it is important to bear in mind his remark that rabbit ears listen "for something . . . beyond words."

26. Celan's sensitivity to the rope-like status of the *Gedankenstrichel* left hanging in suspense "between yes and no" in *Woyzeck* is reflected in his poem "Sprich Auch Du" ("Speak You Too") in which it is said: "Sprich—/Doch scheide das Nein nicht vom Ja. /Gib deinem Spruch auch den Sinn: /gib ihm den Schatten.//Gib ihm Schatten genug, /gib ihm so viel, /als du um dich verteil weisst zwischen/Mittnacht und Mittag und Mittnacht" (Speak—/But don't split off No from Yes. /Give your say this meaning too; /give it the shadow.//Give it shadow enough, /give it as much/as you see spread round you between/midnight and midday and midnight). Tellingly, the shadow mentioned in these lines shrinks precisely at the moment of the meridian: "Nun aber schrumpt der Ort, wo du stehst:/Wohin jetzt, Schattenentblösster, wohin?" (But now the place shrinks, where you stand:/Where now, shadow-stripped, where?). Now stripped of its shadow, the *Du* thins out—*Dünner wirst du*—becoming a tenuous connective. And it is upon this attenuated, stretched out thread—not so much that of the *Du* but of the word *Dünner* it will have become, the very word into which it will have been finely drawn out—that the shadow-deprived addressee of the poem may ascend: "Steige. Taste empor. /Dünner wirst du, unkenntlicher, feiner! /Feiner:" (Climb. Grope upwards. /Thinner you grow, less knowable, finer! /Finer:). And it is upon this same thread that the star above may in its turn descend: "ein Faden, /am dem er herab will, der Stern" (a thread on which the star wants to descend). That *der Stern* is preceded by the pronoun *er* reminds us of the way the threadword *Dünner* literally connects the *Du* and *er*, the *you* and *he*, at each of its ends (*SPP* 76–7).

27. "Does the poem," Levinas asks, "perhaps allow the 'I' to separate from itself? In Celan's terms: discover 'a place in which the person, in grasping himself as a stranger to himself, emerges.'" Emmanuel Levinas, "Paul Celan: From Being to the Other" in *Proper Names*, trans. Michael B. Smith (Stanford University Press: 1996), 43.

28. Of relevance here is Jonathan Lear's notion of the "lucky break." Happiness, he reminds us, has an older sense of happenstance: "the experience of chance things working out well rather than badly. Happiness, on this interpretation, is not the ultimate goal of our teleologically organized strivings, but the ultimate ateleological moment: a chance event going well for us—quite literally a lucky break. Analysis puts us in a position to take advantage of certain kinds of chance occurrences: those breaks in psychological structure which are caused by too much of too much. This isn't a teleological occurrence, but a taking-advantage of the disruption of previous attempts to construct a teleology." Jonathan Lear, *Happiness, Death, and the Remainder of Life* (Cambridge: Harvard UP,

2000), 129. It is particularly significant in this respect that the lucky break Celan happens upon in the form of Franzos's editorial slip occurs just at the end of *Leonce and Lena*, at the point, that is, where the play is brought teleologically to a close. For a further discussion of Lear, see Eric Santner's excellent mongraph *On The Psychotheology of Everyday Life* (Chicago: University of Chicago Press, 2001), 99.

29. Consider the following examples: "And poetry? Poetry which, of course, must go the same way of art?" (*CP* 44; *GW* 3:193); "Poetry is perhaps this: an *Atemwende*, a turning of our breath. Who knows, perhaps poetry goes its way—the way of art—for the sake of just such a turn?" (*CP* 47; *GW* 3:195); "Perhaps after this, the poem can be itself . . . can in this now art-less, art-free manner go other ways, including the ways of art, time and again?" (*CP* 47; *GW* 3:196).

30. The altered translation here follows to a large extent the one appearing in Jacques Derrida, *Sovereignties in Question*, 120.

31. Jacques Derrida, "The Majesty of the Present," trans. Alessia Ricciardi and Christopher Yu, *New German Critique* 91 (Winter 2004): 26.

32. Celan calls increasing attention to this movement as he approaches the end of his speech. "Ladies and gentlemen, I have come to the end—I have come back to the beginning" (*CP* 51; *GW* 200). "Ladies and gentlemen, allow me, since I have come back to the beginning, to ask once more, briefly and from a different direction, the same question" (*CP* 52; *GW* 3:200–1). "Ladies and gentlemen, I am coming to the end, I am coming, along with my acute accent, to the end of . . . *Leonce and Lena*" (*CP* 53; *GW* 3:201).

4. ON THE STROKE OF CIRCUMCISION I: DERRIDA, CELAN, AND THE COVENANT OF THE WORD

1. Derrida, "Shibboleth: For Paul Celan," 3; *Schibboleth pour Paul Celan*, 11. Henceforth all references will appear in the body of the text as *S* followed first by the English page number and then by *SPC* and the French page number.

2. In his reading of Freud's *Beyond the Pleasure Principle*, Derrida explicitly treats the text's seven chapters as though each were a day of the week. See Jacques Derrida, "To Speculate—on 'Freud'," in *The Postcard: From Socrates to Freud and Beyond*, trans. Alan Bass (Chicago: University of Chicago Press, 1987), 299 ff.

3. For a further discussion of the term Vielstelligkeit in Celan and Rilke, see Werner Hamacher's essay "Häm: Ein Gedicht Celans mit Motiven Benjamins," in *Jüdisches Denken in einer Welt ohne Gott: Festschrift für Stéphane Mosès*, ed. Jens Mattern, Gabriel Motzkin, and Shimon Sandbank (Berlin: Vorwerk 8, 2000), 173–97.

4. For a further discussion of the term *Kontur*, see Chapter 3.

5. In a note to *Poetry as Experience*, Philippe Lacoue-Labarthe cites Roger Munier's response to an inquiry on experience in *Mise en page*,

First there is etymology. Experience comes from the Latin *experiri*, to test, try, prove. The radical is *pereri*, which one also finds in *periculum*, peril, danger. The Indo-European root is *per*, to which are attached the ideas of crossing and, secondarily, of trial, test. In Greek, numerous deviations evoke a crossing or passage; *peirô*, to cross; *pera*, beyond; *peraô*, to pass through; *perainô*, to go to the end; *peras*, end, limit. For Germanic languages, Old High German *faran* has given us *fahren*, to transport, and *führen*, to drive. Should we attribute *Erfahrung* to this origin as well, or should it be linked to the second meaning of *per*, trail, in Old High German *fara*, danger, which became *Gefahr*, danger, and *gefährden*, to endanger? The boundaries between one meaning and the other are imprecise. The same is true for the Latin *periri*, to try, and *periculum*, which originally means trial, test, then risk, danger. The idea of experience as a crossing is etymologically and semantically difficult to separate from that risk. From the beginning and no doubt in a fundamental sense, experience means to endanger. (128n15)

6. There it is asked of the Jew: "what does he have that is really his own, that is not borrowed, taken and not returned?" (*CP* 17; *GW* 3: 169).

7. For my English translation of the poem, I consulted the translations appearing in *Selected Poems and Prose of Paul Celan*, 170–1, and in Derrida's "Shibboleth: For Paul Celan," 61, 62, 63, 65.

5. ON THE STROKE OF CIRCUMCISION II: CELAN, KAFKA, AND THE WOUND IN THE NAME

1. For an eloquent discussion of this passage from a different perspective see Geoffrey Hartman, "'Breaking Every Star': On Literary Knowledge," Comparative Criticism 18 (1996): 3–20.

2. The stone or flint was an instrument of circumcision used not only by Abraham but also by Joshua, who circumcised the entire generation of Hebrews born after the exodus from Egypt before entering the Promised Land. Cf. Joshua 5: 7–8. Commenting in *The Book of J* on the phrase "It was that day Yahweh cut a covenant with Abram," Harold Bloom writes, "Nothing is weirder than the ceremony that celebrates the covenant that has been cut between Abram and Yahweh.... For J, a word, whether Yahweh's or Abram's, is also an act and a thing." *Book of J*, trans. David Rosenberg, interp. Harold Bloom (New York: Grove Weidenfeld, 1990), 201.

3. Gershom Scholem, "The Idea of the Golem," in *On the Kabbalah and its Symbolism*, trans. Ralph Mannheim (New York: Schocken Books, 1969), 161. All references will henceforth appear in parentheses in the body of the text as *IG* followed by page number.

4. Hamacher, *Premises*, 309–10. All references to this text will henceforth appear in parentheses in the body of the text as *Premises* followed by page number.

5. The poem, written on May 20, 1965, closes the fourth cycle of the 1967 collection *Atemwende (Breathturn)* and "corresponds," in the words of Badiou, "to a caesura in the life of Paul Celan," his release from the psychiatric hospital in Vésinet, where, following a period of severe depression at the end of April 1965, he had stayed from May 8 to 21 (*CCL* II: 222, trans. mine). While in the hospital, he read Bergson, Camus, Kafka, Lichtenberg, and Shakespeare and wrote poems that were often intimately connected to his readings of these authors (*CCL* II:555).

6. For a detailed discussion of the legal questions raised by Kafka's parable, see Jacques Derrida, "Devant la loi," trans. Avital Ronell, in *Kafka and the Contemporary Critical Performance: Centenary Readings*, ed. Alan Udoff (Bloomington, Indiana University Press, 1987), 309–55.

7. Franz Kafka, *Letter to His Father / Brief an den Vater* bilingual edition, trans. Ernst Kaiser and Eithne Wilkins (NY: Schocken Books, 1966), 88–91.

8. "Without forebears, without marriage, without heirs," Kafka writes in a diary entry of January 21, 1922, "with a fierce longing for forebears, marriage, and heirs. They all of them stretch out their hands to me: forebears, marriage and heirs, but too far away from me. There is an artificial, miserable substitute for everything, for forebears, marriage and heirs. Feverishly you contrive these substitutes, and if the fever has not already destroyed you, the hopelessness of the substitutes will." *The Diaries of Franz Kafka, 1914-1923*, ed. Max Brod, trans. Joseph Kresh (New York: Schocken, 1948), 207. Later published in German as *Tagebücher* (Frankfurst am Main: Fischer, 1990).

9. Franz Kafka, *Letters to Friends, Family, and Editors*, trans. Richard and Clara Winston (New York: Schocken Books, 1977), 138.

10. The phrase, meaning a gushing or welling up from the throat, appears in one of Kafka's last letters to Felice, dated September 7, 1917. Franz Kafka, *Letters to Felice*, trans. Eric Heller and Jürgen Born (New York: Schocken, 1973), 543; *Briefe an Felice* (Frankfurst am Main: Fischer Taschenbuch Verlang, 1983), 753.

11. This moment is evoked in the 1966 lyric "In Prague," which speaks of "wordblood born / in the night bed [wortblutgeboren / im Nachtbett]" (Celan, *SPP*, 258–9).

12. For a brilliant reading of this correspondence, see Elias Canetti, *Kafka's Other Trial: The Letters to Felice*, trans. Christopher Middleton (New York: Schocken, 1974).

13. For a comprehensive discussion of Kafka's illness, viewed in the context of the medical and ideological discourses of the time, see Sander Gilman, *Franz Kafka, the Jewish Patient* (New York: Routledge, 1995).

14. I discuss this poem at length in *The Belated Witness* (Stanford: Stanford University Press, 2006), 169–88.

15. Celan's poem "In Prague" evokes this mass in the lines directly following the ones cited above: "larger and larger / we grew through one another, there

was no name for / what drove us" (grösser und grösser / wuchsen wir durcheinander, es gab / keinen Namen für / das, was uns trieb) (Celan, *SPP*, 258–9).

16. The previous year Kafka had written a story of almost the same name. Organized around a play of names and wounds, "A Country Doctor" describes in lurid detail a "rosy" stigma blossoming "near the hip" of the doctor's patient. "Rose-red [Rosa], in many variations of shade, dark in the hollows, lighter at the edges, softly granulated, with irregular clots of blood, open as a surface mine to the daylight," this gaping wound opens as the revenant of a violated name. For what returns in it is the rape of the doctor's servant girl, Rosa, whom he had abandoned to the brutish force of a groom found living, to his own apparent surprise, in his "own house." Driven from his home by a team of horses hitched up and dispatched by the groom, he drives to the house of a "seriously ill patient" only to encounter in the boy's rose-colored wound the violated body of the maiden he had left behind." "A Country Doctor," in *The Complete Stories*, trans. Willa and Edwin Muir (New York: Schocken), 220–6. Not only does the unlocatable trauma oscillating in the gap between these two scenes resonate in the title of *Die Niemandsrose*, but, as Felstiner and Badiou note, a refrain from the story "It's only a doctor" (Sist nur ein Arzt) was altered by Celan into "It's only a Jew" (s'ist nur ein Jud) and used in lieu of his own name to sign a letter to Reinhard Federman dated February 23, 1962. See John Felstiner, *Paul Celan: Poet, Survivor, Jew* (New Haven: Yale University Press), 185–86. While the Celanian signature "s'ist nur ein Jud" resonates with a refrain from "A Country Doctor," it also echoes Kafka's response to Milena Jesenská's question "Jste zid?" (Are you Jewish?) "Don't you see," Kafka writes, "how in the *Jste* the fist is withdrawn to gather muscle-strength? And then in the *zid* the cheerful, unfailing, forward-flying blow?" Franz Kafka, *Letters to Milena*, ed. Willy Haas, trans. Tania and James Stern (New York: Vintage, 1999), 42.

See also a letter Celan wrote approximately a month earlier to the French translator and Kafka scholar Marthe Robert, in which he requests a meeting to speak with her about the "Goll affaire," describing it as "une campagne de diffamation qui, après être passée par des phase aussi incroyable que révélatrice—les choses, en Allemagne, ont beaucoup évolué, l'antise- [sic] mitisme, sous une forme plus ou moins savamment déguisé [sic] par le double jeu (qui se joue à 'gauche' (comme ailleurs) a abouti—grace à une belle participation nazie, 'philosémite' et hélas—'juive') . . . à mon abolition pure et simple comme personne et comme auteur. . . . cette affaire, . . . croyez-moi, est une vraie affaire Dreyfus" [A campaign of defamation which, having passed through phases as unbelievable as they are revealing—matters, in Germany, have evolved a lot, anti-Semitism, in a form more or less cleverly disguised by the double game (which is being played on the 'left' (as elsewhere) has resulted, thanks to lively Nazi participation, 'philosemitic' and, alas, 'Jewish,') . . . in my destruction, pure and simple, as a person and as a writer . . . this affair, . . . believe me, is a real Dreyfus Affair"] (qtd. in *CCL* II: 533, my trans.).

Notes to pages 91–94   145

17. See Celan, *Die Niemandesrose: Vorstufen–Textgenese—Endfassung*, ed. Heino Schmull (Frankfurt am Main: Suhrkamp, 1996), 64. See also Otto Pöggeler, *Spur des Wortes: Zur Lyrik Paul Celans* (Munich: Karl Alber, 1986), 342–50; Sigrid Mayer, *Golem: Die literarische Rezeption eines Stoffes* (Frankfurt am Main: Peter Lang, 1975), 85–90; Bernt Witte, "Der zyklische Charakter der Niemandsrose von Paul Celan," in *Argumentume silentio*, ed. Amy Colin (Berlin–New York: Walter de Gruyter, 1987) 78–79; Peter Horst Neumann, *Zur Lyrik Paul Celans: Eine Einführung* (Göttingen: Vandenhoeck and Ruprecht, 1968), 44–55.

18. For Celan, the ornithonym *Taube*, meaning pigeon or dove, is always associated with what is *taub*: not merely deaf, but oblivious, unfeeling, callous, and numb; empty and hollow; dead, sterile, and barren. Thus, for example, in the poem "In Front of a Candle" ("Vor einer Kerze") published in the 1955 collection *From Threshold to Threshold*, he relates *die Taube* to an "Amen, das uns übertäubt." "I speak you free/," he writes, in Felstiner's translation, "of the Amen that deafens us, /of the icy light that edges it/where it steps towers-high into the sea,/where the gray one, the dove/pecks up names/this side and that side of dying" (*SPP* 60–3). Celan may thus have read Kafka's "poor *Taubenhälse*," these two birdlike throats cut by one and the same knife, as the double and divided space of a vibrantly oscillating wound. Between the initial drafts of "To One Who Stood Before The Door," begun in May 1961, and the final revisions it underwent in September of the same year, Celan wrote a poem on August 7 entitled "Muta" that remained unpublished during his lifetime. Resonances of the wounded vibrancy of Kafka's constricted glottis may be heard in the poem's opening lines: "Seul —: zu dreien gesprochen, stummes/Vibratio des Mitlauts" (Seul —: spoken to three, the silent/vibratio of the consonant). Celan, *Die Gedichte aus dem Nachlaß*, (Frankfurt am Main: Suhrkamp, 1997), 63, trans. and emphasis mine. Published under the title "Erratisch" ("Erratic") in *Die Niemandsrose*, this poem speaks of "syllables—beautiful, /soundless circle" (Silben—schönes/lautloses Rund); they "help the *Kriechstern*/in their midst" (helfen dem Kriechstern/in ihre Mitte), and this middle (*Mitte*) "opens itself" (tut sich auf) in the unoccupied, silent interval between the poem's two strophes, in an interval apostrophized by the poem's last word as "aether" (*GW* 1:235) As Hamacher notes, "it is this silent 'middle' [Mitte] of the poem, the *Muta*, out of which its words and images emerge and into whose medium they are by dint of the poem reabsorbed. —The extent to which the *Muta* and its relationship to the *liquida* entered Celan's poetological reflection may be gauged from a note to a preliminary draft of his *Meridian* address which speaks of 'That which is voiced in the poem today; in the initial sound; *muta cum liquida* [Das Stimmhafte des Gedichts heute; im Anlaut: muta cum liquida]'" (Hamacher, "Häm" 177–8n5; my trans.).

19. That this wound resurfacing at the edge of the poem as an intersection of text and body also gathers in the place and in the very body of the name *Kafka* is further suggested by the "two sharp *k*'s that," as Felstiner notes, "cut

through" the terms *Kielkropf* and *Kriegsknechts*. John Felstiner, "Kafka and the Golem," *Prooftexts* 6, no. 2 (1986), 174. If the *Kielkropf* is a brother born in the mercenary's dung-caked boot ("im kotigen Stiefel des Kriegsknechts/geborenen Bruder"), it is in one sense born—like the golem and indeed like Adam himself—of the element that clings to the boot of the foot soldier. Yet, insofar as this element is described as *kotig*, it is associated not merely with adamic earth or golemic mud but, more specifically, with excrement. It is this infantile *Kacke*, closely related to the Latin *cacare* and the Russian *kákat*, that is onomatopoetically sounded out in the fraternal pairing of the twin *k*'s resonating in *Kielkropf*, *Kriegsknechts*, *Kehlkopf*, and *Ka(f)ka*, making the letters rather than the mud the true element of creation. As though to accentuate the insistence of this initial *k*-sound (and here one should recall the importance Celan placed on the *Anlaut* in the note cited above [n18]), he changed the phrase "Rabbi, mummelt ich..." (Rabbi, I mumbled...), which appeared in an earlier draft of the poem dated May 20, 1961, to "Rabbi, knirschte ich..." (Rabbi, I gnashed...) in the final version. Similarly, the words *verkrüüppelten Finger*, appearing in that draft, were later condensed into the capitalized composite *Krüppelfinger*, which now opens the twenty-third line of the published text.

20. For a further "metastasis" of this unmutable silence see the late poem from the 1971 collection *Schneepart* entitled "Largo." There it is said that "the pair of blackbirds [Das Amselpaar] hangs/beside us, under/our whitely drifting/companions up there, our/meta-/stases." *Poems of Paul Celan*, trans. Michael Hamburger (New York: Persea, 1988), 326—7; *GW* 2: 356. In his sensitive discussion of this poem, Paul Auster hears in the *Amsel* echoes of Celan's own name, without, however, pursuing the link to Kafka's *Amschel-Amsel*. Instead, he relates the poem's pair of blackbirds to Günter Grass's novel *Dog Years*, which chronicles the love-hate relationship between a Jew and a Nazi during the war. The Jewish character is named Amsel. "Toward the end of the poem," Auster notes, "the presence of 'our whitely drifting/companions up there' is a reference to the Jewish victims of the Holocaust: the smoke of the bodies burned in crematoria. From early poems such as 'Todesfuge'... to later poems such as 'Largo,' the Jewish dead in Celan's work inhabit the air, are the very substance we are condemned to breathe: souls turned into smoke, into dust, into nothing at all—'our/meta-/stases.'" Paul Auster, *Ground Work: Selected Poems and Essays 1970–1979* (London: Faber and Faber, 1990), 159–61.

21. This translation is a slightly modified version of the one appearing in Rainer Nägele, *Reading after Freud* (New York: Columbia University Press, 1987), 136.

22. In his discussion of Celan's poem "Aus Dem Moorboden" ("From The Swampy Soil"), which appeared in the 1971 collection *Scheepart* (*Snow Part*) and begins with a quotation from Benjamin's 1934 Kafka essay, Hamacher follows Benjamin in assigning Josefine to the same intermediate world, or *Mittelwelt*, to

which Kafka's assistants and messengers are said to belong, describing her as the "singing, but perhaps inaudibly singing mouse" and noting how this singing is evoked in an earlier poem from *Scheepart* which begins, "Mit Der Stimme Der Feldmaus/quiekst du herauf" (With The Voice Of A Field Mouse/you pipe up or squeak forth). *Snow Part*, trans. Ian Farley (Riverdale-on-Hudson: The Sheep Meadow Press, 2007), 24–5; *GW* 2: 343. Recalling Celan's claim in *The Meridian* that "every poem remains dedicated to its own '20th of January'"; that "Conversation in the Mountains," in which he "commemorated a missed encounter in the Engadine," was "written from a '20th of January,' from my '20th of January,'" from a time in which as he says, "I had . . . encountered myself" (*CP* 47, 53; *GW* 3: 196, 201), it is important to note that both "With The Voice Of A Field Mouse" and the poem immediately preceding it in *Scheepart* were written on January 20, 1968. Indeed, the preceding poem—whose opening line "Ich Höre, Die Axt Hat Geblüht" resonates strongly with the axe strokes and blossoming wounds of Kafka's "A Country Doctor" and whose last line, "die einzige Zuflucht," is a barely altered citation of a line from Benjamin's Kafka essay—initially bore the title "Der zwanzigste Jänner 1968" ("The Twentieth of January 1968") (Hamacher, "Häm," 178–9). Like Danton's "September" and the other meridians of the Büchnerian text, Kafka's singing glottal stop remains for Celan a wound around which his own texts will continue to gather, a date from which, as of which, and toward which he writes. The wound, Kafka says, is so massive, so turbulent, so mutable and ever-growing that there is no seeing it whole. Yet it is precisely in the repeated misses of Celan's failed encounter with this silently mutating wound, in the very midst of this vortex of throttling silence, that he will have stumbled upon his own innermost alterity, that he will, as if by accident, have encountered himself as another, his own *Antschel* as an *Amschel-Amsel*, as the birdlike twittering of a constricted glottis, as the squeaky silence of a singing mouse.

23. The reference here is, of course, to the Altneu Synagogue of Prague, which was located in the vicinity of Kafka's home. This synagogue has a curious tradition directly associated with the figure of Rabbi Löw and the legend of the Golem. As was noted earlier, the rabbi once forgot to remove the divine *shem* from his golem's mouth on the eve of the Sabbath. The golem caused such a disturbance, however, that the rabbi had to be called away from the *Schul* just as the Sabbath psalm was being recited so that he could remove the shem. Since that time the Sabbath psalm is always sung twice in the Altneu Synagogue. Elke Günzel, *Das wandernde Zitat: Paul Celan im jüdischen Kontext*. (Würzburg: Königshausen and Neumann, 1995). 21.

Apropos of his own house, household deity, and house of god, Kafka wrote the following in his diary on February 1, 1922: "Strange that the god of pain was not the chief god of the earliest religions (but first became so in the later ones, perhaps). For each invalid his household god, for the tubercular the god of suffocation [Jedem Kranken sein Hausgott, dem Lungenkranken der Gott des Erstickens]. How can one bear his approach [sein Herankommen] if one does not partake of him in advance of the terrible union?" (*Diaries* 217–8; *Tagebücher* 899).

24. In the open-endedness of the "Ra- —" is also inscribed an endlessly interrupted beginning, the beginning not just of a name broken off in the mouth of a speaker or of a sound trapped in the throat, but of the *Radius* Kafka repeatedly sought to draw out in the course of his life. "A feeling of fretfulness again," a diary entry dated January 23, 1922, begins.

> From what did it arise? From certain thoughts which are quickly forgotten but leave my fretfulness unforgettably behind. Sooner than the thoughts themselves I could list the places in which they occurred to me; one, for example, on the little path that passes the Altneu Synagogue. Fretful too because of a certain sense of contentment that now and then drew near me, though timidly enough and sufficiently far off. Fretful too that my nocturnal resolve remains merely a resolve. Fretful that my life till now has been merely marking time [ein stehendes Marschieren war], has progressed at most in the sense that decay progresses in a rotten tooth. I have not shown the faintest firmness of resolve in the conduct of my life. It was as if I, like everyone else, had been given a point [Kreismittelpunkt] from which to prolong the radius of a circle, and had then, like everyone else, to describe my perfect circle round this point [den entscheidenden Radius zu gehen und dann den schönen Kreis zu ziehen]. Instead, I was forever starting my radius only constantly to be forced at once to break it off [Statt dessen habe ich immerfort einen Anlauf zum Radius genommen, aber immer wieder gleich ihn abbrechen müssen]. (Examples: piano, violin, languages, Germanics, anti-Zionism, Zionism, Hebrew, gardening, carpentering, writing, marriage attempts, an apartment of my own.) The center of my imaginary circle bristles with the beginnings of radii [Es starrt im Mittelpunkt des imaginären Kreises von beginnenden Radien], there is no room left for a new attempt; no room means old age and weak nerves, and never to make another attempt means the end. If I sometimes prolonged the radius a little farther than usual, in the case of my law studies, say, or engagements, everything was made worse rather than better just because of this little extra distance.
>
> (*Diaries* 208–9; *Tagebücher* 887–8)

25. Celan and Celan-Lestrange, *Correspondance*, 2: 472. See also Celan, *glottal stop: 100 poems*, trans. Nikolai Popov and Heather McHugh (Hanover: Wesleyan University Press, 2000), xiii.

6. POETRY'S DEMANDS AND ABRAHAMIC SACRIFICE: CELAN'S POEMS FOR ERIC

1. See the letter from Gisèle dated January 29, 1952, in which she writes, "ça sera très merveilleux de vivre à *côté* de toi—plus merveilleux encore *peut-être* quand François hurlera tout le jour et toute la nuit—Nous serons heureux—malgré les cris—et toi aussi, n'est-ce pas?" (It will be marvelous to live *by your side* – even more so *perhaps* with François wailing all day and night–We'll be happy–despite the crying–you too, right?) (*CCL* II : 18). Badiou adds a note here stating that "GL est sans doute enceinte" (GL is no doubt pregnant) (*CCL* II: n.2, 55). Given the fact that François was born October 7, 1953, the pregnancy referred to here is presumably one that resulted in a miscarriage.

2. Celan's *demande de naturalisation* was submitted along with a *demande de francization du nom Antschel en Celan* on July 17, 1953. For details *see CCL* II: 490, 500–1.

3. Although *Schneepart* was only first published in 1971, a year after the author's death, it was finished and prepared for publication during his lifetime. While the present chapter focuses only on the three poems for Eric written in the spring and summer of 1968, it should be noted that "Ich habe Bambus geschnitten," contained in *Die Niemandsrose* (GW 1: 264; *SSP* 184–5) and "Die Unze Wahrheit," in *Fadensonnen* (GW 2: 128) also contain addresses to him. Paul Celan, *Threadsuns*, trans. Pierre Joris (Los Angeles: Sun and Moon Press, 2000).

4. "C'était . . . très dur pour moi de me trouver . . . devant une si terrible alternative" (It was . . . very difficult to find myself . . . confronted with such a dreadful alternative) (*CCL* I: 324).

5. The term *kilodrame* is a neologism coined by Celan to suggest a drama of overwhelming, "thousandfold" proportion. For further discussion of it, see Thomas Schestag, "Men Schen Schnitte durch in ein Gedicht Paul Celans," *MLN German Issue*, 119, no. 3 (2004): 580–607; esp. fn. 25, 601.

6. ". . . qu'il imagine en train de faire du mal à son fils" (who he imagined was in the process of hurting his son) (*CCL* II: 427).

7. The attack took place on November 14, 1968 (*CCL* II: 427).

8. As my colleague Fatima Naqvi reminded me, the past participle *gepestet* is itself a neologism obviously modeled on the noun *Pest* (plague, pestilence, pest). In coining it, Celan seems to suggest that the *Gleichung* (equation) modified by it is not merely precarious but inherently unstable and that it is this instability afflicting and infecting the *Gleichung* from the very first that threatens to spread uncontrollably throughout the poem.

9. "Für Eric," composed in 1968, reads in many ways like a rewriting of the poem "BEIM HAGELKORN" (IN THE HAILSTONE) published in the 1967 collection *Atemwende* (*Breathturn*). Both are organized around the sign *Schütze*, or Sagittarius. In the earlier poem the phrase *meine Pfeilschrift* appears in the same

place as the latter's "meine . . . pfeilende / Hand"—that is, in the second-to-last line. Yet in contrast to the earlier poem, in which "your arrow-writing" is released from "a bowstring," the later poem focuses attention on the archer's hand and the undischarged tension gathering within its grip.

> BEIM HAGELKORN, *im*
> *brandigen Mais-*
> *kolben, daheim,*
> *den späten, den harten*
> *Novembersternen gehorsam:*
>
> *in den Herzfaden die*
> *Gespräche der Würmer geknüpft—:*
>
> *eine Sehne, von der*
> *deine Pfeilschrift schwirrt,*
> *Schütze.*
>   (qtd. in Gadamer,
>   *Gadamer on Celan* 543)

> IN THE HAILSTONE, in the
> blighted corn
> cob, at home, obeying
> the late, the hard
> November stars:
>
> in your heart-thread the
> conversations of worms are knit—:
>
> a string, from which
> your arrow-writing whirs,
> Archer.
>   (qtd. in Gadamer,
>   *Gadamer on Celan*)

Gadamer discusses this poem in his essay "Who Am I and Who Are You" without any consideration of the astrological associations of the terms Novembersternen and Schütze. See Hans-Georg Gadamer, *Gadamer on Celan: Who Am I and Who Are You? And Other Essays,* trans. Richard Heinemann and Bruce Krajewski (Albany: SUNY Press, 1997), 102–4; Hans-Georg Gadamer, *Wer bin Ich und wer bist Du? Ein Kommentar zu Paul Celans Gedichtfolge "Atemkristall."* Frankfurt am Main: Suhrkamp, 1986.

  10. On the interruption of the sacrifice, see "Rams" and in particular the very rich passage in which Derrida writes,

Caesura, hiatus, ellipsis—all are interruptions that at once open and close. They keep access to the poem ["GREAT GLOWING VAULT"] forever at the threshold of its crypts (one among them, only one, would refer to a singular and secret experience, wholly other, whose constellation is accessible only through the testimony of the poet and a few others). The interruptions also open, in a disseminal and non-saturable fashion, onto unforeseeable constellations, onto so many other stars, some of which would perhaps still resemble the seed that Yahweh told Abraham, after the interruption of the sacrifice, he would multiply like the stars. (*Sovereignties* 157).

This passage is preceded by a discussion of the role of the ram in the sacrificial scene, a discussion prompted not only by the poem's question, "Wo-/gegen/rennt er nicht an?," but also by Michael Hamburger's "judicious translation" of it as "In-/to what/does he not charge?" Picking up on the ambiguity of the English word "charge," Derrida asks:

> Is not this charge [. . .] also an accusation or a price to pay [. . .] and thus the discharge of a debt or the atonement of a sin? Doesn't the ram charge the adversary, a sacrificer or a wall, with every crime? For the question, as we noted earlier, is in the interro-negative form: Against what does he not strike? Against what does he not charge? Able to butt in order to attack or to seek revenge, the ram can declare war or respond to sacrifice by protesting in opposition against it. Its burst of indignant incomprehension would not spare anything or anyone in the world. No one in the world is innocent, not even the world itself. One imagines the anger of Abraham's or Aaron's ram, the infinite revolt of the ram of all holocausts. But also, figuratively, the violent rebellion of all scapegoats, all substitutes. Why me? Their adversity, their adversary, would be everywhere. The frontline, the forehead of this protest would hurl the ram against sacrifice itself, against men and God. The ram would, finally, want to put an end to their common world. It would charge against everything and against whomever, in all directions as if blinded by pain. (*Sovereignties* 156–7)

11. See also Gerhart Baumann, *Erinnerungen an Paul Celan* (Frankfurt am Main: Suhrkamp Verlag, 1986), 55–7. Recalling a walk with the poet around the Latin Quarter on April 26, 1968, he writes,

> Auf Strassen und Plätzen Unrat, zerknüllte Flugschriften, an den Wänden herausfordernde Aufrufe. Das Ganze mutete wie eine verlassene Bühne an; ungewiss blieb, ob sie für den nächsten Akt geräumt worden war, ob man das Drama abgesetzt oder nur vorläufig beendet hatte. Die unflätigen und anzüglichen Parolen legten den Schluss nahe, dass nicht eine grosse

Tragödie abgehandelt worden war, vielmehr eine Schmierenkomödie oder ein zweideutiges Stegreifspiel. Bei Celan regten sich zunächst Anflüge von schwarzem Humor; dann aber gab er sich schweigsamer und seine knappen Bemerkungen gewannen an Schärfe. Mit einer Unerbittlichkeit . . . entlarvte er die hohlen Schlagwörter, die anmassenden Lügen, welche sich geistvoll-kritisch gebärdeten. [. . .] Er verdammte jede leichtfertige Herausforderung, das gewissenlose Abenteuer, das sich nicht Rechenschaft darüber gab, zu welchem Ende der angezettelte Aufstand führen konnte. [. . .] Vor allem peinigte ihn jedoch die Sorge, dass Vergangenes wiederkehren konnte,— ein Umschlag vom Allzumenschlichen in das Unmenschliche. [. . .] Celans eigener Sohn Eric war von dem Strudel mitgerissen worden und noch nicht zur Besinnung gekommen. Das Gespräch zwischen den Generationen [. . .] war abgebrochen oder in Beschimpfungen ausgeartet. (55–6)

(On the streets and squares there was garbage and crumpled pamphlets, on the walls, calls to action. It all looked like an abandoned stage—though whether it had been cleared for the next act, whether the drama had been definitively canceled or merely put on hold, was unclear. The lewd and salacious slogans suggested that what had been played out was not so much a great tragedy as a knockabout comedy or some ambiguous bit of improv. While at first responding with flashes of black humor, Celan turned increasingly taciturn, his terse remarks becoming ever more acerbic. He systematically analyzed the vapid slogans and pretentious lies that sought to pass themselves off as profound critique. [. . .] He condemned every frivolous provocation and the recklessness of a makeshift uprising that seemed to give little thought to where it might be heading [. . .] Above all, it was the fear that the past might return—that the all-too-human might abruptly turn inhuman—that tormented him [. . .] Celan's own son Eric had been caught up in the whirl of events and had not yet come to his senses. The intergenerational dialogue [. . .] had collapsed or had at best become little more than an exchange of insults.) (trans. mine)

12. In his commentary on the first cycle of poems from this collection, published separately as *Atemkristall* (*Breath Crystal*), Gadamer draws attention to the *Maul* (mouth) within the term *Maulbeerbaum* (mulberry tree) appearing in the first poem. "Already here in one's first approach to the poem," he notes,

one must understand as concretely as possible. This means correctly accounting for the poet's awareness of language, since he not only uses words in their clear reference to objects, but also constantly plays with the meanings and associations that sound in them. One can thus ask whether the poet here is playing with the syllable *Maul* [meaning "mouth"] by referring to the *Maulheld des Wortes* [the loudmouth] whose shouting he can no longer bear.

(Gadamer, *Who Am I*, 71, 76; *Wer bin Ich* 15, 21)

While Gadamer will ultimately decide in favor of a different interpretation of the mulberry tree and its crying or shouting leaf, the first suggestion is still plausible and worth considering not only because of the connection between the *Maul* (mouth) of the *Maulbeerbaum* (mulberry tree) and the oral qualities attributed to its crying leaf in the poem ("schrie sein jüngstes/Blatt" (qtd. in Gadamer, *Who Am I*, 70) but also because Gadamer opens his discussion of the next poem, "Von Ungeträumten," with the identification of another *Maul*. "Ein Maulwurf ist tätig" (A mole is at work), he says, even though such an animal is never explicitly named (an observation that will be important for what follows). While neither the *Maulwurf* Gadamer sees at work in the second poem nor the *Maulbeerbaum* mentioned in the first is necessarily associated with the figure of the *Maulheld*, what is clear is that the signifier *Maul* cannot simply be taken on its own terms but must instead be read in the context of a signifying chain whose links run from *Maul* through *Maulbeerbaum* to *Maulwurf*, *Maulheld*, and beyond. It is this "beyond" that my own reading of Celan's poems for Eric seeks to trace.

13. The *FAZ* article by Robert Held is discussed in "Die Kunst der Verwebung: Von der Zeitung zum Gedicht—Paul Celan und der Pariser Mai 68" which appeared in the *Neue Zürcher Zeitung* on December 17, 2005. While the NZZ article does not refer to the use of the term *Flüstertüte* in the poem "Für Eric" composed on June 2, the day on which the Cohn-Bendit article appeared in the *FAZ*, it does document how the same article became the source of another poem written on that day, "Dein Blondschatten" ("Your Blond Shadow"). Published in the posthumous collection *Schneepart* (*Snow Part*), "Dein Blondschatten" appears immediately after the poem "Für Eric." I am grateful to Anna Glazova for bringing this article to my attention. See also Paul Celan, *Die Gedichte: Kommentierte Ausgabe*, ed. Barbara Weidemann (Frankfurt am Main: Suhrkamp, 2005), 847.

14. The child of a German-Jewish father and French-Jewish mother who had fled Nazism in 1933, he was officially stateless at birth, only choosing German citizenship in 1959 at the age of fourteen in order to avoid conscription.

15. Karl Marx and Friedrich Engels, *Marx-Engels Reader*, ed. Robert C. Tucker (New York: Norton, 1978), 606. As Freddie Rokem notes in *Philosophers and Thespians: Thinking Performance* (Stanford: Stanford University Press, 2010), Marx takes up the figure again in a 1856 speech in which he claims that "the old mole that can work in the earth so fast, that worthy pioneer [is] the Revolution." Karl Marx, "Speech at the Anniversary of the *People's Paper*," (1856), http://www.marxists.org/archive/marx/works/1856/04/14.htm.. As Rokem further

Notes to page 107

notes, Marx's comments "echo Hegel's explication of the ghost of Hamlet's father in his *Lectures on the Philosophy of History*." There Hegel writes,

> It [the old mole, the ghost] always comes forward and to the fore, because spirit also is progression. Often it seems to have forgotten who it is, to have gotten lost. But, internally divided, it works its way forward—as Hamlet says of his father's spirit, 'Well done [or well labored], old mole' [brav gearbeitet, wackerer Maulwurf]—until, having gathered strength it pushes through the crust of earth that has separated it from its sun, its concept, and the crust collapses. When crust collapses, like a rundown, abandoned building, spirit takes on new youthful form and dons seven-league boots. This labor of spirit to know itself, find itself, this activity is spirit, the life of spirit itself. Its result is the concept that it grasps of itself: the history of spirit yields the clear insight that spirit willed all of this in its history. (qtd. in Rokem 80–1)

As he and others have noted, both Hegel and Marx are misquoting Shakespeare. The most extensive discussion of these misquotations is Martin Harries, "Homo Alludens: Marx's *Eighteenth Brumaire*," *New German Critique* 66 (1995), 35–64. There he notes:

> That Marx has called the revolution "gründlich" ["thoroughgoing"] now appears as something of a pun. It is not only thorough, as one definition of the word would suggest, but thoroughly of the earth, of the ground. "Brav gewühlt, alter Maulwürf!" Well subverted, old mole! Well undermined, old mole! It is difficult to know how to translate this phrase: "wühlen" can mean to burrow, to dig, to undermine, or to grub; a "Wühler" may be an agitator or subversive. [. . .] Marx alludes to a phrase from Schlegel's translation of *Hamlet*: "Brav, alter Maulwürf! Wühlst so hurtig fort?" Schlegel translates Shakespeare: "Well said, old mole! Canst work i' th'earth so fast?" (54)

Yet, as Harries later adds,

> Marx does not simply use Schlegel's translation; his slight alteration makes a past participle ("gewühlt") of Schlegel's present tense verb ("wühlst"), and moves it from the beginning of the second phrase of Schlegel's line to the second position in the first phrase. There is a strange restoration here. A parallel to Shakespeare not found in Schlegel appears in Marx: Marx "translates" Shakespeare's "said" with "gewühlt," it is true, but there is at least some word that takes the place of "said." (59)

Of particular relevance to my reading of Celan is Harries' observation:

Revolution, opposed to executive power, never finds pure expression; its forms are parodic or allusive. Marx describes a paradoxical revolution that has no visible features yet nevertheless does its invisible, subterranean work. Marx analyzes a historical formation—Bonaparte's coup d'état—that seems, on the surface, to spell the revolution's doom; the historian's analysis discovers what that formation represses and finds that the symptoms of the surface, properly considered, reveal a depth, a tunneling, a burrowing, a mole. The linguistic tactic of allusion, then, may figure the disjunction between surface and depth that is the historian's subject. The moment in *Hamlet* to which Marx alludes offers an exemplary instance of such a disruption in the field of theatrical action. It draws attention to an unsuspected representational space beneath the stage. Marx, similarly, draws attention to an unsuspected field of historical action. Allusion figures not only the farce that is Bonaparte's recapitulation of Napoleonic history, but the materialist analysis of history that insists on reading contradictions not simply as conflict on the surface but as symptoms of what that conflict represses. (55)

16. Ctd. in Rokem, 81; trans. mod.

17. William Shakespeare, *Hamlet*, in *Complete Works*, eds. Jonathan Bate and Eric Rasmussen (New York: Random House, 2007).

18. Prompting Hamlet from his position just off or below the stage, the ghost functions theatrically as a *souffleur*, one whose whispers are associated with that which speaks softly and grubs away in the *Flüstertüte* or "whisper bag" of Celan's poem. I am grateful to Gabriele Schwab for suggesting this additional connection to *Hamlet*.

19. Rokem, 179. For more on this scene and its Marxian afterlife, see Rokem, 59–86, esp. 77–86.

20. It should also be noted that Günter Eich had begun to publish his *Maulwürfe* around this time. Having read a number of these pieces at the last meeting of the Gruppe 47 in 1967, he published the first of them that same year in the journal *Merkur*. In 1968, a collection of these short prose pieces was published under the title *Maulwürfe*. The topos already appears in the Büchner Preis speech Eich delivered in 1959, a year before Celan was to deliver his famous *Meridian* address upon receipt of the same prize.

21. The arrangement was as follows:

Geschichte buddeln
Bereitschaftswagen
Leitwege
untergehakt
Absperrketten

Flüstertüte
Raupenhelme
(history to grub away
rapid-response vehicle
routes
linked arms
cordon
megaphone
helmet with caterpillar-shaped decoration)

The draft is itself followed by a quote from Valéry: "Toute vue des choses qui n'est pas étrange est fausse" (Any view of things that is not strange is false), to which we will return below (Celan, *Schneepart*, 82). The assertion that Celan coined the verb *raupen* is not quite correct since it does in fact exist in German. The novelty of Celan's usage consists in its association with a caterpillar-like creeping movement. Otherwise, according to *Grimm Deutsches Wörterbuch*, it is used to describe the act of getting rid of or exterminating caterpillars or larvae ("von raupen befreien, raupen tilgen")." Jacob and Wilhelm Grimm, *Deutches Wörterbuch*. 8.14 (Leipzig: Hirzel, 1942).

22. To view the forces pitted against each other in these lines as inverted mirror images is not to collapse the differences between them but rather to see them as joined in a tense stand-off.

23. As Benjamin notes in Convolute C of his *Arcades Project*,

> Paris is built over a system of caverns from which the din of the Métro and railroad mounts to the surface, and in which every passing omnibus or truck sets up a prolonged echo. And this great technological system of tunnels and thoroughfares interconnects with the ancient vaults [. . .] and catacombs [. . .] [T]his subterranean city had its uses, for those who knew their way around it. [. . .] [I]n the sixteenth and seventeenth centuries smuggling operations went on for the most part below ground. We know also that in times of public commotion mysterious rumors traveled very quickly via the catacombs to say nothing of the prophetic spirits and fortunetellers duly qualified to pronounce upon them. [. . .] And a few years later a rumor suddenly spread through the population that certain areas of town were about to cave in.
>
> (*AP C2.1: 85*)

24. The cocoon-like wrapping resonates with the *Tüte* (bag) contained in the word *Flüstertüte* which is perhaps another reason Celan chose to use it rather than the more familiar terms *Megaphon* and *Sprachrohr*.

25. On sight, spinning, and the begetting of hybrid offspring, see Celan's 1959 excursus, "Gespräch im Gebirg" ("Conversation in the Mountains"), in which he writes,

> Aber sie, die Geschwisterkinder, sie haben, Gott sei's geklagt, keine Augen. Genauer: sie haben, auch sie, Augen, aber da hängt ein Schleier davor, nicht davor, nein, dahinter, ein beweglicher Schleier; kaum tritt ein Bild ein, so bleibts hängen im Geweb, und schon ist ein Faden zur Stelle, der sich da spinnt, sich herumspinnt ums Bild, ein Schleierfaden; spinnt sich ums Bild herum und zeugt ein Kind mit ihm, halb Bild und halb Schleier.
>
> (But they, those cousins, have no eyes, alas. Or, more exactly: they have eyes, but with a veil hanging in front of them, no, not in front, behind them, a moveable veil. No sooner does an image enter than it gets caught in the web, and a thread starts spinning, spinning itself around the image, a veil-thread; spins itself around the image and begets a child, half image, half veil.)
>
> (GW 3: 170; CP 18)

The phrase *beweglicher Schleier* (moveable veil) may be an allusion to the figure of the *bewegte Schleier* (agitated veil) of Benjamin's Baudelaire essay. It is through this veil that is not simply before the eyes, Benjamin suggests, that Baudelaire sees. I have discussed this mode of vision in a chapter entitled "En garde! Benjamin's Baudelaire and the Training of Shock Defense" in *Writing Through Repression*. The *Geweb* (web) behind the eye of which Celan speaks would appear to be an allusion to the *Netzhaut* (retina). My attention was first drawn to this passage in "Conversation in the Mountains" by Derrida's discussion of Cixous' eye operation in conjunction with the English phrase "contact lens" and the name *Lenz* appearing in "Conversation." The figure of the moveable veil returns at the end of "Conversation," linked once again to the name *Lenz*.

> ... und in meinem Aug, da hängt der Schleier, der bewegliche, da hängen die Schleier, die beweglichen, da hast du den einen gelüpft, und da hängt schon der zweite, und der Stern—denn ja, der steht jetzt überm Gebirg—, wenn er da hineinwill, so wird er Hochzeit halten müssen und bald nicht mehr er sein, sondern halb Schleier und halb Stern ...
>
> (and in my eyes there is that moveable veil, there are veils, moveable veils, you lift one, and there hangs another, and the star there—yes, it is up there now, above the mountains—if it wants to enter it will have to wed and soon it won't be itself, but half-veil and half-star ...)
>
> (Celan GW 3:172; CP 22)

26. One of the ineluctable passages through which we enter Celan's poem today is Derrida's very beautiful 1997 text "Un vers à soie: Points de vue piqués sur l'autre voile," which appears in Hélène Cixous and Jacques Derrida, *Voiles* (Paris: Galilée, 1997), 23–85; and Jacques Derrida, "A Silkworm of One's Own: Points of View Stitched on the Other Veil," trans. Geoffrey Bennington, *Acts of Religion*, ed. Gil Andijar (New York: Routledge, 2002), 311–355. While it at no point directly addresses the poem "Für Eric," there are four citations of Celan in the text. The first a reference to "Conversation in the Mountains" that is accompanied by a long footnote (Cixous and Derrida 36; Derrida, *Acts* 320-1) The second and third citations are from poems published respectively in *Schneepart* (*Snow Part*) and *Zeitgehöft* (*Timesteads*) and appear as epigraphs at the beginning of the third section of Derrida's text (Cixous and Derrida, 71; Derrida, *Acts*, 344). The fourth citation is from the poem "Aschenglorie" (Ash-Aureole): "'Aschenglorie' [. . .] grub ich mich in dich und in dich" ("Ash-Aureole" [. . .] I dug me into you and you) (Cixous and Derrida 84; Derrida, *Acts*, 353–4). The last citation appears in the most explicitly autobiographical section of Derrida's text, which begins: "Avant mes treize ans, avant d'avoir jamais porté un talith et d'avoir me^me revé de posséder le mien, j'ai cultivé (mais quel rapport?) des vers à soie, ces chenilles ou larves de bombyx." (Before I was thirteen, before ever having worn a *talith* and even having dreamed of possessing my own, I cultivated (what's the link?) silkworms, the caterpillars or larvae of the bombyx.) (Cixous and Derrida 82; Derrida, *Acts*, 352).

What's the link, indeed—the link not only between the *talith* and the silkworm of one's own in Derrida's text but between *Un vers à soie* and Celan's poem? While there is no connection drawn in "Für Eric" between the silkworm and Celan's son's age, we know that the poem was written just before his thirteenth birthday, the time when it would have been traditional to receive a *talith* on the occasion of his bar mitzvah. More directly relevant to Celan's poem is Derrida's description of the four moultings through which his caterpillars would go: "à travers leurs quatre mues, les chenilles, chacune pour soi, n'étaient elles-mêmes, en elles-mêmes, pour elles-mêmes que le temps d'un passage. Elles ne s'animaient qu'en vue de la transformation du mûrier en soie." (Through their four moultings, the caterpillars, every one for itself, were themselves, in themselves, for themselves, only the time of a passage. They were animated only in view of the transformation of the mulberry into silk) (Cixous and Derrida 82; Derrida, *Acts*, 352).

27. Among the terms Celan jots down in an earlier draft of the poem is *untergehakt*, suggesting a resistant human chain of interlinked arms. It is this element of resistance that is stressed by Hans-Michael Speier in "Stehen chez Celan," trans. Jean-Luc Evard, *Po&sie* 69(1994): 102–12. See especially 108–12.

28. What might require further analysis, however, is the rhyme *hableurs/cableurs*. While the connection between *hableurs* and Celan's ongoing critique

of the figure *Maulheld* is clear enough, it is unclear what is at stake for him in this facile end rhyme—unless, of course, it is the very facility of the rhyme and near-identity of the two admonitions he wishes to underscore. See the discussion of seconding below. It is also worth noting the possible encryption of the name *Rainer Kabel* in the term *cableurs*; for it was Kabel, writing at the behest of Claire Goll and under the pseudonym Rainer K. Abel, who authored the article "Umstrittener Ausflug in der Vergangenheit: Anleihe oder Anlehnung?" The article appeared in the *feuilleton* section of the wide-circulation daily *Die Welt* on November 11, 1960, helping to launch the so-called Goll Affair that would have such a debilitating effect on Celan.

29. The verb *gravir*, meaning "to climb a steep slope or wall of rock with great effort using one's hands and feet," is derived from *krawjan*, meaning "to claw one's way up."

30. This no doubt made him acutely sensitive to related issues in Kafka. Cf. Chapter 5.

31. On Celan's familiarity with Benjamin's essay see Paul Celan, *La bibliothèque philosophique*, eds. Alexandra Richter, Patrik Alac, Bertrand Badiou (Paris: Éditions Rue d'Ulm, 2004), 294–8.

32. Hölderlin defines *caesura* as a counter-rhythmic interruption in his "Remarks on Oedipus," *Essays and Letters on Theory*, ed. and trans. Thomas Pfau (Albany, SUNY Press, 1988). There he notes,

> in the rhythmic sequence of the representations wherein transport presents itself, there becomes necessary what in poetic meter is called caesura, the pure word, the counter-rhythmic rupture [Unterbrechung]; namely, in order to meet the onrushing change of representations at its highest point in such a manner that very soon there does not appear the change of representation but representation itself. (102)

33. Werner Hamacher has written eloquently about "the second of inversion" in Celan's poetry. While my own understanding of the splitting of the second in this particular instance is greatly indebted to his work, I want to stress the special connection to Benjamin in this context, a connection I seek to develop below. For the moment I wish simply to note with Susan Buck-Morss and others that Benjamin's theses on the concept of history, which end with the description of the "second" as "the strait gate through which the Messiah might enter," should be read as a kind of suicide note. On "the second of inversion" in Celan, see Hamacher, *Premises*, 337–388.

34. As noted earlier, Celan commemorated this loss in his poem "Epitaph for Francois," which is contained in the 1955 collection *From Threshold to Threshold*. Yet, as I have elsewhere observed, the question of commemoration is particularly complex in this instance; for, as the poet Yves Bonnefoy reported to Ber-

trand Badiou, Celan actually wrote the poem before the child's birth and death, as though he had had already somehow foreseen what was to occur ("y voyant une prémonition des événements") (*CCL* II: 493). See also fn.1.

35. Leon Anisfeld and Arnold D. Richards, "The Replacement Child: Variations on a Theme in Individual and Collective History and Psychoanalysis," *Psychoanalytic Study of the Child* 55 (2000): 303.

36. Gabriele Schwab, *Haunting Legacies: Violent Histories and Transgenerational Trauma* (New York: Columbia University Press, 2010), 124. I am grateful to Professor Schwab for suggesting in private conversation a connection between the *seconde* in Celan's poem and Eric's status as a replacement child.

37. Romain Leick, "Bittere Brunnen des Herzens," *Der Spiegel*, April 2 2011, 206.

38. *CCL* II: 202, 352, 423. I am grateful to Bertrand Badiou for pointing out this recurrent slip as well as his suggestion that Eric may have been named after his paternal grandmother, Fredericke.

39. Alternate ways of translating this line might be: "There must be a way to scale this time" or "This time must be scaled no matter what it takes."

40. Paul de Man, "The Task of the Translator," in *Resistance to Theory* (Mineapolis, University of Minnesota Press, 1986), 104. Here one might also recall the passage in Benjamin's *Trauerspiel* book in which it is said that allegorical intention "would [. . .] fall from emblem to emblem down into the dizziness of its bottomless depths" (*Origin* 232; *GS* I.1: 405).

41. "It is as though," Shoshana Felman comments, "the translator, by the very power of his rendering the silence that inhabits Sophocles' tragedies, were himself exploded and aspired by that very silence" (Felman and Laub 154).

42. I would go so far as to suggest that it is the force of repetition, the translational/transferential dynamic in which Hölderlin, Benjamin, Celan, and de Man will have found themselves enmeshed, that makes insight into the dangers of translation possible in the first place.

43. The exact date on which this poem was composed is July 19, 1968. The connection between Hölderlin and Benjamin alluded to in its title is made explicit in the body of the text, which, as critics have noted, is itself pieced together from citations drawn from Benjamin's 1930 review of a book by Max Kommerell. As can be seen from Celan's citations, the passages of greatest interest to him were those in which Benjamin took issue with Kommerell's reading of Hölderlin. For a book-length study of Celan's poem see Ulisse Dogà, *"Port Bou—deutsch?": Paul Celan liest Walter Benjamin* (Rimbaud Verlag, 2009). See also Anna Glazova's "Opening the Secret: Paul Celan and Walter Benjamin Against 'Secret Germany.'" I am grateful to her for sharing this unpublished manuscript and for drawing my attention to Celan's French poem in the first place.

44. These were indeed the languages in which Benjamin conversed with his fellow refugees, the Spanish police, and staff of the hotel in which he took his life

in the border town of Port Bou. For an account of Benjamin's last days see Lisa Fitko, "The Story of Old Benjamin," in Benjamin, *Arcades*, 946–54.

45. Among these *confrères* one might also count the stateless Jew Daniel Cohn-Bendit. As Glazova notes, in 1968 de Gaulle's government considered Cohn-Bendit, a Jew born in Germany, a disturber of peace and a stranger in the French state. Celan, who was initially very enthusiastic about the riots, wrote a poem, "DEIN BLONDSCHATTEN," full of allusions to the journalists' attacks on Cohn-Bendit and expressing solidarity with this stateless Jew. See also fn. 15 above.

46. As Rainer Nägele pointed out in a private communication, Celan may have heard this lethal possibility resonating in the German version of his son's name, of *Eric* as *Erich*—which is to say, as *Er-ich* (*He-I*).

47. The place of the signature is also held open to others still to come—especially to those translator doubles who will have been belatedly implicated in the chain of traumatic repetitions I have been tracing. Among these translator doubles is Paul de Man who, as Shoshana Felman reminds us, "ends his career in a reflection not merely on translation and on silence but specifically on Walter Benjamin." "Benjamin," she argues, "stands for a change de Man has undergone, and the choice of Benjamin for de Man's last lecture signifies that de Man's testament, his legacy, consists in nothing other than the imperative and implications of this change." Stressing the element of doubling by which their relationship is defined, Felman adds "through his own translation of 'The Task of the Translator' de Man implicitly has recognized in Benjamin a double and brother" (Felman and Laub 157). The phrase "double and brother" is no doubt meant to echo the opening poem of *Les fleur du mal*, in which the poet addresses his reader as "mon semblable, mon frère" and thereby remind us of Baudelaire's own mediating and mirroring role in this relationship among his translators ("The Task of the Translator" being at once the preface Benjamin wrote to his translation of Baudelaire's *Tableux parisiens* and the text de Man in his turn "translates"). Yet, it is also used by Felman to conjure a more traumatic scene of fraternal doubling and uncanny repetition. Thus, she adds parenthetically "(a brother, who can be related to, once more, only belatedly as a dead brother)" (Felman and Laub 157). The allusion here is to the death of de Man's brother Hendrik, who died in a bicycle accident at a railroad crossing; a year later, Felman notes, "his mother committed suicide on the anniversary of his brother's death" (Felman and Laub 124).

Speaking primarily about de Man, Felman here emphasizes only the double and brother he implicitly recognized in Benjamin, the "brother who can be related to, once more, only belatedly, as a dead brother" (Felman and Laub 157). Yet, returning to Benjamin in a subsequent text, Felman takes up his own traumatic relationship to the death of a fraternal double or, as she puts it in this context, of an "alter ego," the poet Fritz Heinle. In her analysis of this relationship, discussed in Chapter 3, Felman seeks to demonstrate how Benjamin's "own suicide will repeat . . . and mirror the suicide of his younger friend, his alter ego, at the outbreak of the First World War" (*JU* 48). If, as she suggests, the repetitive, mirroring relationship in which these two suicides stand is indicative of Benjamin's inconsolability over the loss of his friend, it is not surprising to learn that the figure most immediately associated with his boundless grief was the poet-translator Hölderlin. Indeed, it would appear that Hölderlin haunted not only the impassable linguistic frontier at which Benjamin would eventually take his life but also the work of mourning he sought in vain to perform, the interminable act of grieving by which he would remain inextricably bound to the suicide of his younger friend and alter ego. Felman's account of the initial period of mourning is worth citing at length. Shortly after Heinle's death, she writes,

> Benjamin leaves Germany for Switzerland and resorts to a silence that will last six years, until 1920. During these years he does not publish anything. He writes and circulates among close friends a text on Hölderlin in which he meditates on the nature of the lyric and its relation to the poet's death. The poet's death relates to Heinle's death. Heinle also left poems, which Benjamin reads and rereads in an attempt to deepen his acquaintance with the dead. It is, indeed, as a dead poet that he now comes to know his friend. But Benjamin vows to give the dead poet immortality: to save Heinle from oblivion, to save the suicide from its meaninglessness, by publishing his friend's poetic work. This hope will never be relinquished. In the years of silence following the suicides [of Heinle and his girlfriend], he edits the manuscripts. Benjamin's own text on Hölderlin and the nature of the lyric is also an implicit dialogue with Heinle's work, a dialogue with Heinle's writing as well as with his life and with his death. Hence, Benjamin's specific interest in two poems by Hölderlin, "The Poet's Courage" and "Timidity," which designate the difference between Heinle's (suicidal) "Courage" and the "Timidity" of Benjamin's own (condemnation to) survival: suicide or survival, two existential stances between which Benjamin no doubt has oscillated but that he declares to be, surprisingly and paradoxically, two "versions" of the same profound text. (*JU* 35)

Celan knew Benjamin's essay on Hölderlin extremely well, as is evidenced by the numerous markings he made in his personal copy. That Benjamin would seek to come to terms with the suicide of his dear friend Heinle as well as with "his own (condemnation to) survival" through his writing on Hölderlin takes on particular poignancy when we recall the circumstances of his own suicide. Not only was Celan acutely aware of these circumstances or its Hölderlinian resonances but, as has often been noted, he left a Hölderlin biography open on his desk, leaving it, no doubt, as a kind of suicide note, when he plunged to his own death near the Pont Mirabeau on or around April 20, 1970.

48. While the German *Aber*, which Celan uses repeatedly in this passage, has the dominant sense of "but" or "however," its very repetition reminds us that it may also be used in terms like *abermals* to mean "once again" or "once more." His "but" is but a way of interrupting and objecting to himself even as he continues to speak, persevering and perseverating through these counter-rhythmic self-interruptions.

49. One might note, in conclusion, how the figure of the doubly open door and its relation to the thresholds of birth and death, each of which opens onto and beats at the heart of the other, is the central metaphor around which Celan's "Epitaph for Francois" is organized. "Both doors of the world / stand open: / opened by you / in the twinight. / We hear them beating and beating / and bear the uncertain, / and bear the green into your Ever. // October 1953." This translation is a modified version of the one appearing in Celan, *SPP*, 57.

50. Celan plays on the botanical resonances of his name in several poems, most notably in "Der Geglückte" ("The Successful") in *Fadensonnen* (*GW* 2: 144) (*Threadsuns* 99) in which there is a mention of "a single giant leaf of paulownia." See also the discussion of the poem, "La contrescarpe," in Vivian Liska, "Auf den Plätzen des Schweigens. Späte Begegnungen mit Paul Celan" in *Jahrbuch für internationale Germanistik* 43, no. 1 (2011): 15–34.

BIBLIOGRAPHY

Agamben, Georgio. "The Messiah and the Sovereign: The Problem of Law in Walter Benjamin." In *Potentialities*, trans. Daniel Heller-Roazen. Stanford: Stanford University Press, 1999.
Adorno, Theodor W. "A Portrait of Walter Benjamin." In *Prisms*, trans. Samuel and Shierry Weber, 227–41. Cambridge: MIT Press, 1981.
Anisfeld, Leon and Arnold D. Richards. "The Replacement Child: Variations on a Theme in Individual and Collective History and Psychoanalysis." *Psychoanalytic Study of the Child* 55 (2000): 301–19.
Arendt, Hannah. *Eichmann in Jerusalem: A Report on the Banality of Evil*. New York: Penguin, 1963.
———. *The Life of the Mind*. Vol. 1, *Thinking*. New York: Harcourt Brace Jovanovich, 1977.
———. *Men in Dark Times*. New York: Harcourt, Brace & World, 1968.
Auster, Paul. *Ground Work: Selected Poems and Essays 1970–1979*. London: Faber and Faber, 1990.
Barthes, Roland. *Camera Lucida: Reflections on Photography*. Trans. Richard Howard. New York: Farrar, Straus and Giroux, 1981.
———. *La chambre claire: Note sur la photographie*. Paris: Éditions de l'Étoile, Gallimard, Le Seuil, 1980.
Baudelaire, Charles. *Twenty Prose Poems*. Trans. Michael Hamburger. San Francisco: City Lights Books, 1988.
Baumann, Gerhart. *Erinnerungen an Paul Celan*. Frankfurt am Main: Suhrkamp Verlag, 1986.
Benjamin, Walter. *The Arcades Project*. Trans. Howard Eiland and Kevin McLaughlin. Cambridge: Harvard UP, 2002.
———. *The Correspondence of Walter Benjamin 1910–1940*. Eds. Gershom Scholem and Theodor W. Adorno. Trans. Manfred R. Jacobson and Evelyn M. Jacobson. Chicago: University of Chicago Press, 1994.
———. *Gesammelte Schriften*. Eds. Rolf Tiedemann und Hermann Schweppenhäuser. 7 vols. Frankfurt am Main: Suhrkamp, 1972–89.

―――. *The Origin of German Tragic Drama*. Trans. John Osborne. London: Verso, 1985.

―――. *Reflections*. Trans. Edmund Jephcott. New York: Harcourt Brace Jovanovich, 1978.

―――. *Selected Writings*. Eds. Marcus Bullock, Howard Eiland, Michael Jennings et al. 4 vols. Cambridge, MA: Harvard UP, 1996–2003.

―――. *Über den Begriff der Geschichte*. In *Walter Benjamin: Werke und Nachlaß Kritische Ausgabe*, ed. Gérard Raulet. Berlin: Suhrkamp, 2010.

Book of J. Trans. David Rosenberg. Interpreted by Harold Bloom. New York: Grove Weidenfeld, 1990.

Broderson, Momme. *Walter Benjamin: A Biography*. Trans. Malcolm R. Green and Ingrida Ligers. New York: Verso, 1997.

Buck-Morss, Susan. *The Dialectics of Seeing: Walter Benjamin and the Arcades Project*. Cambridge: MIT Press, 1999.

Büchner, Georg. *Werke und Briefe Münchner Ausgabe*. Eds. Karl Pörnbacher, Gerhard Schaub, Hans-Jochim Simm, and Edda Ziegler. Munich: Carl Hanser, 1988.

―――. *Complete Plays, Lenz and Other Writings*. Trans. John Reddick. New York: Penguin Books, 1993.

Canetti, Elias. *Kafka's Other Trial: The Letters to Felice*. Trans. Christopher Middleton. New York: Schocken, 1974.

Caruth, Cathy. *Unclaimed Experience: Trauma, Narrative, and History*. Baltimore: Johns Hopkins University Press, 1996.

Celan, Paul. *Collected Prose*. Trans. Rosemarie Waldrop. New York: Sheep Meadow Press, 1986.

―――. "Engführung/Stretto." Celan, *SPP*, 2001, 118–31.

―――. "Epitaph for François." Celan, *SPP*, 2001, 56–7.

―――. "Frankfurt, September." Nägele 1987, 136.

―――. "From Beholding the Blackbirds." *Breathturn*. Trans. Pierre Joris. Los Angeles: Sun & Moon, 1995. 227–9.

―――. *Die Gedichte: Kommentierte Ausgabe*. Ed. Barbara Weidemann. Frankfurt am Maine: Suhrkamp, 2005.

―――. *Die Gedichte aus dem Nachlaß*. Frankfurt am Main: Suhrkamp, 1997.

―――. *Gesammelte Werke*. 3 vols. Frankfurt am Main: Suhrkamp, 1986.

―――. *glottal stop: 101 poems*. Trans. Nikolai Popov and Heather McHugh. Hanover: Wesleyan University Press, 2000.

―――. "In Front of a Candle." Celan, *SPP*, 2001, 60–3.

―――. "In One." Celan, *SPP*, 2001, 188–9.

―――. *La bibliothèque philosophique*. Eds. Alexandra Richter, Patrik Alac, Bertrand Badiou. Paris: Éditions Rue d'Ulm, 2004.

―――. *Last Poems*. Trans. Katherine Washburn and Margaret Guillemin. San Francisco: North Point, 1986.

―――. *Der Meridian: Endfassung—Entwürfe—Materialien*. Ed. Bernhard Böschenstein and Heino Schmull. Frankfurt am Main: Suhrkamp, 1999.
―――. *The Meridian: Final Version—Drafts—Materials*. Trans. Pierre Joris. Stanford: Stanford UP, 2011.
―――. *Die Niemandesrose: Vorstufen—Textgenese—Endfassung*. Ed. Heino Schmull. Frankfurt am Main: Suhrkamp, 1996.
―――. *Poems of Paul Celan*. Trans. Michael Hamburger. New York: Persea, 1988.
―――. *Schneepart: Vorstufen, Textgenese, Reinschrift*. Eds. Heino Schmull and Markus Heilmann. Frankfurt am Main: Tübinger Ausgabe, Suhrkamp, 2002.
―――. *Selected Poems and Prose of Paul Celan [SPP]*. Trans. John Felstiner. New York: Norton, 2001.
―――. *Snow Part*. Trans. Ian Farley. Riverdale-on-Hudson: The Sheep Meadow Press, 2007.
―――. "To One Who Stood before the Door" Celan, *SPP*, 2001, 170–1.
―――. "The Vintagers." Celan, *SPP*, 2001, 82–3.
―――. *Threadsuns*. Trans. Pierre Joris. Los Angeles: Sun and Moon Press, 2000.
―――. "Your Dream [Your Waking's]." In *Breathturn*, 80–1. Trans. Pierre Joris. Los Angeles: Sun & Moon, 1995.
Celan, Paul and Gisèle Celan-Lestrange. *Correspondance*. Ed. Bertrand Badiou. 2 vols. Paris: Seuil, 2001.
Cixous, Hélène and Jacques Derrida. *Voiles*. Paris: Galilée, 1997.
The Concise Oxford Dictionary of English Etymology, ed. Terry F. Hoad. Oxford: Oxford University Press, 1996.
de Man, Paul. "The Task of the Translator." *Resistance to Theory*. Minneapolis: University of Minnesota Press, 1986. 73–105.
―――. *The Rhetoric of Romanticism*. New York: Columbia University Press, 1984.
Demetz, Peter. Introduction to *Reflections*, by Walter Benjamin, trans. Edmund Jephcott. New York: Harcourt Brace Jovanovich, 1978.
Derrida, Jacques. "A Silkworm of One's Own: Points of View Stitched on the Other Veil." Trans. Geoffrey Bennington. *Acts of Religion*, ed. Gil Andijar, 311–355. New York: Routledge, 2002.
―――. "Devant la loi." Trans. Avital Ronell. *Kafka and the Contemporary Critical Performance: Centenary Readings*, ed. Alan Udoff, 309–55. Bloomington: Indiana University Press, 1987.
―――. "The Majesty of the Present." Trans. Alessia Ricciardi and Christopher Yu. *New German Critique* 91 (Winter 2004): 17–40.
―――. *Sovereignties in Question: The Poetics of Paul Celan*, ed. Thomas Dutoit and Outi Pasanen, 135–63. NY: Fordham University Press, 2005.

———. *Schibboleth pour Paul Celan*. Paris: Galilée, 1986.

———. "To Speculate—on 'Freud.'" In *The Postcard: From Socrates to Freud and Beyond*, trans. Alan Bass, 257–407. Chicago: University of Chicago Press, 1987.

Deuber-Mankowsky, Astrid. "'. . . das Bild von Glück, das wir hegen': Zur messianischen Kraft der Schwäche bei Herman Cohen, Walter Benjamin und Paulus." In *Die Entdeckung des Christentums in der Wissenschaft des Judentums*, ed. Görge K. Hasselhoff. Berlin: de Gruyter, 2010.

"Die Kunst der Verwebung: Von der Zeitung zum Gedicht—Paul Celan und der Pariser Mai 68." *Neue Zürcher Zeitung* Dec. 17 2005. http://www.nzz.ch/2005/12/17/li/articleD0990.html

Dogà, Ulisse. *"Port Bou—deutsch?": Paul Celan liest Walter Benjamin*. Rimbaud Verlag, 2009.

Douglas, Lawrence. *The Memory of Judgment: Making Law and History in the Trials of the Holocaust*. New Haven: Yale University Press, 2001.

Eich, Günter. *Gesammelte Maulwürfe*. Frankfurt am Main: Suhrkamp, 1972.

Felman, Shoshana. *The Juridical Unconscious*. Cambridge: Harvard University Press, 2002.

———, and Dori Laub. *Testimony: Crises of Witnessing in Literature, Psychoanalysis, and History*. New York: Routledge, 1992.

Felstiner, John. "Kafka and the Golem—Translating Paul Celan." *Prooftexts* 6, no. 2 (1986): 172–83.

———. *Paul Celan: Poet, Survivor, Jew*. New Haven: Yale University Press, 1995.

Fittko, Lisa. "The Story of Old Benjamin." In *The Arcades Project*, by Walter Benjamin, trans. Howard Eiland and Kevin McLaughlin. Cambridge: Harvard UP, 2002.

Freud, Sigmund. *The Standard Edition of the Complete Psychological Works of Sigmund Freud*. Trans. James Strachey. Vol. 18, *Beyond the Pleasure Principle*. London: Hogarth, 1973.

Gadamer, Hans-Georg. *Gadamer on Celan: Who Am I and Who Are You? and Other Essays*. Trans. Richard Heinemann and Bruce Krajewski. Albany: SUNY Press, 1997.

———. *Wer bin Ich und wer bist Du? Ein Kommentar zu Paul Celans Gedichtfolge "Atemkristall."* Frankfurt am Main: Suhrkamp, 1986.

Gilman, Sander. *Franz Kafka, the Jewish Patient*. New York: Routledge, 1995.

Glazova, Anna. "Opening the Secret: Paul Celan and Walter Benjamin Against 'Secret Germany.'" Unpublished manuscript.

Grab, Walter. "Der hessische Demokrat Wilhelm Schulz und seine Schriften über Georg Büchner und Friedrich Ludwig Weidig." *Georg Büchner Jahrbuch* 2 (1982): 227–48.

Grimm, Jacob and Wilhelm Grimm. *Deutsches Wörterbuch*. Leipzig: Hirzel, 1942.

Grimm, Reinhold. *Love, Lust, and Rebellion: New Approaches to Georg Büchner.* Madison, WI: University of Wisconsin Press, 1985.
Günzel, Elke. *Das wandernde Zitat: Paul Celan im jüdischen Kontext.* Würzburg: Königshausen and Neumann, 1995.
Hamacher, Werner. "Häm: Ein Gedicht Celans mit Motiven Benjamins." In *Jüdisches Denken in einer Welt ohne Gott: Festschrift für Stéphane Moses,* ed. Jens Mattern, Gabriel Motzkin, and Shimon Sandbank, 173–97. Berlin: Vorwerk 8, 2000.
———. "'Now': Walter Benjamin on Historical Time." Trans. N. Rosenthal. In *Walter Benjamin and History,* ed. Andrew Benjamin, 38–68. London: Continuum, 2006.
———. "'Jetzt.' Benjamin zur historischen Zeit" in Benjamin Studien/Studies 1, eds. Helga Geyer-Ryan, Paul Koopman, and Klaas Yntema (Amsterdam: Rodopi, 2002),
———. *Premises: Essays on Philosophy and Literature from Kant to Celan.* Trans. Peter Fenves. Cambridge, MA: Harvard University Press, 1996.
Harries, Martin. "Homo Alludens: Marx's *Eighteenth Brumaire.*" *New German Critque* 66 (1995): 35–64.
Hartman, Geoffrey. "'Breaking Every Star': On Literary Knowledge." *Comparative Criticism* 18 (1996): 3–20.
Heidegger, Martin. *Being and Time..* Trans. John MacQuarrie and Edward Robinson. New York: Harper & Row, 1962.
Held, Robert. "Revolutionäre Frühling." *Frankfurter Allgemeine Zeitung,* June 1–2 1968.
Hinderer, Walter. *Büchner Kommentar zum dichterischen Werk.* Munich: Winkler, 1977.
Hölderlin, Friedrich. *Essays and Letters on Theory.* Ed. and trans. Thomas Pfau. Albany: SUNY Press, 1988.
Jacobs, Carol. *In the Name of Walter Benjamin.* Baltimore: Johns Hopkins University Press, 1999.
Kafka, Franz. "A Country Doctor." In *The Complete Stories,* trans. Willa and Edwin Muir, 220–26. New York: Schocken, 1976.
———. *Amerika: The Missing Person.* Trans. Mark Harman. NY: Schocken, 2008.
———. *Briefe an Felice.* Frankfurt am Main: Fischer Taschenbuch Verlag, 1983.
———. *The Diaries of Franz Kafka, 1914–1923.* Ed. Max Brod. Trans. Joseph Kresh. New York: Schocken, 1948. Later published as *Tagebücher* (Frankfurt am Main: Fischer, 1990).
———. *Gesammelte Werke in zwölf Bänden.* Vol. 1, *Ein Landarzt und andere Drucke zu Lebzeiten.* Ed. Hans-Gerd Koch. Frankfurt am Main: Fischer Taschenbuch Verlag, 2002.
———. "Josefine, the Singer, or The Mouse People." In *Kafka's Selected Stories,* trans. Stanley Corngold, 94–108. New York: Norton, 2007.

———. *Kafka's Selected Stories*. Trans. Stanley Corngold. New York: Norton, 2007.
———. *Letters to Felice*. Trans. Eric Heller and Jürgen Born. New York: Schocken, 1973.
———. *Letters to Friends, Family, and Editors*. Trans. Richard and Clara Winston. New York: Schocken Books, 1977.
———. *Letter to His Father / Brief an den Vater*. Trans. Ernst Kaiser and Eithne Wilkins. New York: Schocken, 1966.
———. *Letters to Milena*. Ed. Willy Haas. Trans. Tania and James Stern. New York: Vintage, 1999.
———. *The Metamorphosis*. Trans. Stanley Corngold. New York: Bantam, 1972.
Klotz, Volker. *Geschlossene und offene Form im Drama*. München: Carl Hanser Verlag, 1969.
Knapp, Gerhard P. *Georg Büchner*. Stuttgart: Metzler, 2000.
Lacoue-Labarthe, Philippe. *Poetry as Experience*. Trans. Andrea Tarnowski. Stanford: Stanford University Press, 1999.
Lear, Jonathan. *Happiness, Death, and the Remainder of Life*. Cambridge: Harvard University Press, 2000.
Leick, Romain. "Bittere Brunnen des Herzen." *Der Spiegel*, April 2 2001.
Levinas, Emmanuel. "Paul Celan: From Being to the Other." *Proper Names*, trans. Michael B. Smith, 40–6. Stanford: Stanford University Press, 1996.
Levine, Michael G. *The Belated Witness: Literature, Testimony, and the Question of Holocaust Survival*. Stanford: Stanford University Press, 2006.
———. *Writing through Repression: Literature, Censorship, Psychoanalysis*. Baltimore: Johns Hopkins University Press, 1996.
Liska, Vivian. "Auf den Plätzen des Schweigens. Späte Begegnungen mit Paul Celan." *Jahrbuch für internationale Germanistik* 43, no. 1(2011): 15–34.
Marx, Karl and Friedrich Engels. *Marx-Engels Reader*. Ed. Robert C. Tucker. New York: Norton, 1978.
———. "Speech at the Anniversary of the *People's Paper*." 1856. http://www.marxists.org/archive/marx/works/1856/04/14.htm
Mayer, Sigrid. *Golem: Die literarische Rezeption eines Stoffes*. Frankfurt am Main: Peter Lang, 1975.
Mosès, Stéphane. "Celan Wins Büchner Prize." *Yale Companion to Jewish Writing and Thought*, eds. Sander Gilman and Jack Zipes. New Haven: Yale UP, 1997. 716–22.
Müller-Sievers, Helmut. *Desorientierung: Anatomie und Dichtung bei Georg Büchner*. Gottingen: Wallstein, 2003.
———. "Of Fish and Men: The Importance of Georg Büchner's Anatomical Writings." *MLN* 118 (2003): 704–18.
Nägele, Rainer. *Reading after Freud: Essays on Goethe, Hölderlin, Habermas, Nietzsche, Brecht, Celan, and Freud*. New York: Columbia University Press, 1987.

Neumann, Peter Horst. *Zur Lyrik Paul Celans: Eine Einführung.* Göttingen: Vandenhoeck and Ruprecht, 1968.
Pöggeler, Otto. *Spur des Wortes: Zur Lyrik Paul Celans.* Munich: Karl Alber, 1986.
Rokem, Freddie. *Philosophers and Thespians: Thinking Performance.* Stanford: Stanford University Press, 2010.
Santner, Eric. *On The Psychotheology of Everyday Life.* Chicago: University of Chicago Press, 2001.
Schestag, Thomas. "Men Schen Schnitte durch in ein Gedicht Paul Celans." *MLN. German Issue.* 119, no. 3 (2004): 580–607.
Scholem, Gershom. *The Kabbalah and Its Symbolism.* Trans. Ralph Manheim. New York: Schocken, 1965.
———. *Walter Benjamin: Story of a Friendship.* Philadelphia: Jewish Publication Society of America, 1981.
Schwab, Gabriele. *Haunting Legacies: Violent Histories and Transgenerational Trauma.* New York: Columbia University Press, 2010.
Segev, Tom. *The Seventh Million.* New York: Henry Holt and Co., 1991.
Shakespeare, William. *Hamlet.* In *Complete Works.* Ed. Jonathan Bate and Eric Rasmussen. New York: Random House, 2007.
Sieburth, Richard "Benjamin the Scrivener." In *Benjamin: Philosophy, Aesthetics, History,* ed. Gary Smith, 13–37. Chicago: University of Chicago Press, 1989.
———. Translator's Afterword to *Lenz,* by Georg Büchner, 165–97. New York: Archipelago Books, 2004.
Solomon, Andrew. *The Noonday Demon: An Atlas of Depression.* New York: Scribner, 2001.
Speier, Hans-Michael. "Stehen chez Celan." Trans. Jean-Luc Evard. *Po&sie* 69 (1994): 102–12.
Taussig, Michael. *Walter Benjamin's Grave.* Chicago: University of Chicago Press, 2006.
Weber, Samuel. *Benjamin's -abilities.* Cambridge, MA: Harvard University Press, 2008.
———. "Genealogy of Modernity: History, Myth and Allegory in Benjamin's *Origin of the German Mourning Play.*" *MLN* 106, no. 3 (1991): 465–500.
Witte, Bernt. "Der zyklische Charakter der Niemandsrose von Paul Celan." In *Argumentume Silentio,* ed. Amy Colin, 72–86. Berlin–New York: Walter de Gruyter, 1987.
Wohlfarth, Irving. "On the Messianic Structure of Walter Benjamin's Last Reflections." *GLYPH: Johns Hopkins Textual Studies* 3 (1978): 72–86.
Woolf, Virginia. *The Lady in the Looking-Glass.* London: Penguin Classics, 2011.

INDEX

20th of January, 19–20

Adorno, Gretel, Benjamin's letter to, 1–2
all poets are Jews, 66–67
allegory, Benjamin, Walter, 131
alliance, "To One Who Stood Before the Door" (Celan), 72
Altneu Synagogue (Prague), 147–48
antonomasia, Kafka and, 88–89
AP (*The Arcades Project*), 128
The Arcades Project (Benjamin), 15–16; splitting the atom, 25
Arendt, Hannah, *Eichmann in Jerusalem*, 31–32
Atemkristall (Gadamer), 152–53
"Aus dem Moorboden" (Celan), 146–47

Barthes, Roland, *Camera Lucida: Reflections on Photography*, 126
Bauer, Felice: Kafka, Franz and, 89–90
Baumann, Gerhart, *Erinnerungen an Paul Celan*, 151–52
becoming, origin and, 6–7
"Beim Hagelkorn" (Celan), 149–50
being-towards-death (Heidegger), 129
bells, Kafka and, 129
Benjamin, Walter: Adorno, Gretel, letter to, 1–2; allegory, 131; *The Arcades Project*, 15–16, 25; *Berlin Chronicle*, 26, 28–29; blasting/wrenching, 130–31; burial, 30–31; Catholic cemetary burial, 134; *Central Park*, redemption, 132–33; comparison of Baudelaire and Joshua, 131; constellation, 21–22; Dauthendey photograph, 4–5; Heinle, Fritz: papers, 26–30, 133; Heinle, Fritz: suicide, 28–30; Heinle, Wolf, 26–30, 133; Judgment Day, 26; Konstellation, 17, 18–19, 23–24; last will and testament and, 27–28; *A Little History of Photography*, 4; Messiah, coming, 25–26; "The Metaphysics of Youth," 36; *mit-* prefix, 17–18; nesting future, 4–5; origin, becoming and, 6–7; *Origin of the German Tragic Drama*, 6–7; secret appointment, 2–4, 7, 25; secret meeting place for thoughts, 1–2; Sekunde, 24–25; suicide, 25–30; theses as last will and testament, 26–28; on translation, 118–19; unactualized possibilities, 3–4; *Walter Benjamin: Selected Writings*, 2–3
Berlin Chronicle (Benjamin), 26–30
Brod, Max, Kafka's letter to, 89–90
Büchner, Georg: *Danton's Death*, 38–39, 44–45, 48–51; head placement, 45–46; *The Hessian Messenger*, 21; *Leonce and Lena*, 39–41, 44, 55–59; *Leonce and Lena*, Franzos' error, 53–62; Weidig, Friedrich Ludwig, and, 51; *Woyzeck*, 41–48
Büchner Prize for Literature, Paul Celan, 37–38

173

caesura, 139
calendars, 131
Camera Lucida: Reflections on Photography (Barthes), 126
caterpillar in "Für Eric" (June 1968), 108–9
CCL I (Celan and Celan-Lestrange correspondence), 127–28
CCL II (Celan and Celan-Lestrange correspondence), 127–28
Celan, Paul: all poets are Jews, 66–67; "Aus dem Moorboden," 146–47; "Beim Hagelkorn," 149–50; Büchner Prize for Literature, 37–38; coming, 114–15; coming back, 9–11; coming between, 9–11; constellation, 18–19; *Danton's Death* (Büchner), 38–39; dates, 19–20; "Deathfugue," 134; "Engführung," 81–82; "Epitaph for François," 90, 159–60; Eric anagram, 117; failed homecoming, 58–59; François (son), 97–98; François (son), as replacement child, 116–17; "Frankfurt, September," 94–96; Franzos, Karl Emil, and, 10–11; French, poem in, 13, 98, 112–16; French citizenship, 113; "Für Eric" (June 1968), 105–11; "Für Eric" (May 1968), 100–4; "Gespräch im Gebirg," 157; Golem, 82–83; human presence, 41; "In One," 17–18, 20–23; Kafka's name, 85–88; Kafka's throat, 95–96; Kielkropf, 90–94; kilodrama, 99, 149; Kontur, 23; language, 98; letter to Marthe Robert, 144; mental breakdowns, 98–99; *Meridian* speech, 9–11, 37–62, 135–41; *Die Niemandsrose*, 21; *The No-one's Rose*, 63; "Ô les hableurs" manuscript, 122, 123; "Peace to the cottages!", 21; the poem, 60–61; poems, true, 65; poems' 20th of January, 19–20; poems dedicated to son, 13; poems' legacy to son, 120–21; precision, 81; repetition, 61; sacrifice of Abraham, 99–100; "Shibboleth: For Paul Celan" (Derrida), 11, 17–18; signatures of poems to son, 121; sons, 97; sons, French citizenship and, 113; "Sprich Auch Du," 140; star reference in Bremen address, 18–19; "The Vintagers," 70; time in poem to son, 112–14; "To One Who Stood Before the Door," 63, 67–9; "Todtnauberg," 21; *Wiederkomen* versus *Dazwischenkommen*, 114–15

Celan-Lestrange, Gisèle, François (son), 97, 116–17
Central Park (Benjamin), redemption, 1, 132–33
circling dates, 19–20
circumcision: date, 63–64; Derrida, Jacques, 11–12; naming and, 70–71; reading-wound, 65–66; "Shibboleth: For Paul Celan" (Derrida), 63–65; stone/flint, 142; tropic of, 65–67
circumcision of the word, 63, 67–79; Derrida, Jacques, 73–79, 82; Rabbi Löw, 82
citability, 8, 23, 27, 125
CLPOW (*Complete Plays, Lenz and Other Writings*), 135
constellation, 21–22; Derrida, Jacques, 130; star clusters and, 129–30. *See also* Konstellation
"A Country Doctor" (Kafka), 144
CP (*Collected Prose*), 127
Creation, Golem and, 82–84

Danton's Death (Büchner), 38–39; meridian, 44–45; September, 49–51; window scene, 48–49
dates: circling, 19–20; "In One" (Celan), 20–21
"Deathfugue" (Celan), 134
Derrida, Jacques: circumcision, 11–12; circumcision of the word, 73–79; Golem in "To One Who Stood Before the Door," 80–81; shibboleth as circumcised word, 82
dialectical images, 134–35
Dinoor, Yehiel, 34–35
doors of the world, 90, 163

Eich, Günter, *Maulwürfe*, 155–56
Eichmann in Jerusalem (Arendt), 31–32
Eichmann trial, 31; Arendt, Hannah, 31–32; Dinoor, Yehiel, 34–35; Judgment Day, 31, 35–36; K-Zetnik, 32–35
Eighteenth Brumaire (Marx), revolution, 107–8
ellipsis, "In One" (Celan), 22–23
empty time, 24
"Engführung" (Celan), 81–82
"Epitaph for François" (Celan), 90, 97, 159–60
equinox in "Für Eric" (May 1968), 102, 104
Erinnerungen an Paul Celan (Baumann), 151–52

February 13, 1962, 20–21, 22
Felman, Shoshana: Benjamin and Heinle's death, 162–63; Benjamin's suicide plan, 26–27; Heinle's suicide, *Berlin Chronicle* and, 28–31; *The Juridical Unconscious*, 26; K-Zetnik loss of consciousness, 32–35
film, 131–32
"Frankfurt, September" (Celan), 94–96
Franzos, Karl Emil, 10–11; *Leonce and Lena* error, 53–62
Frente Nationale, 21
Frente Popular, 20–21
Freud, Sigmund: return to, 8–9; *Woyzeck* (Büchner), and, 137
Front of the Right, 20
Front Populaire, 20–21
"Für Eric" (Celan): June 1968, 105–11, 158; May 1968, 100–4

Gadamer, Hans-Georg, *Atemkristall*, 152–53
"Gespräch im Gebirg" (Celan), 157
glass that fills itself with silk in "Für Eric" (June 1968), 109–10, 158
Golem, 80–86, 90–94
GS (*Gesammelte Schriften*), 125, 128
GW (*Gesammelte Werke*), 127

Hamacher, Werner; *Häm*, 145, 146–47; redemption, 3–4; second of inversion, 159
Hamlet (Shakespeare), revolution and, 107–8
happiness: *The Arcades Project* (Benjamin), 15–16; lucky break, 140–41
head placement in Büchner's work, 45–46
Hegel, misquoting Shakespeare, 154–55
Heidegger, Martin, being-towards-death, 129
Heinle, Fritz, 26–30, 133
Heinle, Wolf, 26–27, 133
The Hessian Messenger (Büchner), 21
historical materialism, 7–8, 127
history, unconscious and, 8–9, 32–36
homogeneous, empty time, 24
hunchback of theology, 3
hunchbacked time, 3, 7, 126–27

IG ("The Idea of the Golem"), 142
"In One" (Celan), 17–18, 22–23; dates, 20–21; ellipsis, 22–23; history and, 22
"In the Penal Colony" (Kafka), 75
interruptions, sacrifice of Abraham, 150–51

Jetztzeit, 27
Jewish exclusiveness, "To One Who Stood Before the Door" (Celan), 72
"Josefine, the Singer, or the Mouse People" (Kafka), 92, 95–96
JU (*The Juridical Unconscious*), 133
Judgment Day: Benjamin, Walter, 26; Eichmann trial and, 31, 35–36
The Juridical Unconscious (Felman), 26, 133
justice, Hannah Arendt, 32

Kafka, name origins, 86–88
Kafka, Franz: Altneu Synagogue, 147–48; antonomasia and, 88–89; Bauer, Felice and, 89–90; bells, 129; "A Country Doctor," 144; forebears, marriage, and heirs, 143; "Frankfurt, September" (Celan), 94–96; Golem

Kafka, Franz (*continued*)
  and, 85–86; "In the Penal Colony," 75; "Josefine, the Singer, or the Mouse People," 92, 95–96; Kielkropf and, 92–94, 145–46; Kriegsknecht, 145–46; letter to Max Brod, 89–90; name, Celan and, 86–88; Radius, 148; throat, Celan, and, 95–96; "To One Who Stood Before the Door" (Celan), 85–86; tuberculosis, 89–90
Kielkropf, 90–94, 145–46
kilodrama, 99, 149
Konstellation, 17, 18–19, 23–24
Kontur, 23
Kriegsknechts, 145–46
K-Zetnik (Eichmann trial), 32–35

language: Celan, 98; coming back, 9–11; coming between, 9–11; repetition, 9; rhythm, 9; of sparks, 5
last will and testament, Benjamin's theses as, 26–28
Leonce and Lena (Büchner), 39–41; Franzo's error, 53–62; meridian, 44; Rosetta, 57–58; Valerio, 55–56
A Little History of Photography (Benjamin), 4
lucky break, 140–41

M (*The Meridian: Final Version-Drafts-Materials*), 135
Marx, Karl: *Eighteenth Brumaire*, revolution, 107–8; misquoting Shakespeare, 154–55; revolution, 154–55
megaphone in "Für Eric" (June 1968), 106–7
meridian: *Danton's Death* (Büchner), 44–45; *Leonce and Lena* (Büchner), 40, 44; *Woyzeck* (Büchner), 41–43, 44, 45
Meridian speech (Celan), 9–11, 37–38; *Danton's Death* (Büchner), 38–39; minding, 49; paths of poems, 74–75; *Wiederkunft*, 51–52
"The Metaphysics of Youth" (Benjamin), 36
mit- prefix, 17–18, 61–62, 129

monagonist, 137
Munier, Roger, 141–42

Name of God, 82–4
naming, circumcision and, 70–71
nesting future, 4–5
Die Niemandsrose (Celan), 21
The No-one's Rose (Celan), 63
Nuremberg trials, *versus* Eichmann trial, 31

"Ô les hableurs" (Celan): manuscript, 122, 123
optical unconscious, 4, 126
origin, becoming and, 6–7
Origin of the German Tragic Drama (Benjamin), 6–7

the past, speech of another nature and, 7
paths of poems, 74–75
"Peace to the cottages!", 21
photography, speech of another nature, 4
poems, paths, 74–75
poesis, 80
possibilities, unactualized, 3–4
potential, accumulating, 16–17
precision, 81
the present, standstill, 6
punctum, 126

Rabbi Löw, 80; circumcision of the word, 82; Golem, 81, 83–84
reading-wound of circumcision, 65–66
redemption: *Central Park* (Benjamin), 132–33; secrets and, 3–4
repetition: incomprehension and, 134; language, 9; "To One Who Stood Before the Door" (Celan), 70, 73
revolution: *Eighteenth Brumaire* (Marx), 107–8; *Hamlet* (Shakespeare), 107–8; Marx, Karl, 154–55
rhythmic repetition, 9
Robert, Marthe, Celan's letter to, 144

S (*Sovereignties in Question: The Poetics of Paul Celan*), 130

sacrifice of Abraham: Celan and son, 99–100; interruptions and, 150–51
Scholem, Gershom: Heinle, Fritz, and, 28; "Idea of the Golem," 83–84; posthumous writings, 27; *Walter Benjamin: Story of a Friendship*, 28
secret appointment, 2–4, 7, 25
secret meeting place for thoughts, 2–3
secrets, redemption and, 3–4
seeing through, "Für Eric" (June 1968), 110–11
Sekunde, 24–25
September, *Danton's Death* (Büchner), 49–51
Shakespeare, *Hamlet*, 107–8
shibboleth, 11–12, 22–23; as circumcised word, 82
"Shibboleth: For Paul Celan" (Derrida), 11; Benjamin and, 17–18; circumcision, postponing, 64–65
silence: Golem, 90–91; Kafka and, 95; "To One Who Stood Before the Door" (Celan), 70
sparks, language of, 5
SPC ("Shibboleth: For Paul Celan"), 127, 130
speech of another nature, 4; the past and, 7
"Sprich Auch Du" (Celan), 140
star clusters *versus* constellations, 129–30
studium, 126
suicide: Benjamin, Walter, 25–27; *Berlin Chronicle* (Benjamin), 28–29
SW (*Selected Writings*), 125

Taube, 145
tense: *The Arcades Project* (Benjamin), 15–16; *Berlin Chronicle* (Benjamin), Heinle's suicide, 28–29; K-Zetnik in

Eichmann trial, 33–34; "To One Who Stood Before the Door" (Celan), 69
theology: hunchback of, 3; *versus* materialism, 8
time: calendars, 131; Celan's poem to son, 112–14; homogeneous, empty time, 24; Kant, 127; Sekunde, 24–25
"To One Who Stood Before the Door" (Celan), 63, 67–69; alliance, 72; circumcision of the word, 73–79; doors of the world, 90; Golem, Derrida and, 80–81; Jewish exclusiveness and, 72; Kafka and, 85–86; Rabbi Löw, 69; repetition, 70, 73; silence, 70
"Todtnauberg" (Celan), 21
translation: dangers of, 118–20; de Man, Paul, 161
tropic of circumcision, 65–67

unactualized possibilities, 3–4
unconscious, history and, 8–9

"The Vintagers" (Celan), 70

Walter Benjamin: Selected Writings, 2–3
Walter Benjamin: Story of a Friendship (Scholem), 28
WBMA (*Werke und Briefe, Münchner Ausgabe*), 135
weak messianic power, 14; *The Arcades Project* (Benjamin), 15; as endowment, 8–9; of the subjunctive, 16
Weidig, Friedrich Ludwig, Büchner, Georg, and, 51
Woyzeck (Büchner): Freud and, 137; meridian, 41–43, 44, 45; pond scene, 47–48

zodiac signs in "Für Eric" (May 1968), 101–4

www.ingramcontent.com/pod-product-compliance
Lightning Source LLC
Chambersburg PA
CBHW031247290426
44109CB00012B/476